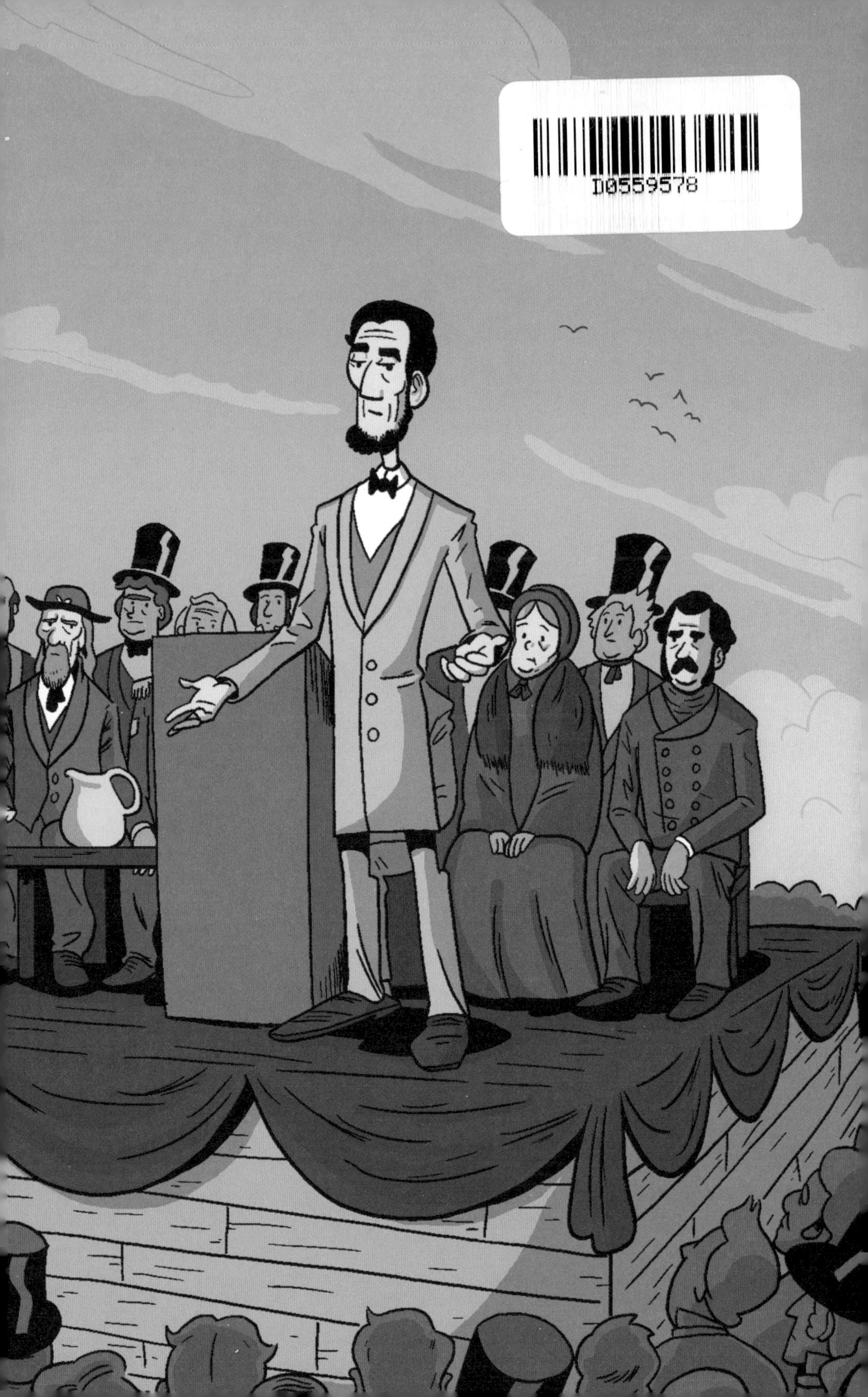

SHOW ME HISTORY!

ABRAHAM LINCOLN

DEFENDER of the UNION!

BY
MARK SHULMAN

ILLUSTRATED BY
TOM MARTIN

LETTERING & DESIGN BY
COMICRAFT

COVER ART BY
IAN CHURCHILL

PORTABLE
PRESS

SAN DIEGO, CALIFORNIA

Portable Press
An imprint of Printers Row Publishing Group
10350 Barnes Canyon Road, Suite 100, San Diego, CA 92121
www.portablepress.com • e-mail: mail@portablepress.com

PORTABLE
PRESS

Printers Row Publishing Group is a division of Readerlink Distribution Services, LLC.
Portable Press is a registered trademark of Readerlink Distribution Services, LLC.

Correspondence regarding the content of this book should be addressed to Portable Press, Editorial Department, at the above address. Author and illustration inquiries should be addressed to Oomf, Inc., www.oomf.com.

Publisher: Peter Norton
Associate Publisher: Ana Parker
Developmental Editor: Vicki Jaeger
Publishing Team: Kathryn C. Dalby, Lauren Taniguchi
Production Team: Jonathan Lopes, Rusty von Dyl

O•MF   Created at Oomf, Inc., www.Oomf.com
Director: Mark Shulman
Producer: James Buckley Jr.

Written by Mark Shulman
Illustrated by Tom Martin
Coloring by YouNeek Studios, Ellie White, Steve Thueson
Lettering & design by Comicraft: John Roshell, Sarah Jacobs, Niklas
   Pousette Harger, Drewes McFarling, Forest Dempsey, Tyler Smith
Cover illustration by Ian Churchill

Library of Congress Cataloging-in-Publication Data

Names: Shulman, Mark, 1962- author. | Martin, Tom, illustrator. | Roshell, John, letterer.
Title: Abraham Lincoln : Defender of the Union! / author: Mark Shulman ;
   interior illustration: Tom Martin ; interior lettering: John Roshell.
Description: San Diego : Portable Press, 2019. | Series: Show me history!
Identifiers: LCCN 2018037869 | ISBN 9781684125449 (hardback)
Subjects: LCSH: Lincoln, Abraham, 1809-1865--Juvenile literature. |
   Presidents--United States--Biography--Juvenile literature. | United
   States--Politics and government--1861-1865--Juvenile literature. | United
   States--History--Civil War, 1861-1865--Juvenile literature. | Lincoln,
   Abraham, 1809-1865--Comic books, strips, etc. | Presidents--United
   States--Biography--Comic books, strips, etc. | United States--Politics and
   government--1861-1865--Comic books, strips, etc. | United
   States--History--Civil War, 1861-1865--Comic books, strips, etc. | Graphic
   novels. | BISAC: JUVENILE NONFICTION / Biography & Autobiography /
   Historical. | JUVENILE NONFICTION / History / United States / Civil War
   Period (1850-1877). | JUVENILE NONFICTION / History / United States / 19th
   Century.
Classification: LCC E457.905 .S49 2019 | DDC 973.7092 [B] --dc23 LC record available
at https://lccn.loc.gov/2018037869

Printed in China

22 21 20 19 18   1 2 3 4 5

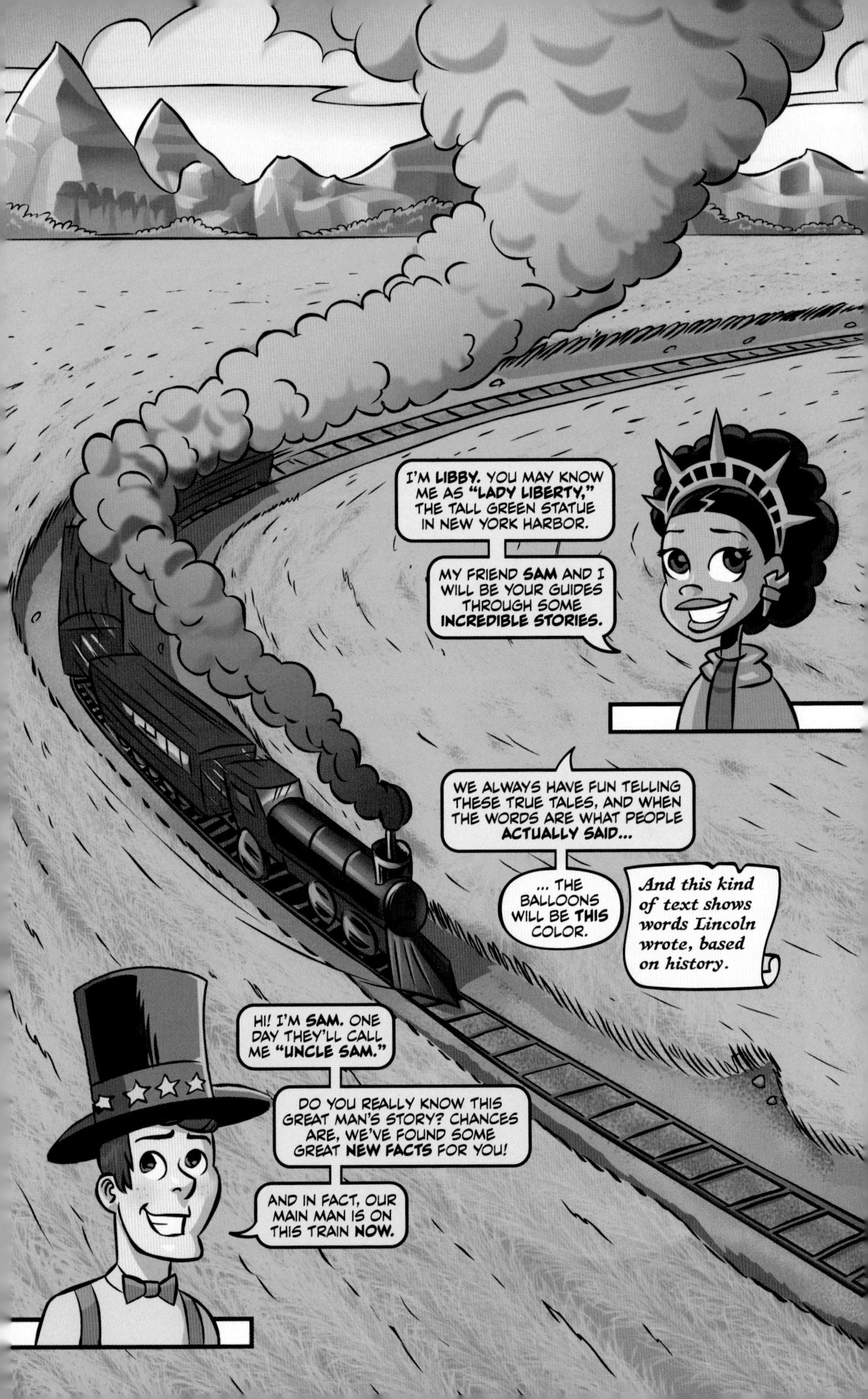
I'M LIBBY. YOU MAY KNOW ME AS "LADY LIBERTY," THE TALL GREEN STATUE IN NEW YORK HARBOR.
MY FRIEND SAM AND I WILL BE YOUR GUIDES THROUGH SOME INCREDIBLE STORIES.
WE ALWAYS HAVE FUN TELLING THESE TRUE TALES, AND WHEN THE WORDS ARE WHAT PEOPLE ACTUALLY SAID...
... THE BALLOONS WILL BE THIS COLOR.
And this kind of text shows words Lincoln wrote, based on history.
HI! I'M SAM. ONE DAY THEY'LL CALL ME "UNCLE SAM."
DO YOU REALLY KNOW THIS GREAT MAN'S STORY? CHANCES ARE, WE'VE FOUND SOME GREAT NEW FACTS FOR YOU!
AND IN FACT, OUR MAIN MAN IS ON THIS TRAIN NOW.

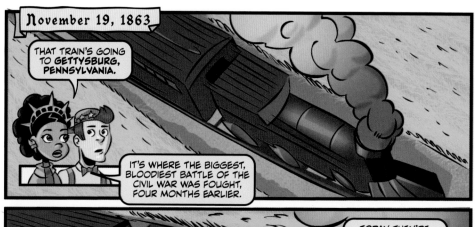

November 19, 1863

THAT TRAIN'S GOING TO **GETTYSBURG, PENNSYLVANIA.**

IT'S WHERE THE BIGGEST, BLOODIEST BATTLE OF THE CIVIL WAR WAS FOUGHT, FOUR MONTHS EARLIER.

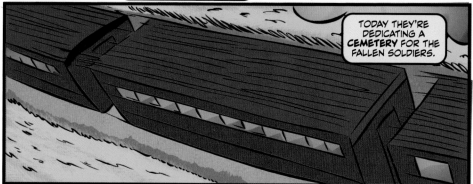

TODAY THEY'RE DEDICATING A **CEMETERY** FOR THE FALLEN SOLDIERS.

MORE THAN **51,000** DIED.

YIKES. AND OUR GUY ON THE TRAIN WANTS TO GO **BACK** THERE?

THAT GUY IS **PRESIDENT LINCOLN.** HE'S WRITING THE FAMOUS **GETTYSBURG ADDRESS.**

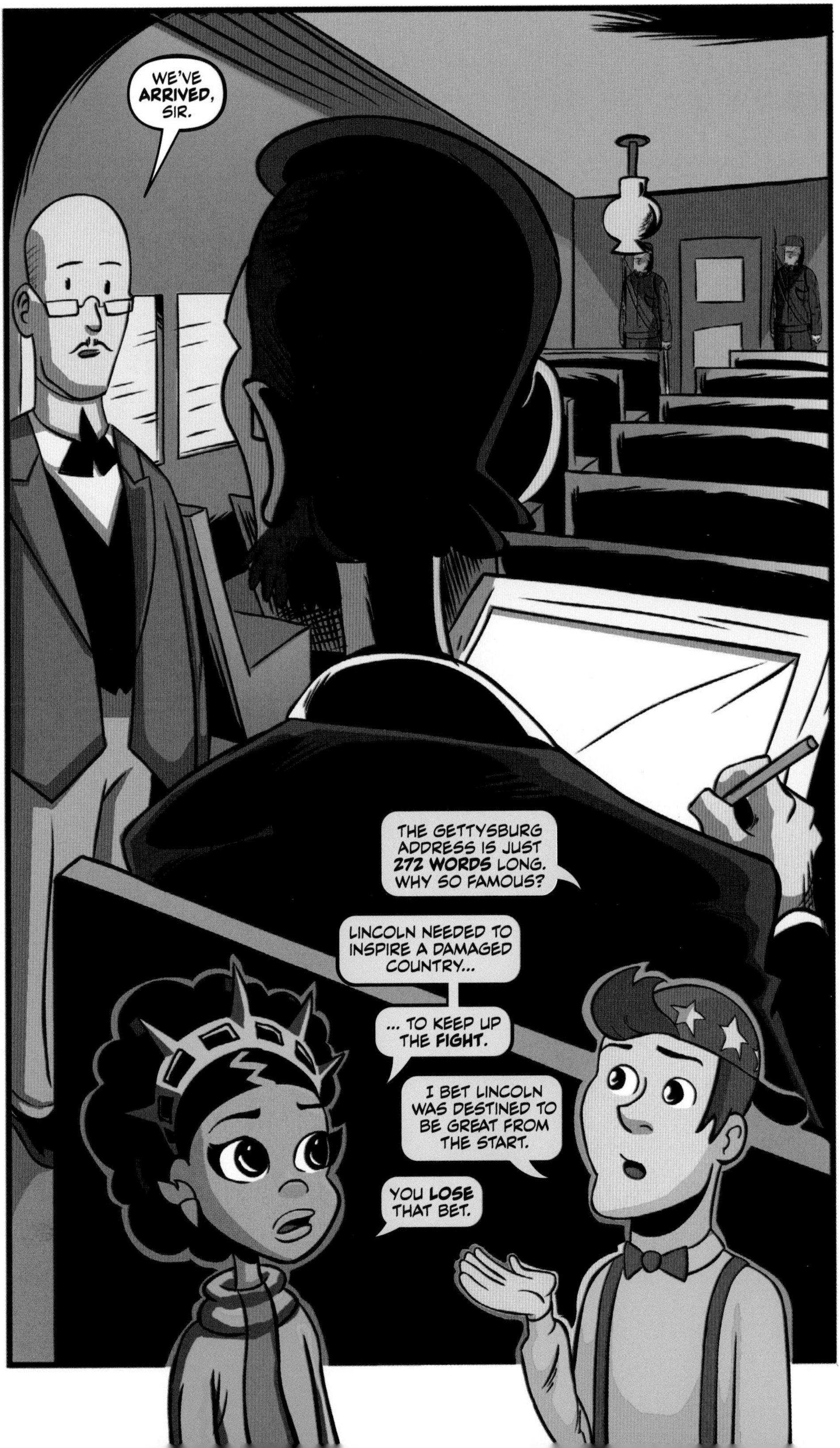
WE'VE ARRIVED, SIR.
THE GETTYSBURG ADDRESS IS JUST 272 WORDS LONG. WHY SO FAMOUS?
LINCOLN NEEDED TO INSPIRE A DAMAGED COUNTRY...
... TO KEEP UP THE FIGHT.
I BET LINCOLN WAS DESTINED TO BE GREAT FROM THE START.
YOU LOSE THAT BET.

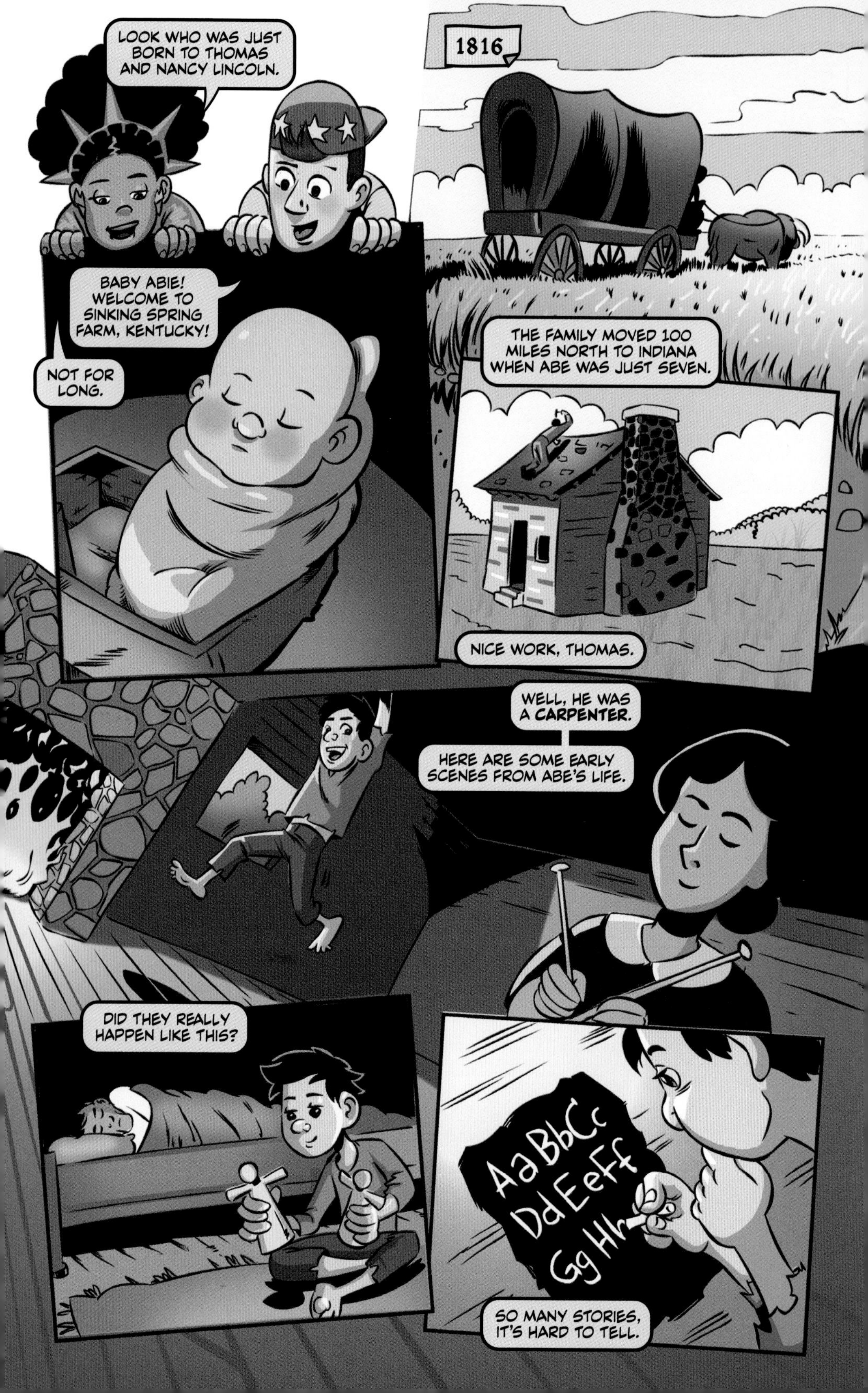
LOOK WHO WAS JUST BORN TO THOMAS AND NANCY LINCOLN.
BABY ABIE! WELCOME TO SINKING SPRING FARM, KENTUCKY!
NOT FOR LONG.
1816
THE FAMILY MOVED 100 MILES NORTH TO INDIANA WHEN ABE WAS JUST SEVEN.
NICE WORK, THOMAS.
WELL, HE WAS A CARPENTER.
HERE ARE SOME EARLY SCENES FROM ABE'S LIFE.
DID THEY REALLY HAPPEN LIKE THIS?
Aa BbCc
Dd EeFf
Gg Hh
SO MANY STORIES, IT'S HARD TO TELL.

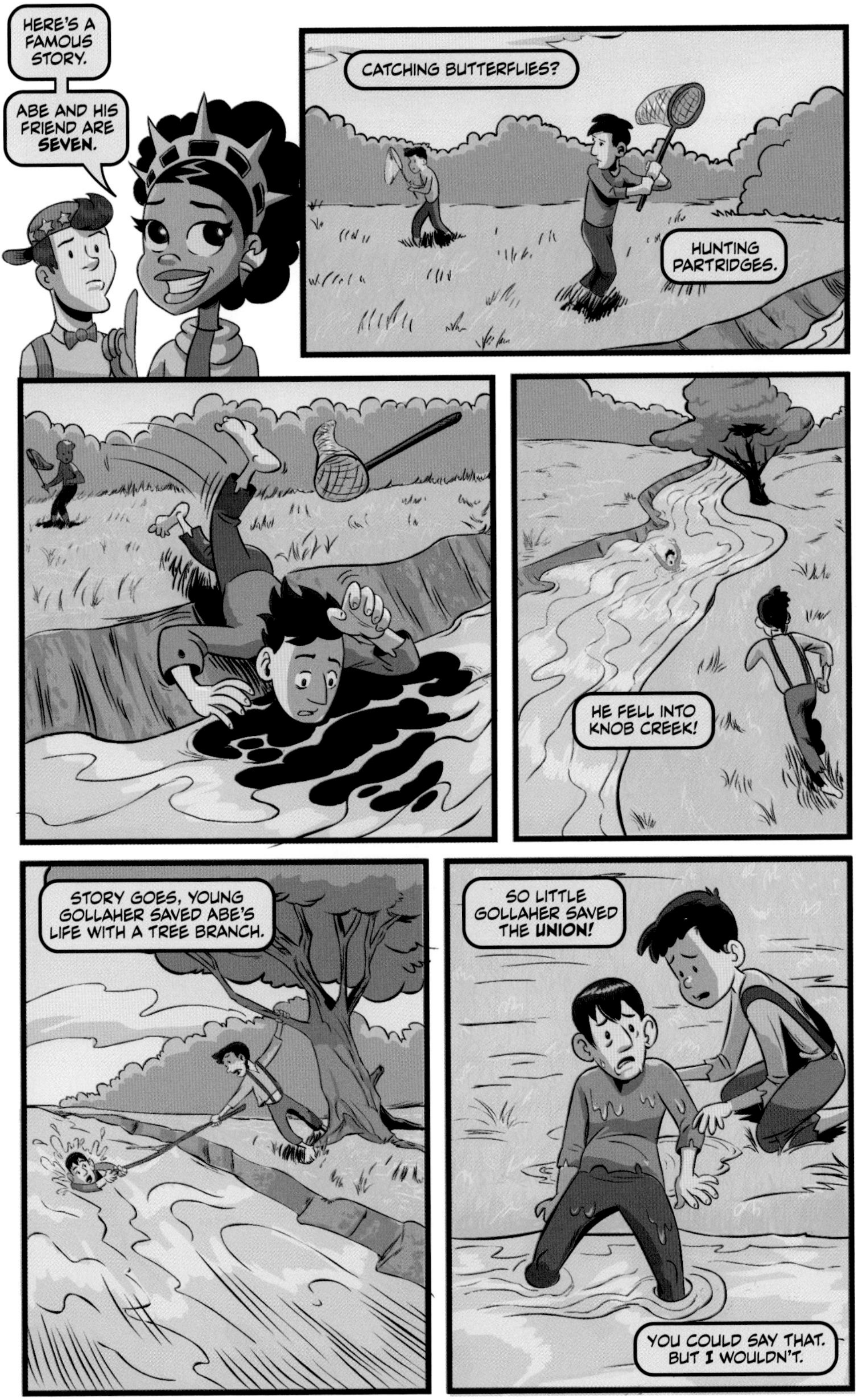
HERE'S A FAMOUS STORY.
ABE AND HIS FRIEND ARE SEVEN.
CATCHING BUTTERFLIES?
HUNTING PARTRIDGES.
HE FELL INTO KNOB CREEK!
STORY GOES, YOUNG GOLLAHER SAVED ABE'S LIFE WITH A TREE BRANCH.
SO LITTLE GOLLAHER SAVED THE UNION!
YOU COULD SAY THAT. BUT I WOULDN'T.

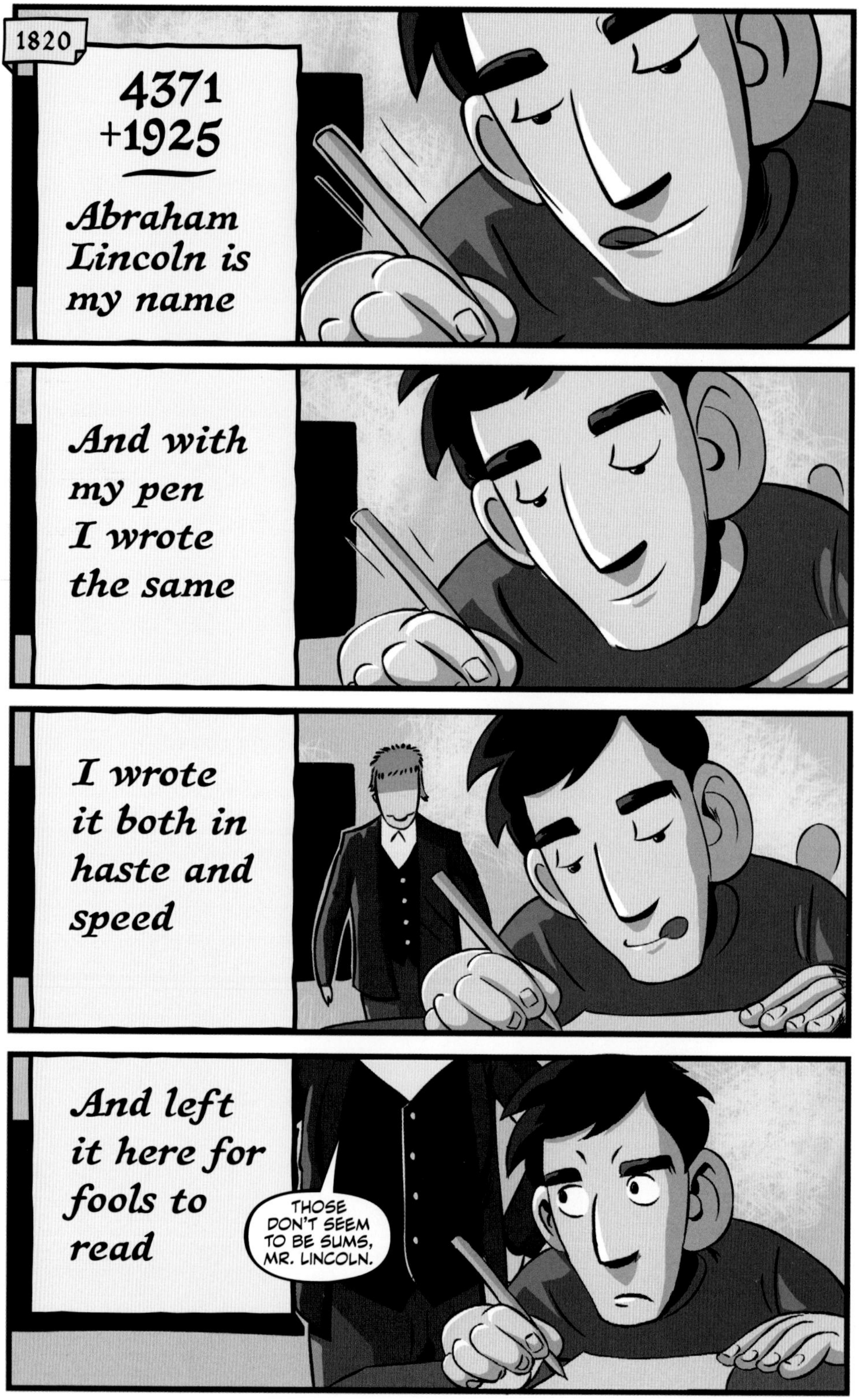
1820
4371
+1925
Abraham Lincoln is my name
And with my pen I wrote the same
I wrote it both in haste and speed
And left it here for fools to read
THOSE DON'T SEEM TO BE SUMS, MR. LINCOLN.

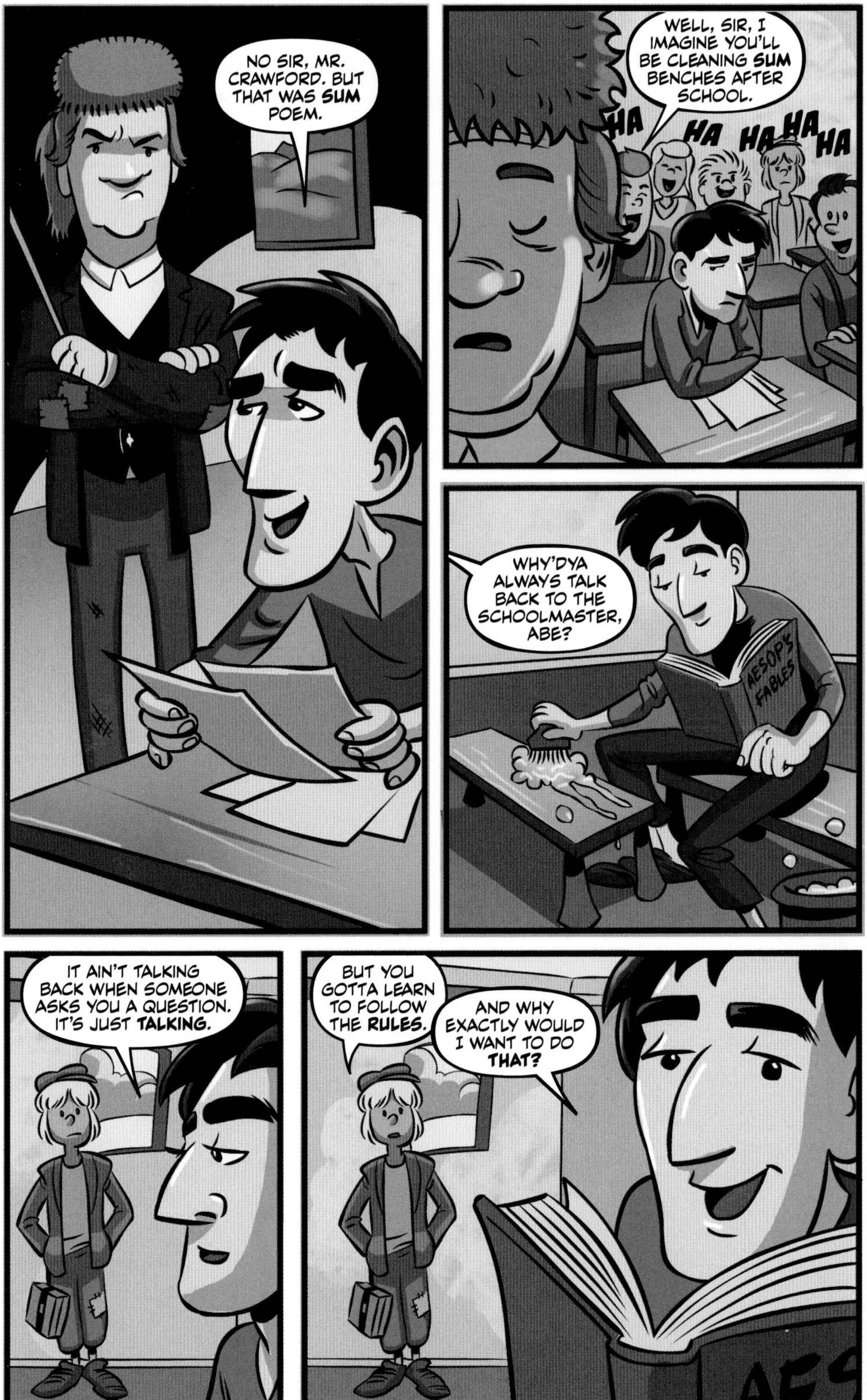
NO SIR, MR. CRAWFORD. BUT THAT WAS **SUM** POEM.
WELL, SIR, I IMAGINE YOU'LL BE CLEANING **SUM** BENCHES AFTER SCHOOL.
HA HA HA HA HA
WHY'DYA ALWAYS TALK BACK TO THE SCHOOLMASTER, ABE?
AESOP'S FABLES
IT AIN'T TALKING BACK WHEN SOMEONE ASKS YOU A QUESTION. IT'S JUST **TALKING.**
BUT YOU GOTTA LEARN TO FOLLOW THE **RULES.**
AND WHY EXACTLY WOULD I WANT TO DO **THAT?**
AES

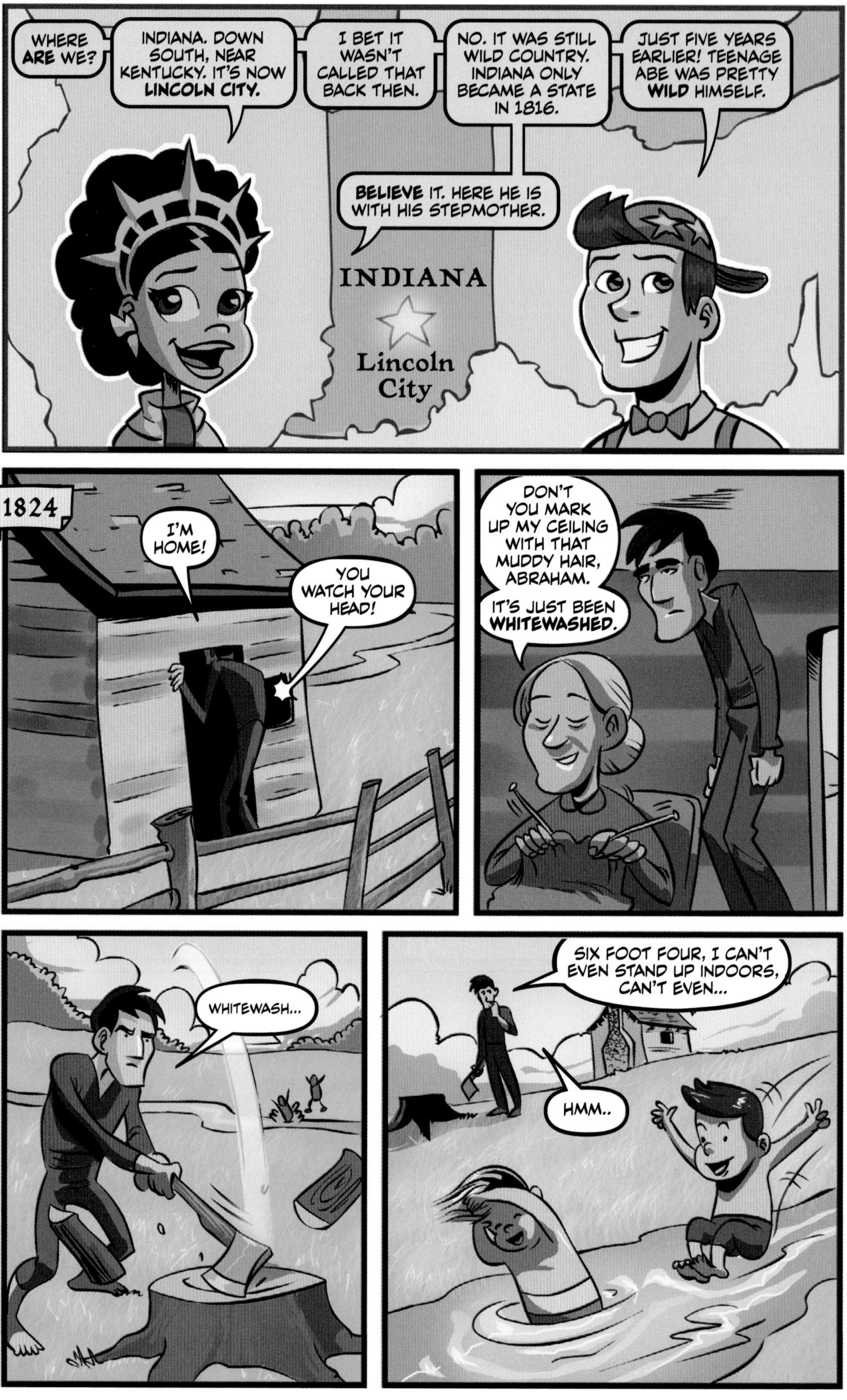
WHERE ARE WE?
INDIANA. DOWN SOUTH, NEAR KENTUCKY. IT'S NOW LINCOLN CITY.
I BET IT WASN'T CALLED THAT BACK THEN.
NO. IT WAS STILL WILD COUNTRY. INDIANA ONLY BECAME A STATE IN 1816.
JUST FIVE YEARS EARLIER! TEENAGE ABE WAS PRETTY WILD HIMSELF.
BELIEVE IT. HERE HE IS WITH HIS STEPMOTHER.
INDIANA
Lincoln City
1824
I'M HOME!
YOU WATCH YOUR HEAD!
DON'T YOU MARK UP MY CEILING WITH THAT MUDDY HAIR, ABRAHAM.
IT'S JUST BEEN WHITEWASHED.
WHITEWASH...
SIX FOOT FOUR, I CAN'T EVEN STAND UP INDOORS, CAN'T EVEN...
HMM..

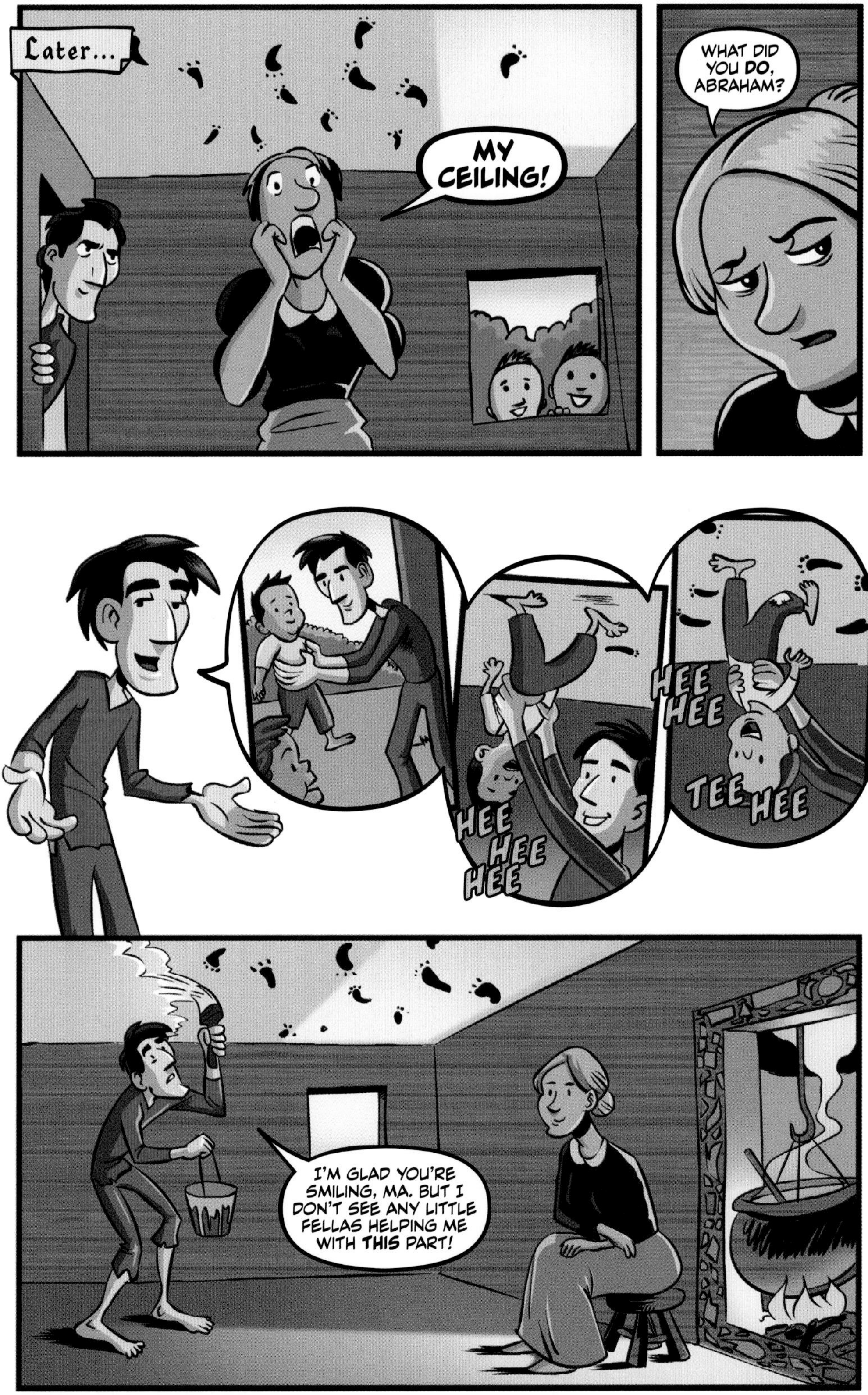
Later...
MY CEILING!
WHAT DID YOU DO, ABRAHAM?
HEE HEE HEE
HEE HEE
TEE HEE
I'M GLAD YOU'RE SMILING, MA. BUT I DON'T SEE ANY LITTLE FELLAS HELPING ME WITH THIS PART!

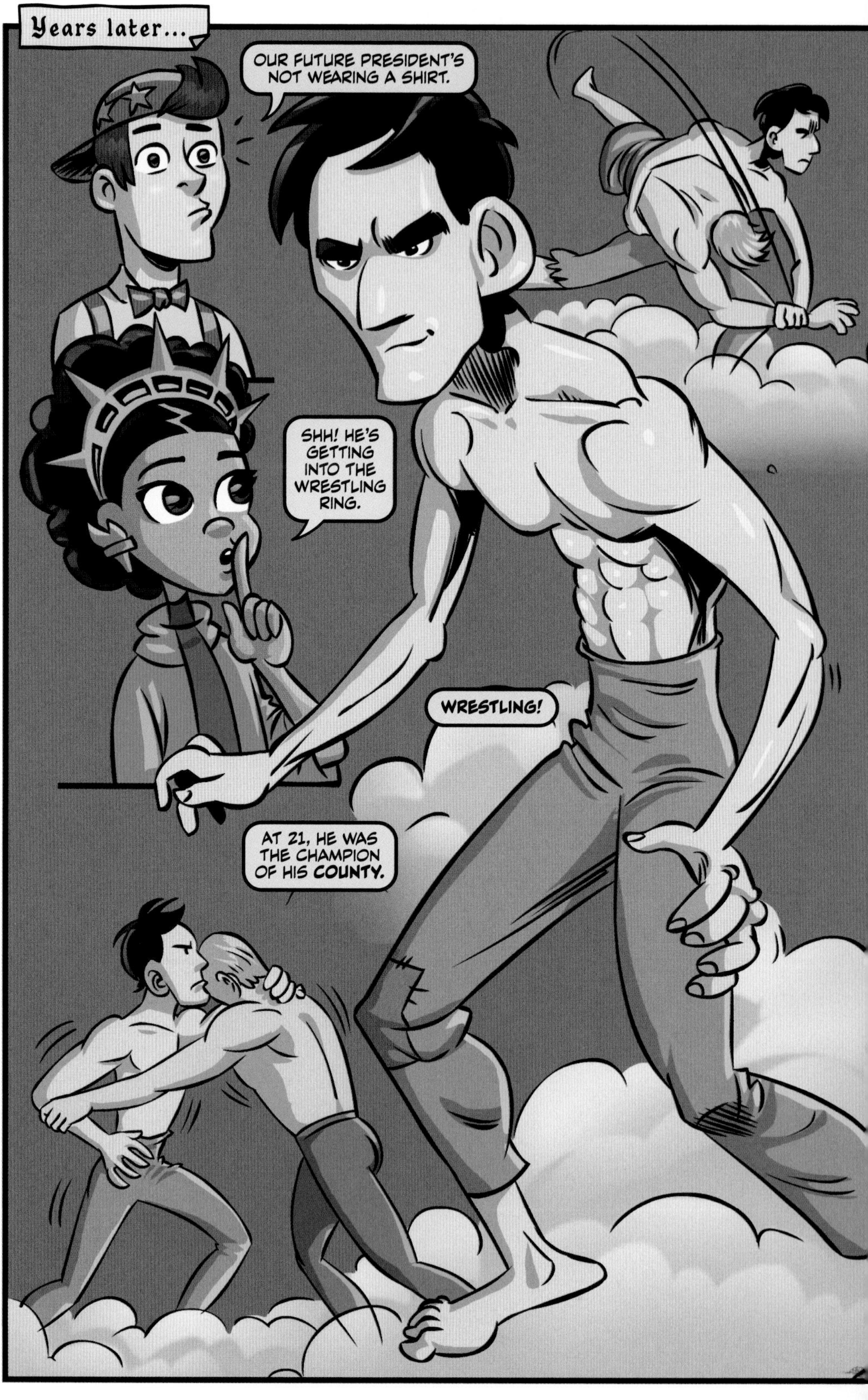
Years later...
OUR FUTURE PRESIDENT'S NOT WEARING A SHIRT.
SHH! HE'S GETTING INTO THE WRESTLING RING.
WRESTLING!
AT 21, HE WAS THE CHAMPION OF HIS COUNTY.

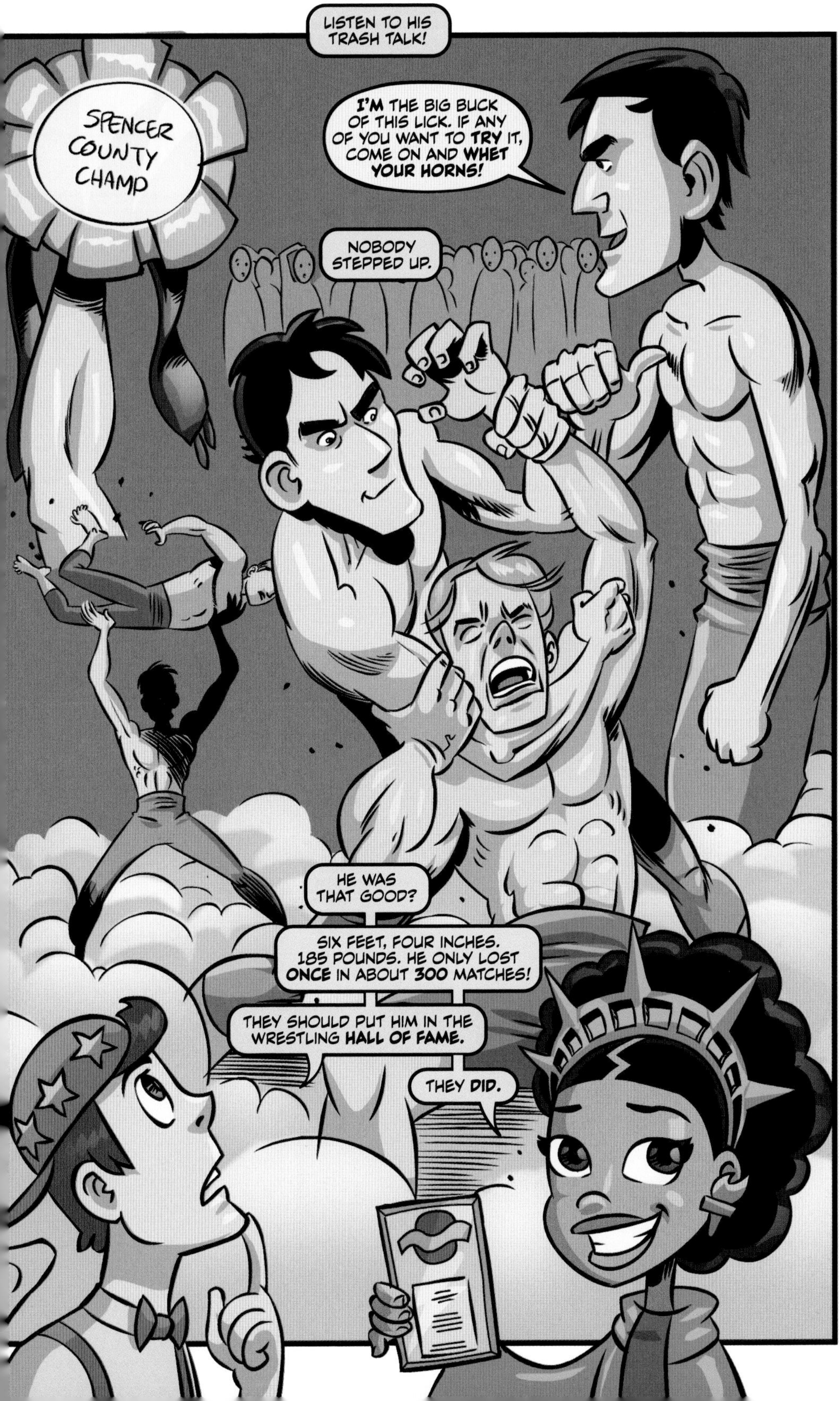
LISTEN TO HIS TRASH TALK!
SPENCER COUNTY CHAMP
I'M THE BIG BUCK OF THIS LICK. IF ANY OF YOU WANT TO TRY IT, COME ON AND WHET YOUR HORNS!
NOBODY STEPPED UP.
HE WAS THAT GOOD?
SIX FEET, FOUR INCHES. 185 POUNDS. HE ONLY LOST ONCE IN ABOUT 300 MATCHES!
THEY SHOULD PUT HIM IN THE WRESTLING HALL OF FAME.
THEY DID.

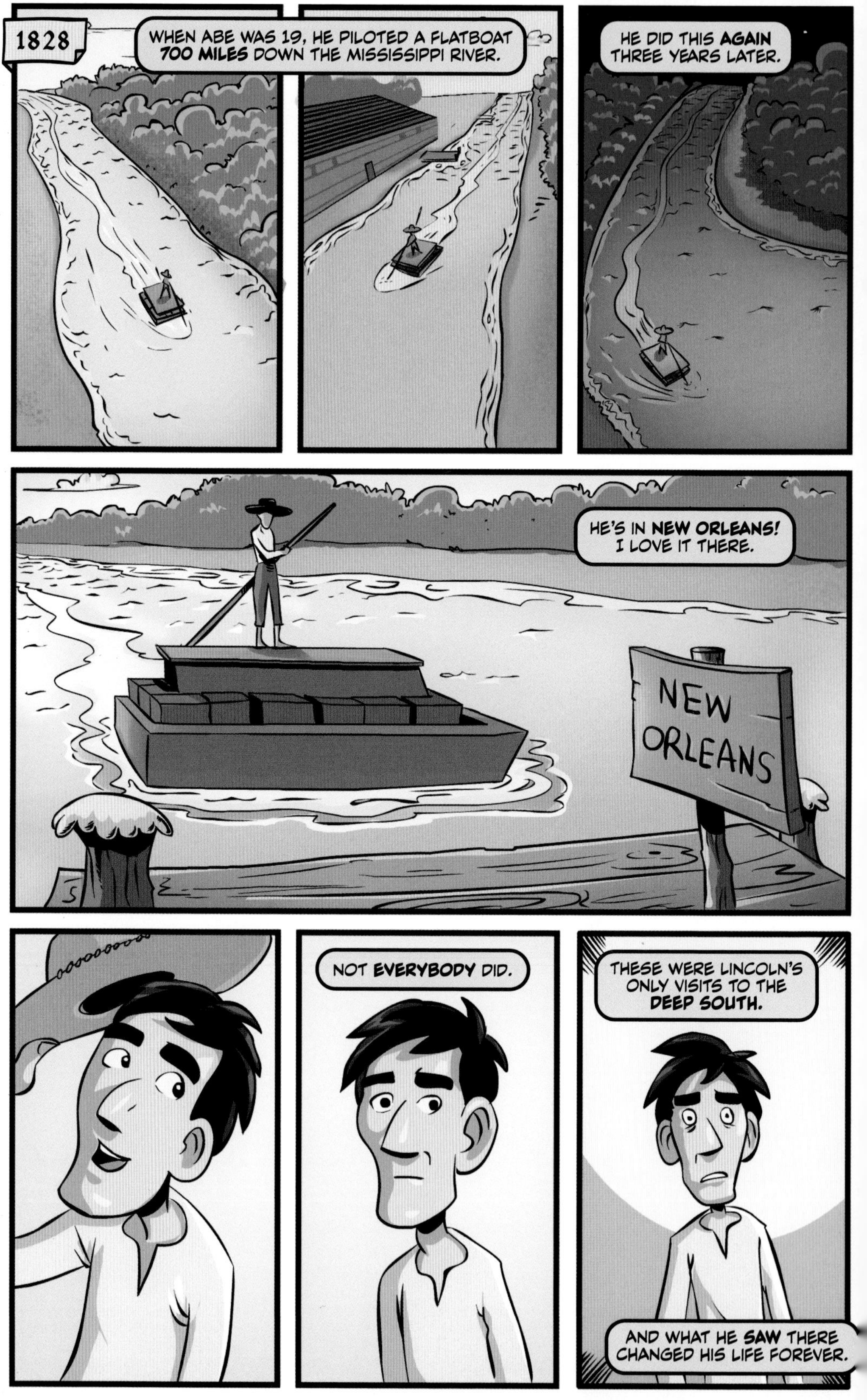

1828
WHEN ABE WAS 19, HE PILOTED A FLATBOAT 700 MILES DOWN THE MISSISSIPPI RIVER.
HE DID THIS AGAIN THREE YEARS LATER.
HE'S IN NEW ORLEANS! I LOVE IT THERE.
NEW ORLEANS
NOT EVERYBODY DID.
THESE WERE LINCOLN'S ONLY VISITS TO THE DEEP SOUTH.
AND WHAT HE SAW THERE CHANGED HIS LIFE FOREVER.

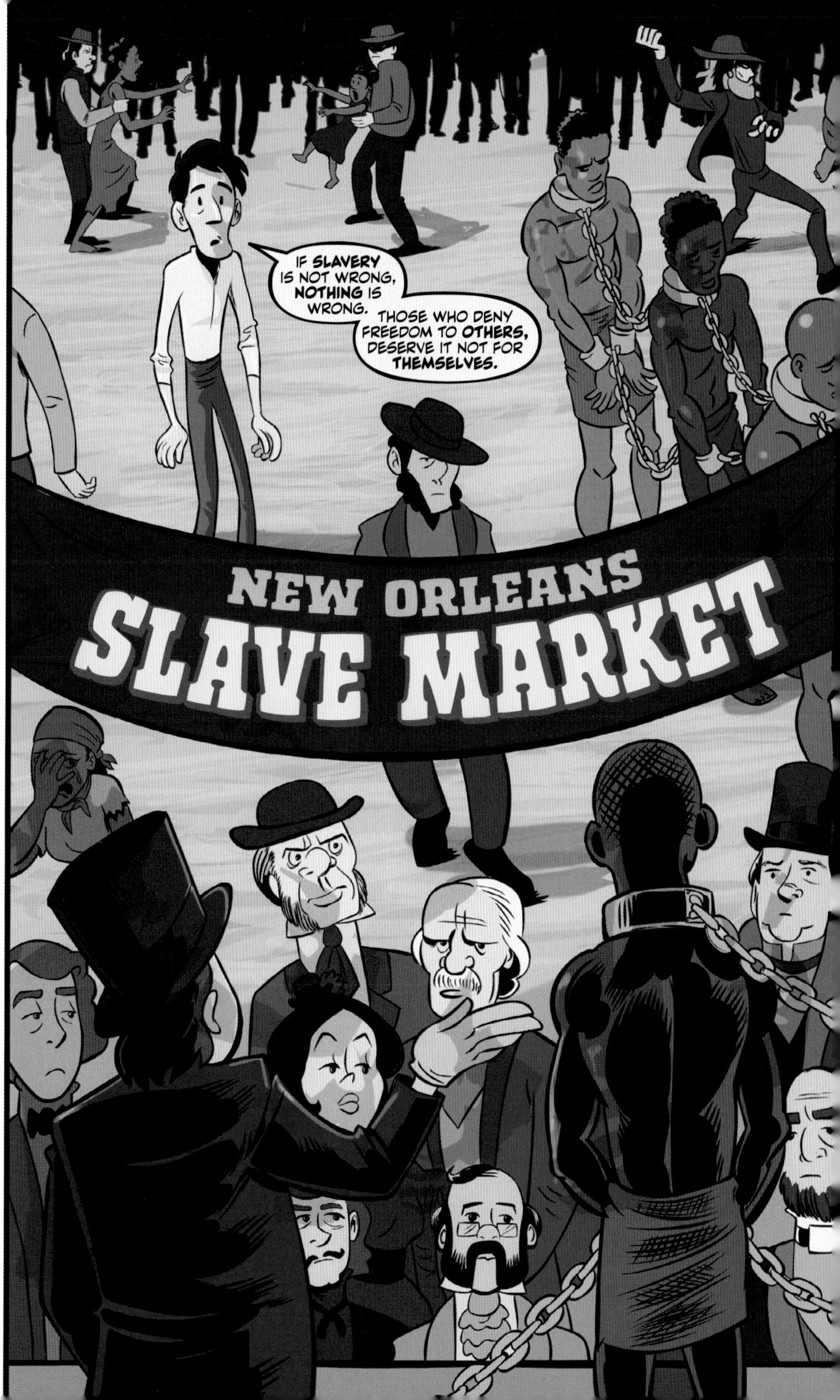
IF **SLAVERY** IS NOT WRONG, **NOTHING** IS WRONG.
THOSE WHO DENY FREEDOM TO **OTHERS**, DESERVE IT NOT FOR **THEMSELVES.**
NEW ORLEANS
SLAVE MARKET

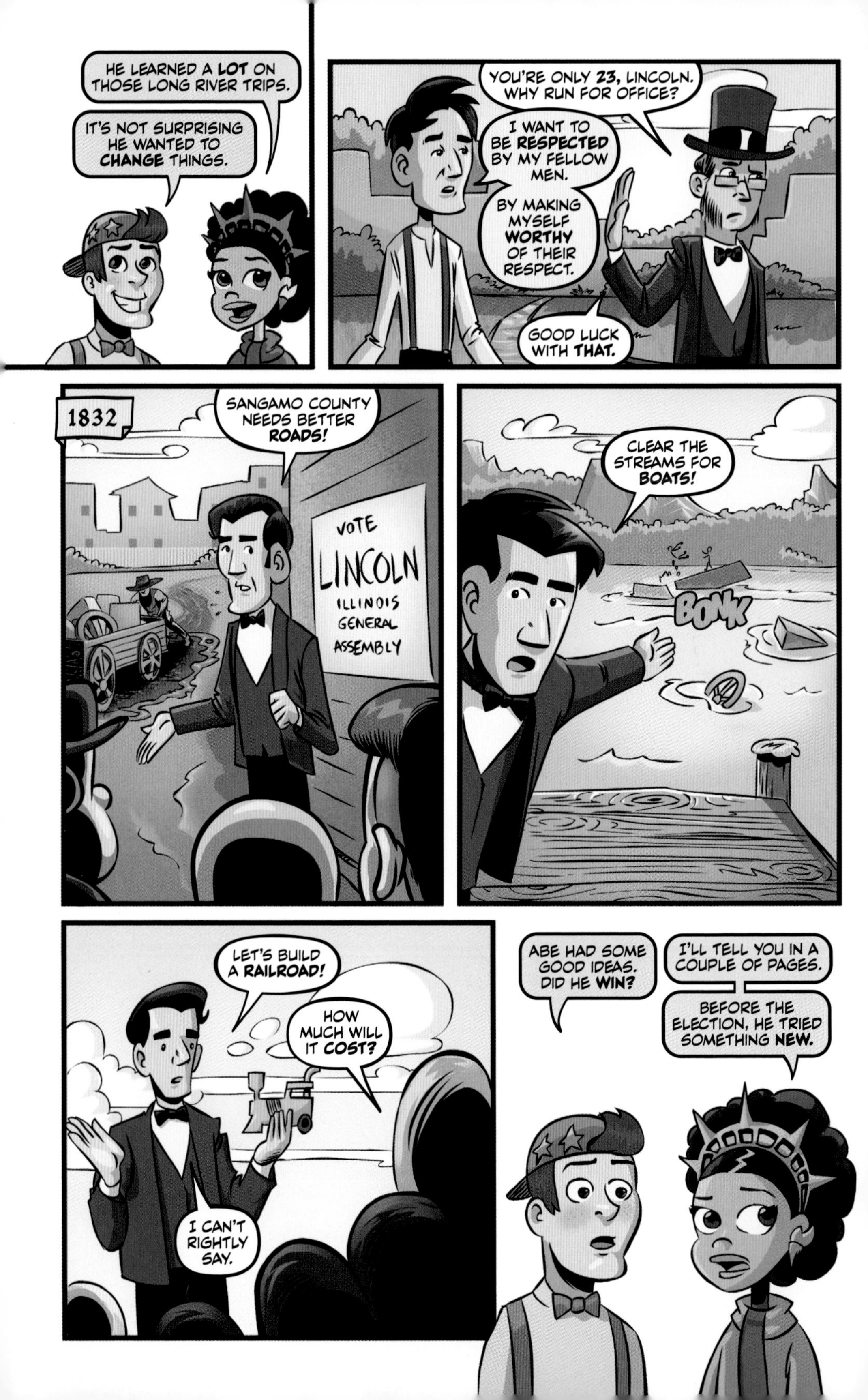
HE LEARNED A LOT ON THOSE LONG RIVER TRIPS.
IT'S NOT SURPRISING HE WANTED TO CHANGE THINGS.
YOU'RE ONLY 23, LINCOLN. WHY RUN FOR OFFICE?
I WANT TO BE RESPECTED BY MY FELLOW MEN.
BY MAKING MYSELF WORTHY OF THEIR RESPECT.
GOOD LUCK WITH THAT.
1832
SANGAMO COUNTY NEEDS BETTER ROADS!
VOTE LINCOLN ILLINOIS GENERAL ASSEMBLY
CLEAR THE STREAMS FOR BOATS!
BONK
LET'S BUILD A RAILROAD!
HOW MUCH WILL IT COST?
I CAN'T RIGHTLY SAY.
ABE HAD SOME GOOD IDEAS. DID HE WIN?
I'LL TELL YOU IN A COUPLE OF PAGES.
BEFORE THE ELECTION, HE TRIED SOMETHING NEW.

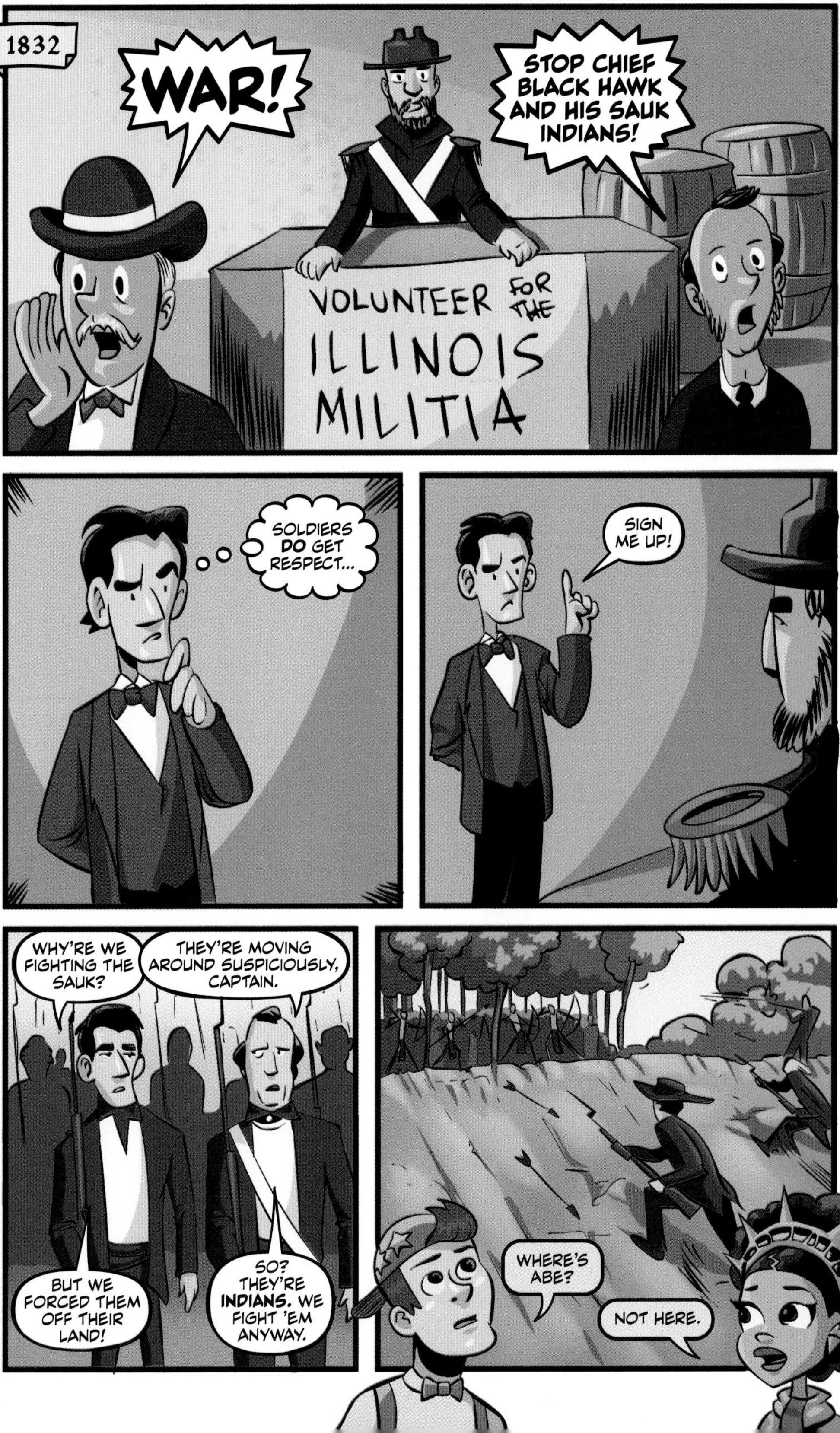
1832
WAR!
STOP CHIEF BLACK HAWK AND HIS SAUK INDIANS!
VOLUNTEER FOR THE ILLINOIS MILITIA
SOLDIERS DO GET RESPECT...
SIGN ME UP!
WHY'RE WE FIGHTING THE SAUK?
THEY'RE MOVING AROUND SUSPICIOUSLY, CAPTAIN.
BUT WE FORCED THEM OFF THEIR LAND!
SO? THEY'RE INDIANS. WE FIGHT 'EM ANYWAY.
WHERE'S ABE?
NOT HERE.

THE BLACK HAWK WAR OF 1832 LASTED FOUR MONTHS. ABE LASTED **THREE**.

DID HE SEE LOTS OF ACTION?

SEE FOR YOURSELF.

HOW COULD IT GET **WORSE**?

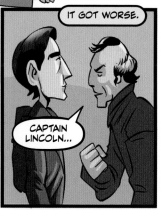

IT GOT WORSE.

CAPTAIN LINCOLN...

... YOU'RE DISCHARGED!

Soon

YOU WANT TO COME BACK? NOW YOU'RE **PRIVATE** LINCOLN!

PRIVATE LINCOLN! YOU'RE DISCHARGED!

YOU WANT TO COME BACK? YOU CAN BE A **SPY**.

AN **INDEPENDENT** SPY.

MY WAR STORIES WILL SOUND A GREAT DEAL BETTER THAN THE REALITY.

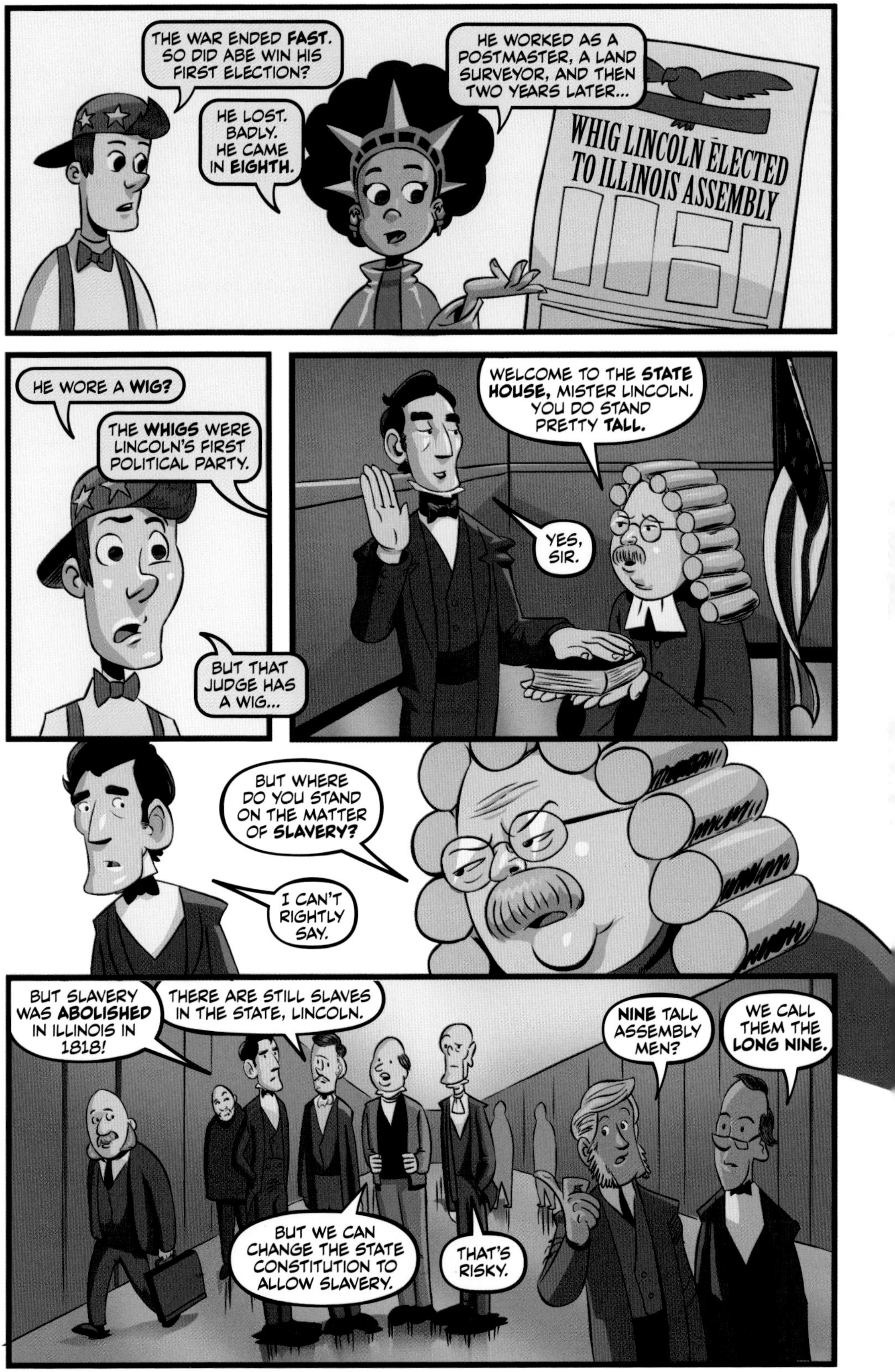

THE WAR ENDED **FAST**. SO DID ABE WIN HIS FIRST ELECTION?
HE LOST. BADLY. HE CAME IN **EIGHTH**.
HE WORKED AS A POSTMASTER, A LAND SURVEYOR, AND THEN TWO YEARS LATER...
WHIG LINCOLN ELECTED TO ILLINOIS ASSEMBLY
HE WORE A **WIG?**
THE **WHIGS** WERE LINCOLN'S FIRST POLITICAL PARTY.
BUT THAT JUDGE HAS A WIG...
WELCOME TO THE **STATE HOUSE,** MISTER LINCOLN. YOU DO STAND PRETTY **TALL.**
YES, SIR.
BUT WHERE DO YOU STAND ON THE MATTER OF **SLAVERY?**
I CAN'T RIGHTLY SAY.
BUT SLAVERY WAS **ABOLISHED** IN ILLINOIS IN 1818!
THERE ARE STILL SLAVES IN THE STATE, LINCOLN.
BUT WE CAN CHANGE THE STATE CONSTITUTION TO ALLOW SLAVERY.
THAT'S RISKY.
NINE TALL ASSEMBLY MEN?
WE CALL THEM THE **LONG NINE.**

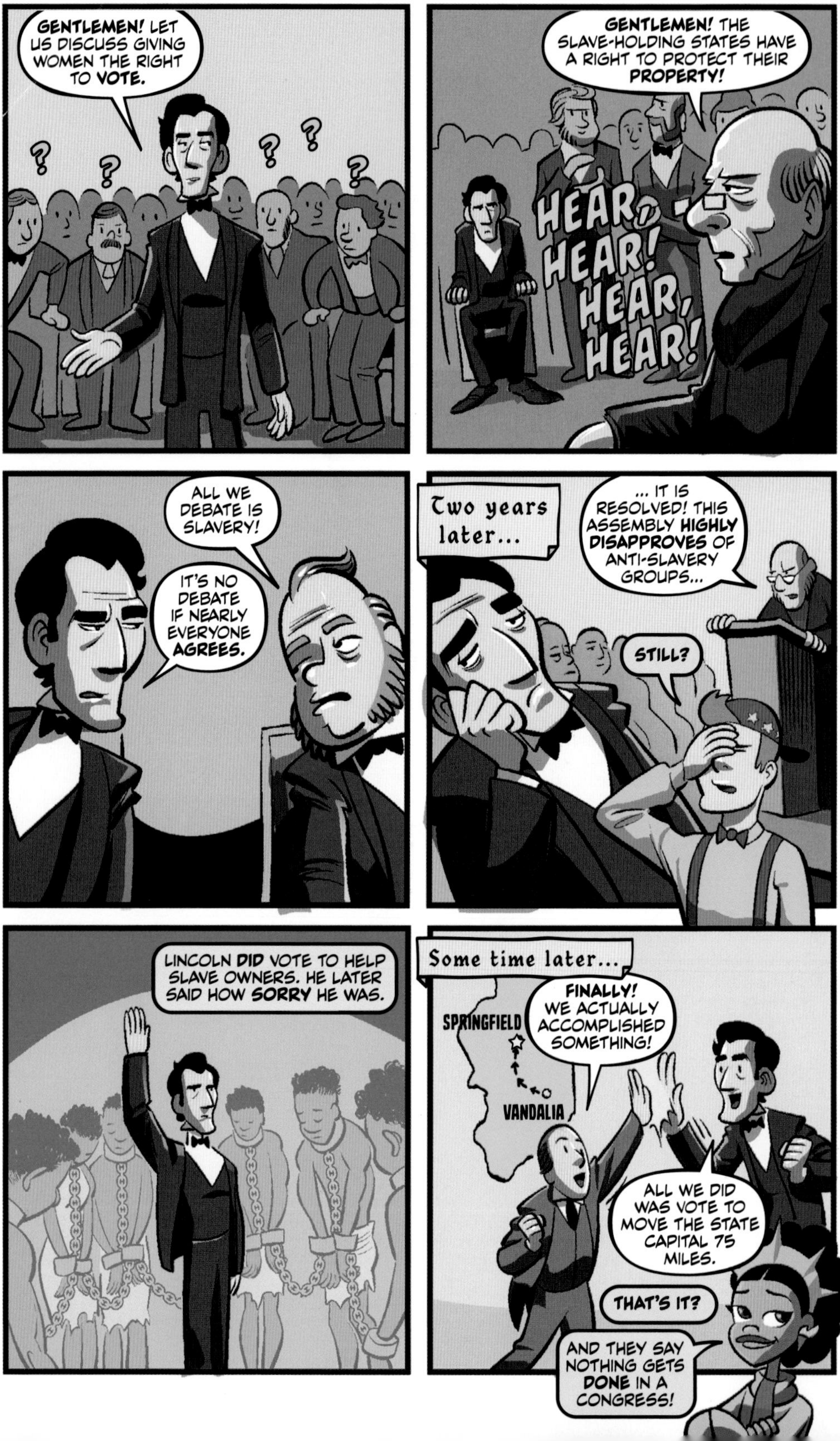
GENTLEMEN! LET US DISCUSS GIVING WOMEN THE RIGHT TO VOTE.
?
GENTLEMEN! THE SLAVE-HOLDING STATES HAVE A RIGHT TO PROTECT THEIR PROPERTY!
HEAR, HEAR! HEAR, HEAR!
ALL WE DEBATE IS SLAVERY!
IT'S NO DEBATE IF NEARLY EVERYONE AGREES.
Two years later...
... IT IS RESOLVED! THIS ASSEMBLY HIGHLY DISAPPROVES OF ANTI-SLAVERY GROUPS...
STILL?
LINCOLN DID VOTE TO HELP SLAVE OWNERS. HE LATER SAID HOW SORRY HE WAS.
Some time later...
SPRINGFIELD
VANDALIA
FINALLY! WE ACTUALLY ACCOMPLISHED SOMETHING!
ALL WE DID WAS VOTE TO MOVE THE STATE CAPITAL 75 MILES.
THAT'S IT?
AND THEY SAY NOTHING GETS DONE IN A CONGRESS!

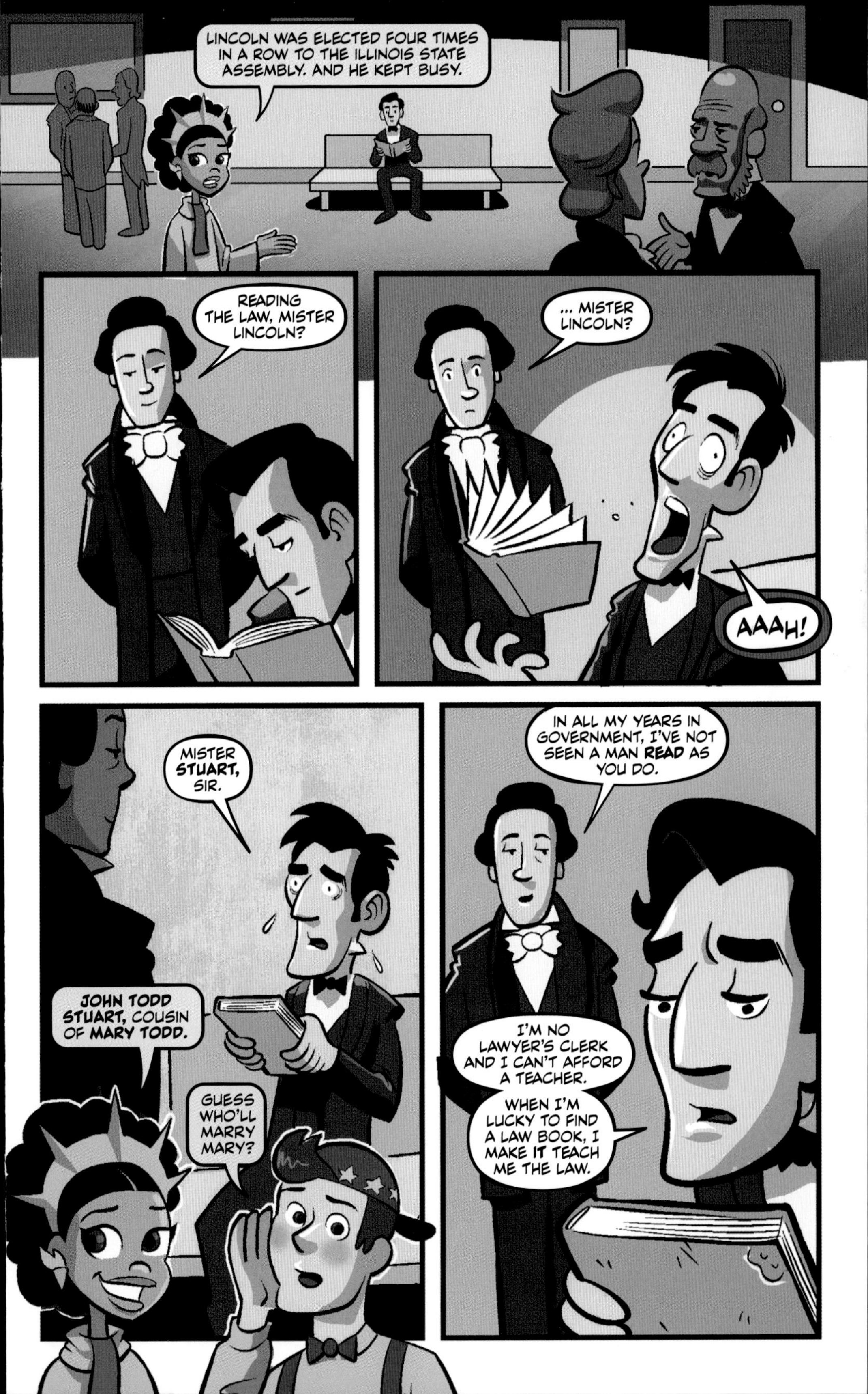

LINCOLN WAS ELECTED FOUR TIMES IN A ROW TO THE ILLINOIS STATE ASSEMBLY. AND HE KEPT BUSY.
READING THE LAW, MISTER LINCOLN?
... MISTER LINCOLN?
AAAH!
MISTER **STUART,** SIR.
JOHN TODD STUART, COUSIN OF **MARY TODD.**
GUESS WHO'LL MARRY MARY?
IN ALL MY YEARS IN GOVERNMENT, I'VE NOT SEEN A MAN **READ** AS YOU DO.
I'M NO LAWYER'S CLERK AND I CAN'T AFFORD A TEACHER.
WHEN I'M LUCKY TO FIND A LAW BOOK, I MAKE **IT** TEACH ME THE LAW.

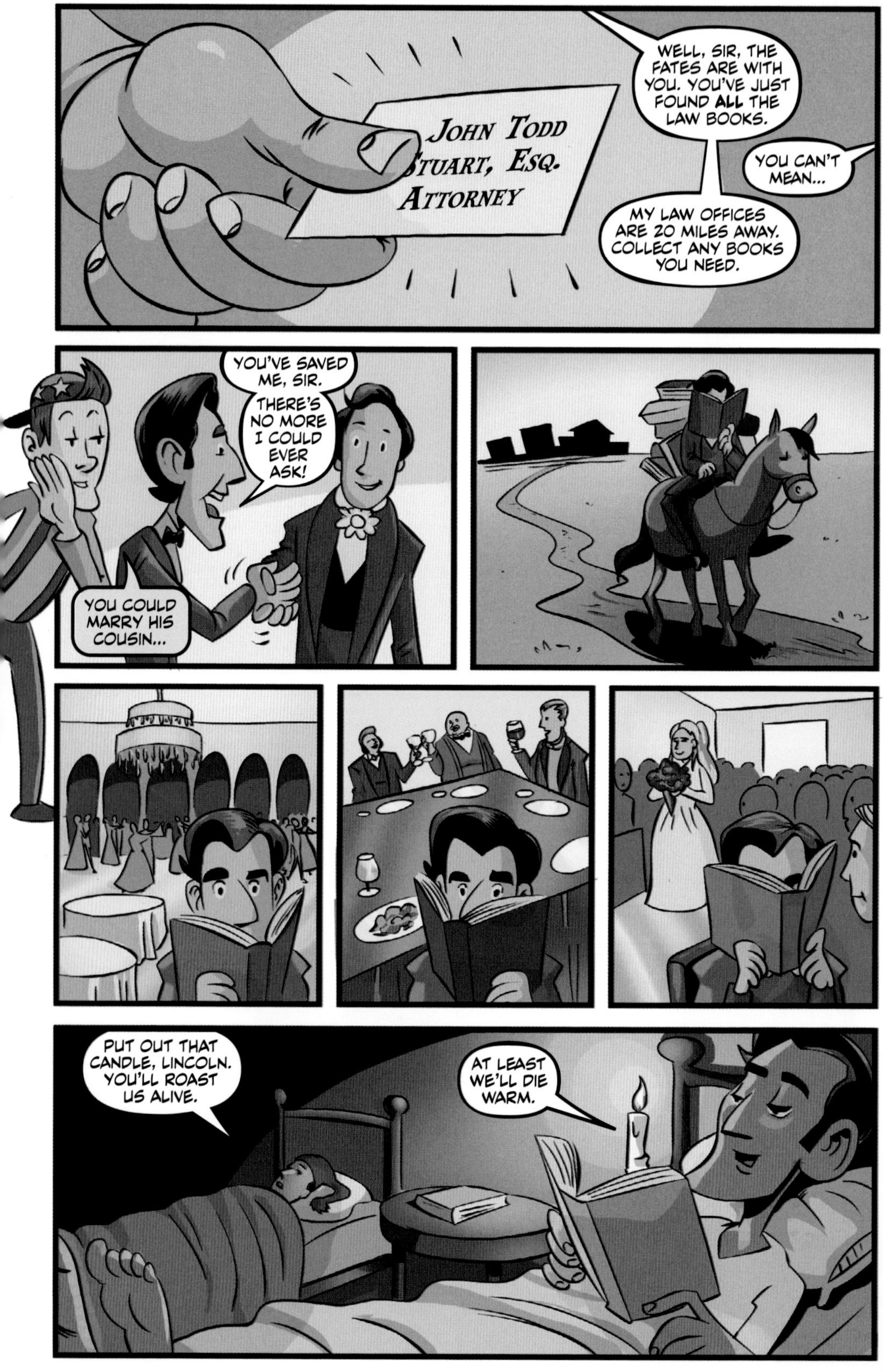
JOHN TODD STUART, ESQ. ATTORNEY
WELL, SIR, THE FATES ARE WITH YOU. YOU'VE JUST FOUND **ALL** THE LAW BOOKS.
YOU CAN'T MEAN...
MY LAW OFFICES ARE 20 MILES AWAY. COLLECT ANY BOOKS YOU NEED.
YOU'VE SAVED ME, SIR.
THERE'S NO MORE I COULD EVER ASK!
YOU COULD MARRY HIS COUSIN...
PUT OUT THAT CANDLE, LINCOLN. YOU'LL ROAST US ALIVE.
AT LEAST WE'LL DIE WARM.

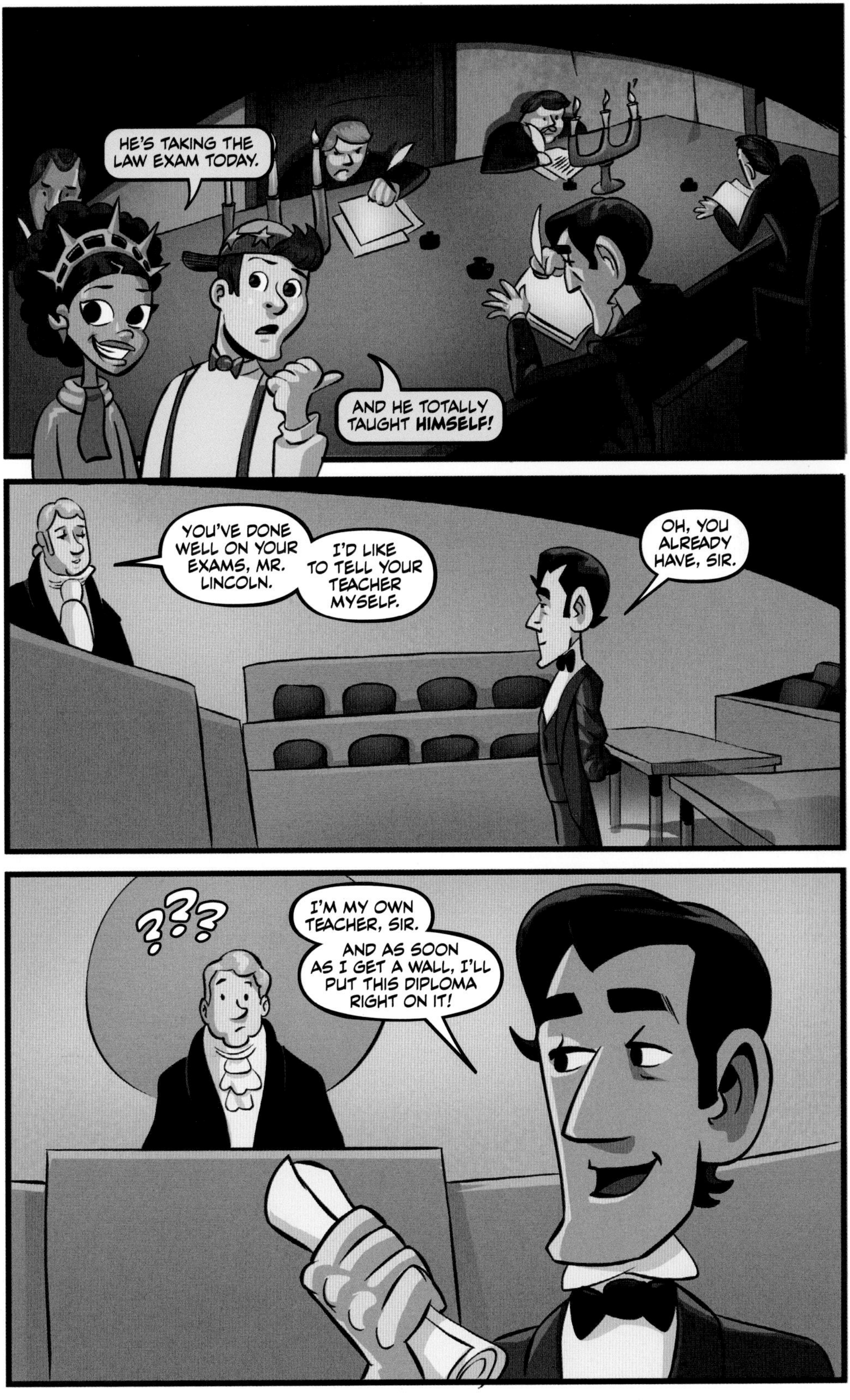
HE'S TAKING THE LAW EXAM TODAY.
AND HE TOTALLY TAUGHT **HIMSELF**!
YOU'VE DONE WELL ON YOUR EXAMS, MR. LINCOLN.
I'D LIKE TO TELL YOUR TEACHER MYSELF.
OH, YOU ALREADY HAVE, SIR.
???
I'M MY OWN TEACHER, SIR.
AND AS SOON AS I GET A WALL, I'LL PUT THIS DIPLOMA RIGHT ON IT!

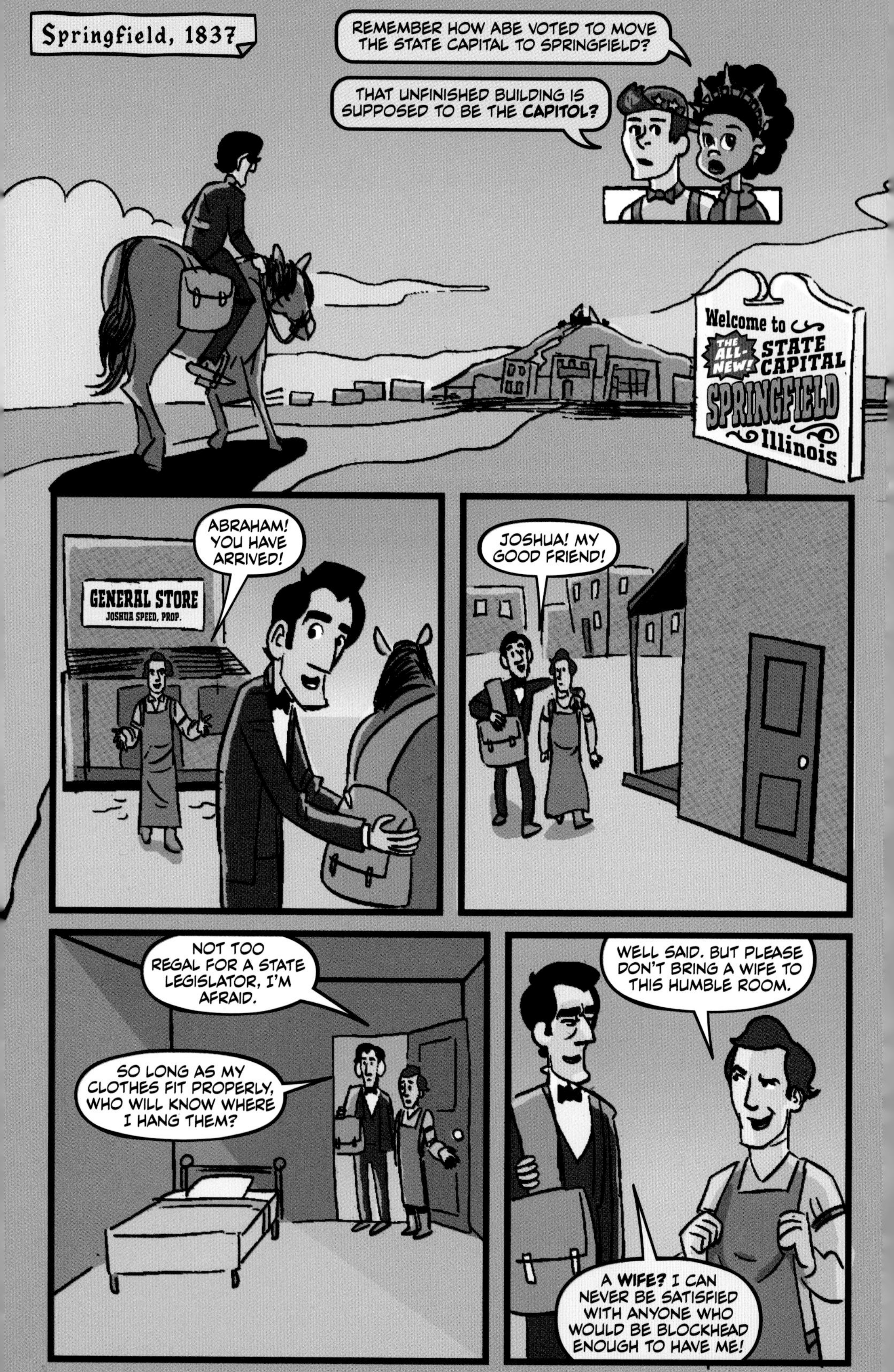
Springfield, 1837
REMEMBER HOW ABE VOTED TO MOVE THE STATE CAPITAL TO SPRINGFIELD?
THAT UNFINISHED BUILDING IS SUPPOSED TO BE THE CAPITOL?
Welcome to THE ALL-NEW! STATE CAPITAL SPRINGFIELD Illinois
ABRAHAM! YOU HAVE ARRIVED!
GENERAL STORE
JOSHUA SPEED, PROP.
JOSHUA! MY GOOD FRIEND!
NOT TOO REGAL FOR A STATE LEGISLATOR, I'M AFRAID.
SO LONG AS MY CLOTHES FIT PROPERLY, WHO WILL KNOW WHERE I HANG THEM?
WELL SAID. BUT PLEASE DON'T BRING A WIFE TO THIS HUMBLE ROOM.
A WIFE? I CAN NEVER BE SATISFIED WITH ANYONE WHO WOULD BE BLOCKHEAD ENOUGH TO HAVE ME!

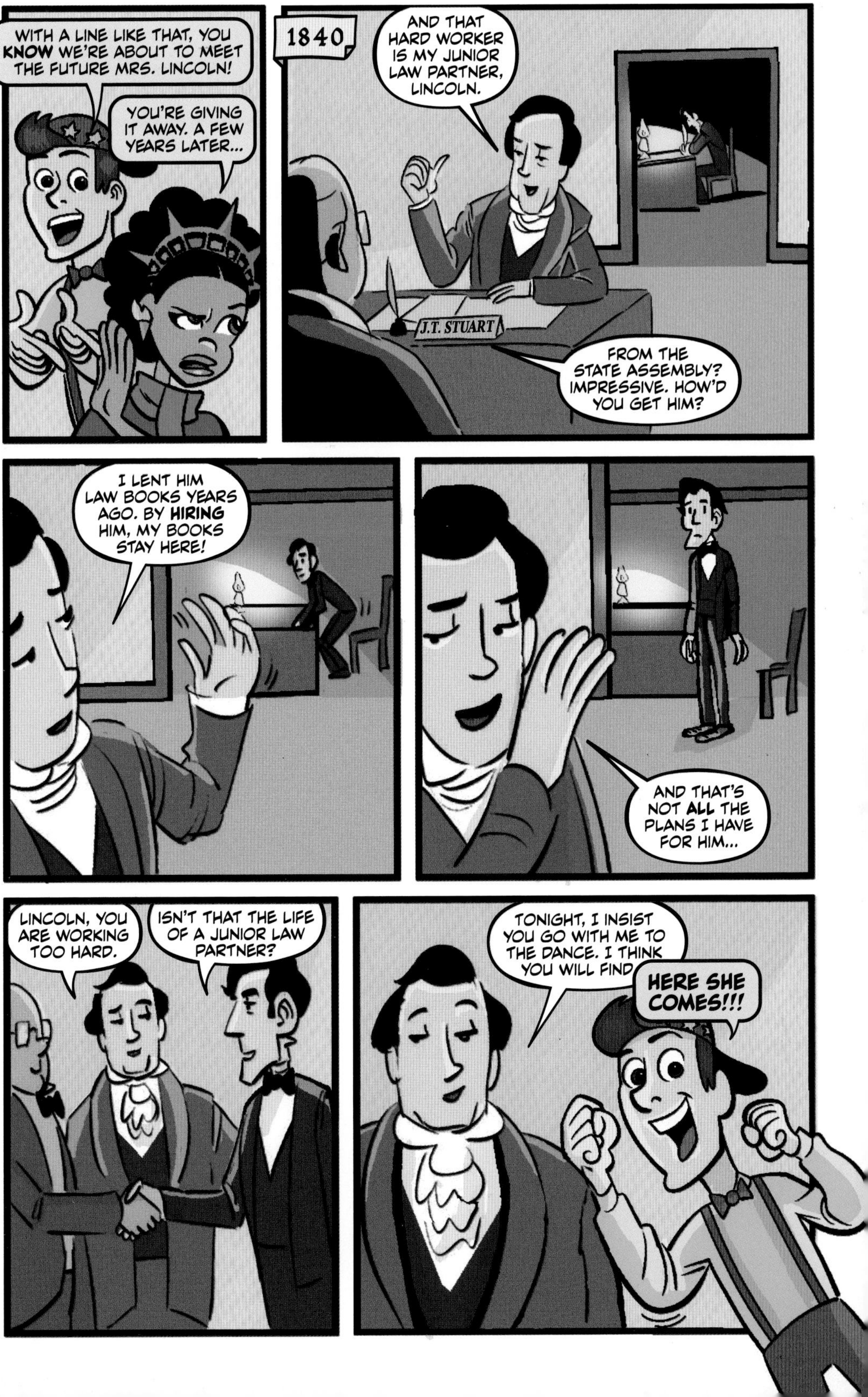
WITH A LINE LIKE THAT, YOU **KNOW** WE'RE ABOUT TO MEET THE FUTURE MRS. LINCOLN!
YOU'RE GIVING IT AWAY. A FEW YEARS LATER...
1840
AND THAT HARD WORKER IS MY JUNIOR LAW PARTNER, LINCOLN.
J.T. STUART
FROM THE STATE ASSEMBLY? IMPRESSIVE. HOW'D YOU GET HIM?
I LENT HIM LAW BOOKS YEARS AGO. BY **HIRING** HIM, MY BOOKS STAY HERE!
AND THAT'S NOT **ALL** THE PLANS I HAVE FOR HIM...
LINCOLN, YOU ARE WORKING TOO HARD.
ISN'T THAT THE LIFE OF A JUNIOR LAW PARTNER?
TONIGHT, I INSIST YOU GO WITH ME TO THE DANCE. I THINK YOU WILL FIND
HERE SHE COMES!!!

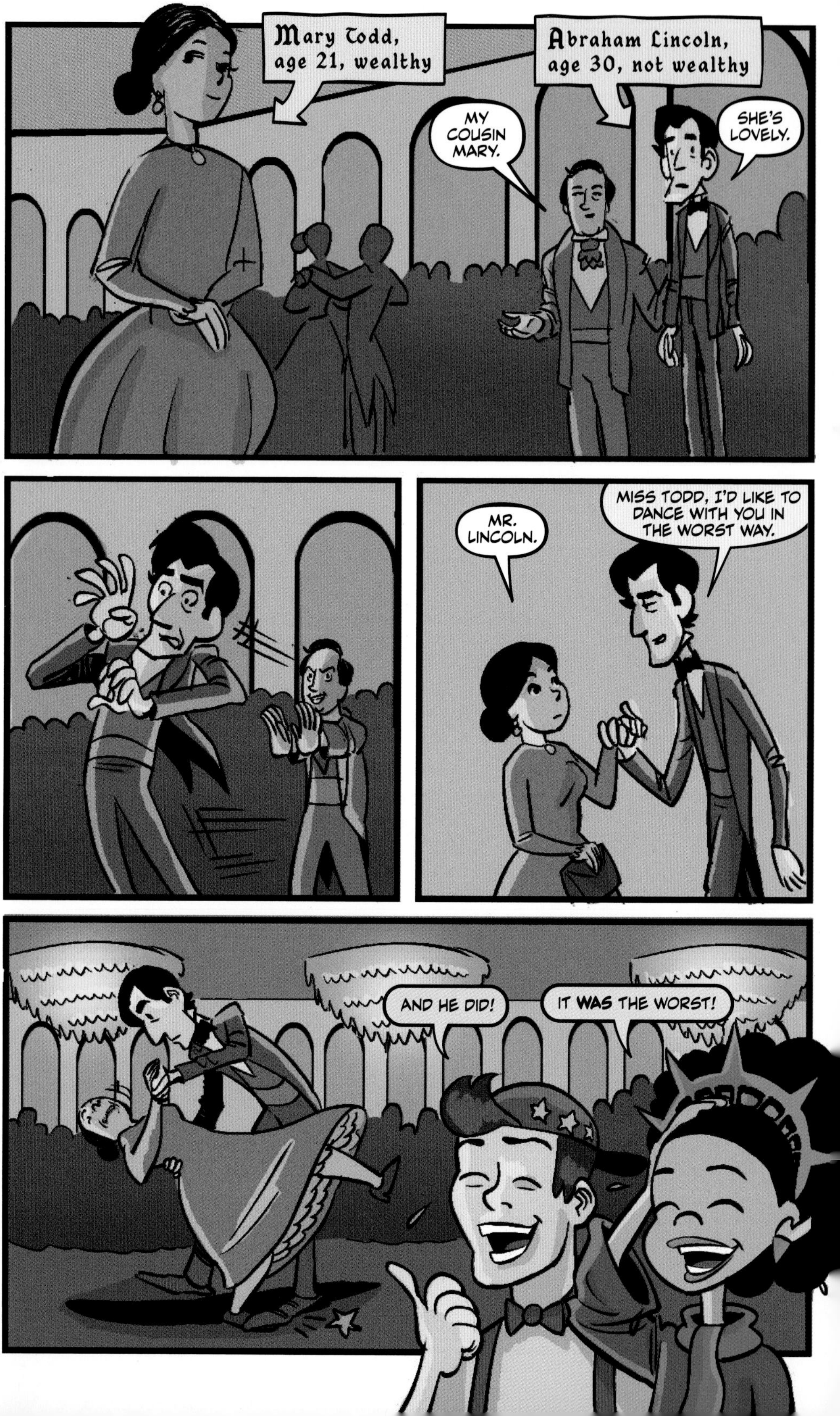
Mary Todd, age 21, wealthy
Abraham Lincoln, age 30, not wealthy
MY COUSIN MARY.
SHE'S LOVELY.
MR. LINCOLN.
MISS TODD, I'D LIKE TO DANCE WITH YOU IN THE WORST WAY.
AND HE DID!
IT WAS THE WORST!

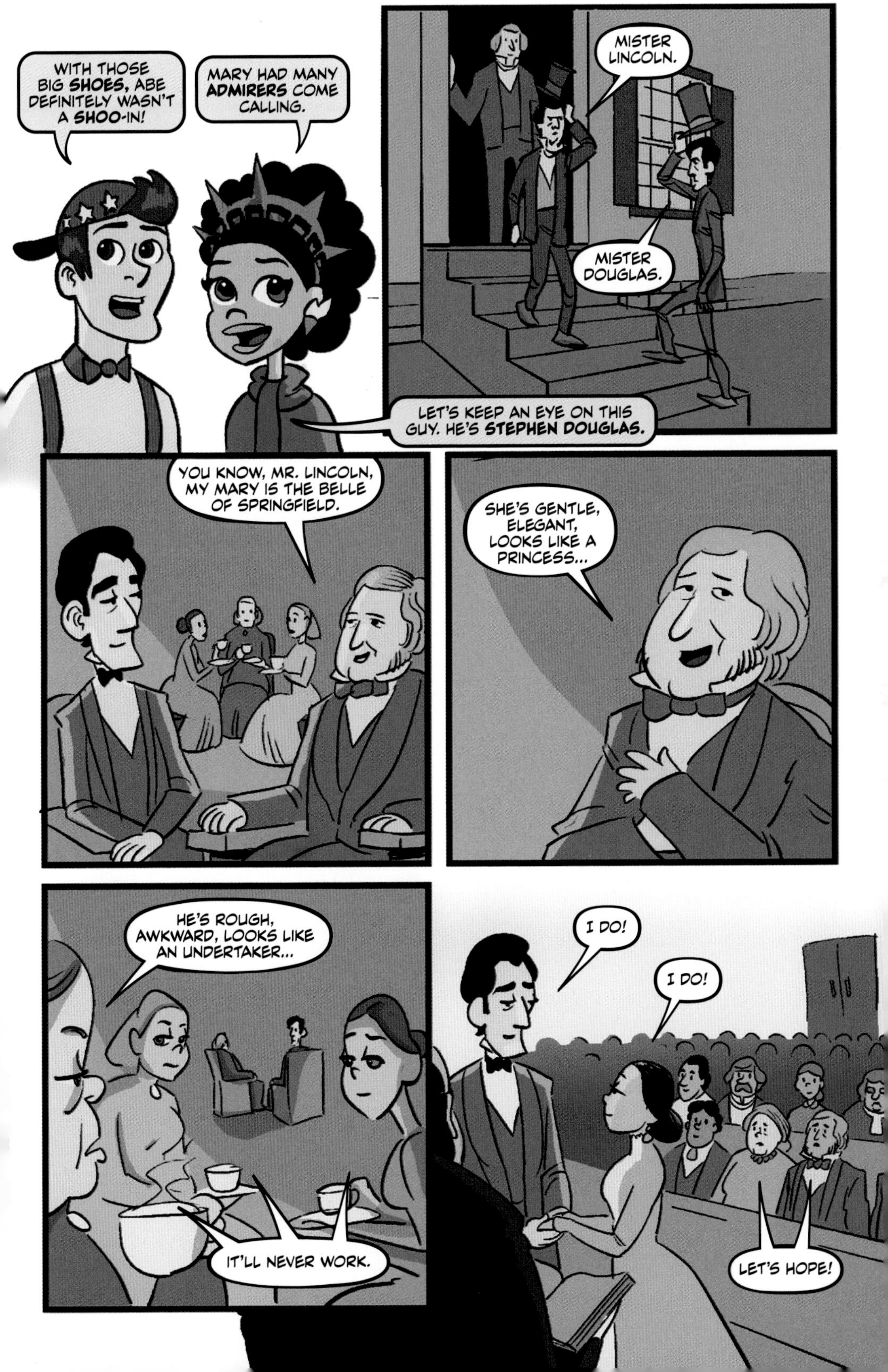
WITH THOSE BIG SHOES, ABE DEFINITELY WASN'T A SHOO-IN!
MARY HAD MANY ADMIRERS COME CALLING.
MISTER LINCOLN.
MISTER DOUGLAS.
LET'S KEEP AN EYE ON THIS GUY. HE'S STEPHEN DOUGLAS.
YOU KNOW, MR. LINCOLN, MY MARY IS THE BELLE OF SPRINGFIELD.
SHE'S GENTLE, ELEGANT, LOOKS LIKE A PRINCESS...
HE'S ROUGH, AWKWARD, LOOKS LIKE AN UNDERTAKER...
IT'LL NEVER WORK.
I DO!
I DO!
LET'S HOPE!

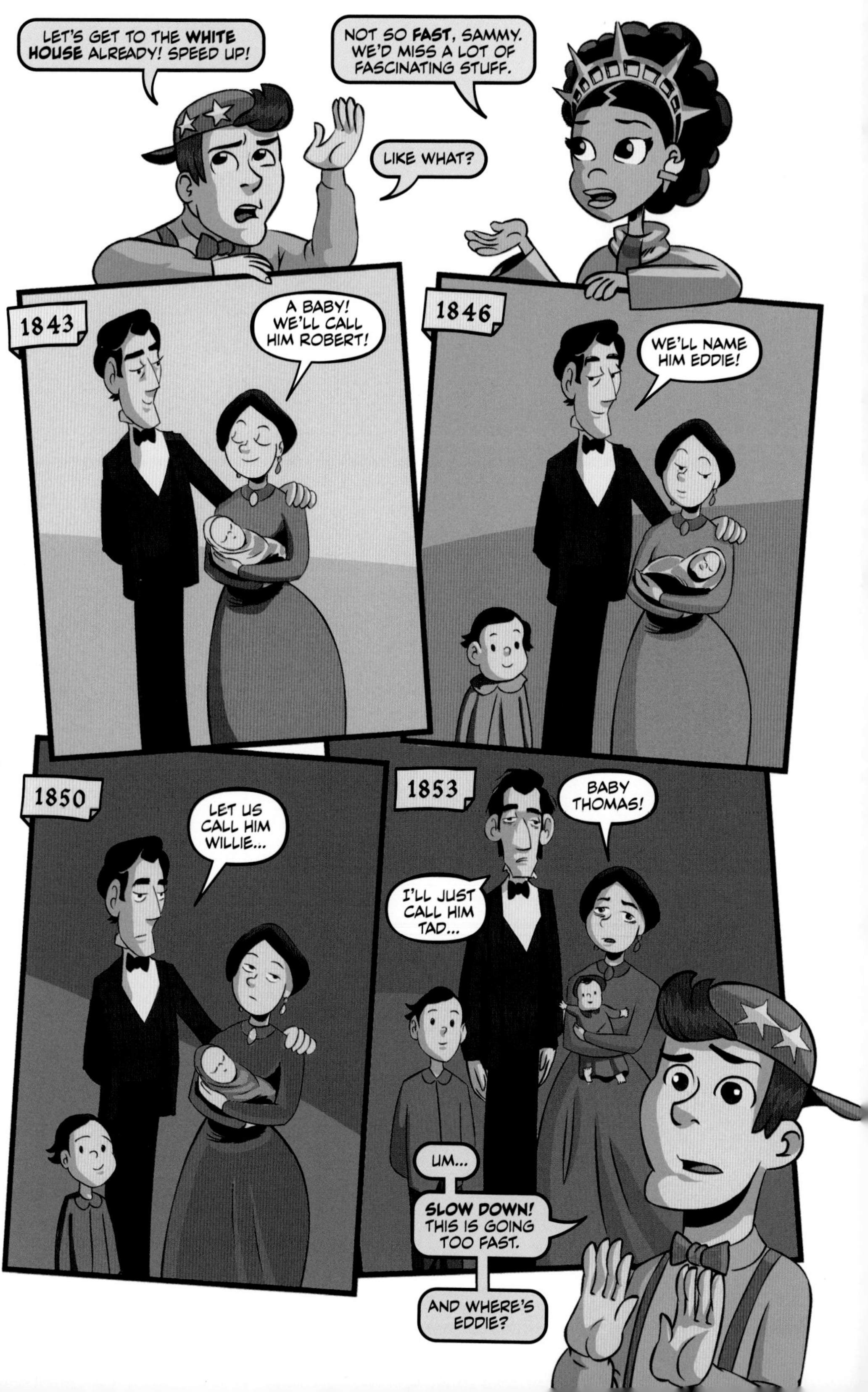
LET'S GET TO THE WHITE HOUSE ALREADY! SPEED UP!
NOT SO FAST, SAMMY. WE'D MISS A LOT OF FASCINATING STUFF.
LIKE WHAT?
1843
A BABY! WE'LL CALL HIM ROBERT!
1846
WE'LL NAME HIM EDDIE!
1850
LET US CALL HIM WILLIE...
1853
BABY THOMAS!
I'LL JUST CALL HIM TAD...
UM...
SLOW DOWN! THIS IS GOING TOO FAST.
AND WHERE'S EDDIE?

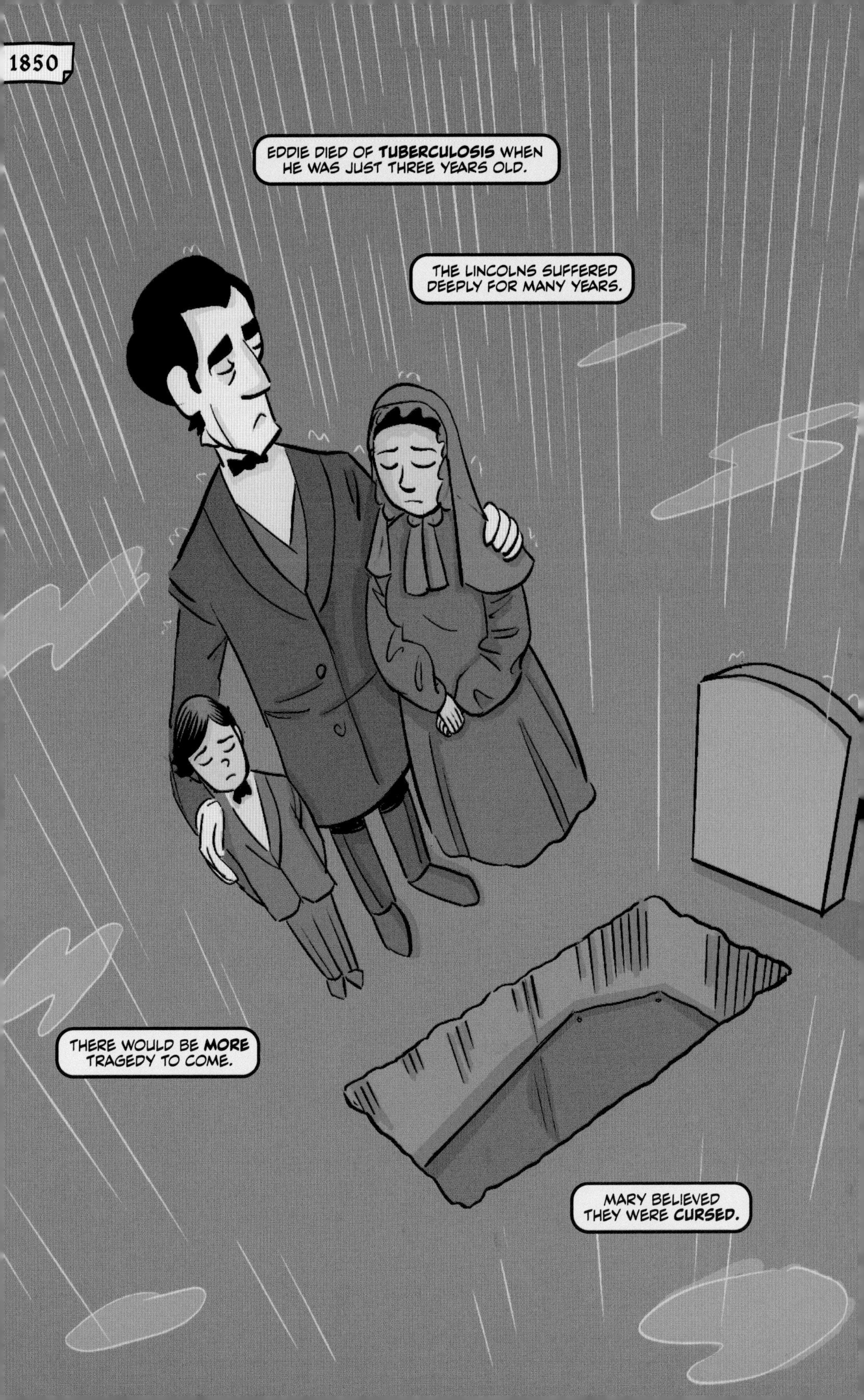
1850
EDDIE DIED OF **TUBERCULOSIS** WHEN HE WAS JUST THREE YEARS OLD.
THE LINCOLNS SUFFERED DEEPLY FOR MANY YEARS.
THERE WOULD BE **MORE** TRAGEDY TO COME.
MARY BELIEVED THEY WERE **CURSED**.

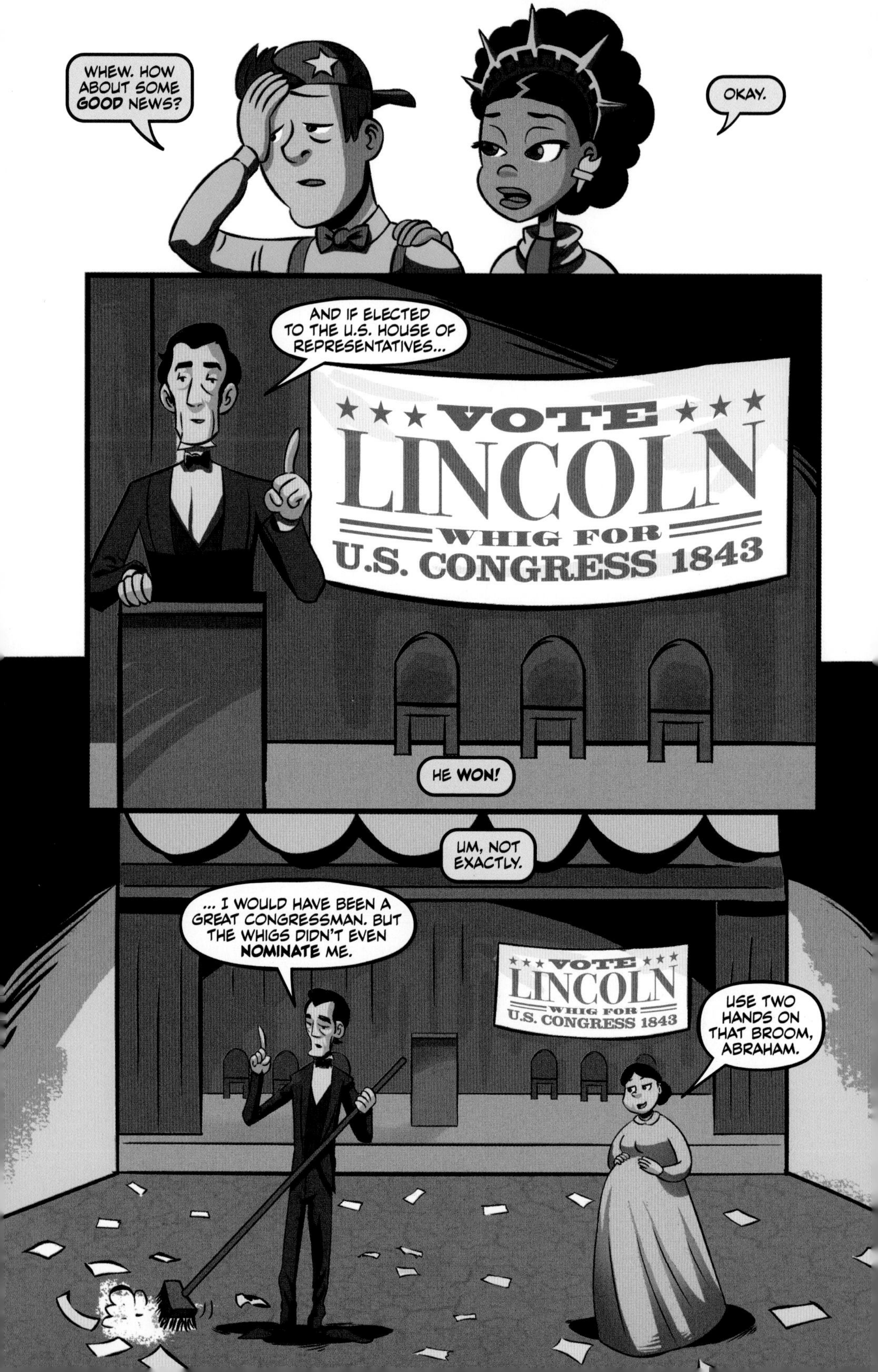

WHEW. HOW ABOUT SOME *GOOD* NEWS?

OKAY.

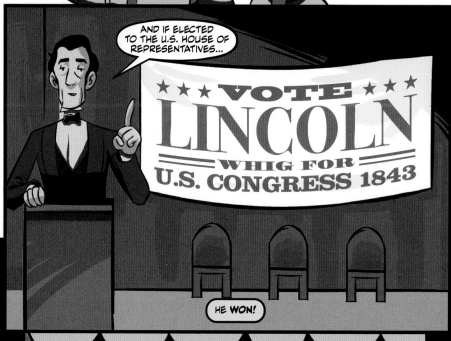

AND IF ELECTED TO THE U.S. HOUSE OF REPRESENTATIVES...

★★★ VOTE ★★★
LINCOLN
WHIG FOR
U.S. CONGRESS 1843

HE WON!

UM, NOT EXACTLY.

... I WOULD HAVE BEEN A GREAT CONGRESSMAN. BUT THE WHIGS DIDN'T EVEN **NOMINATE** ME.

★★★ VOTE ★★★
LINCOLN
WHIG FOR
U.S. CONGRESS 1843

USE TWO HANDS ON THAT BROOM, ABRAHAM.

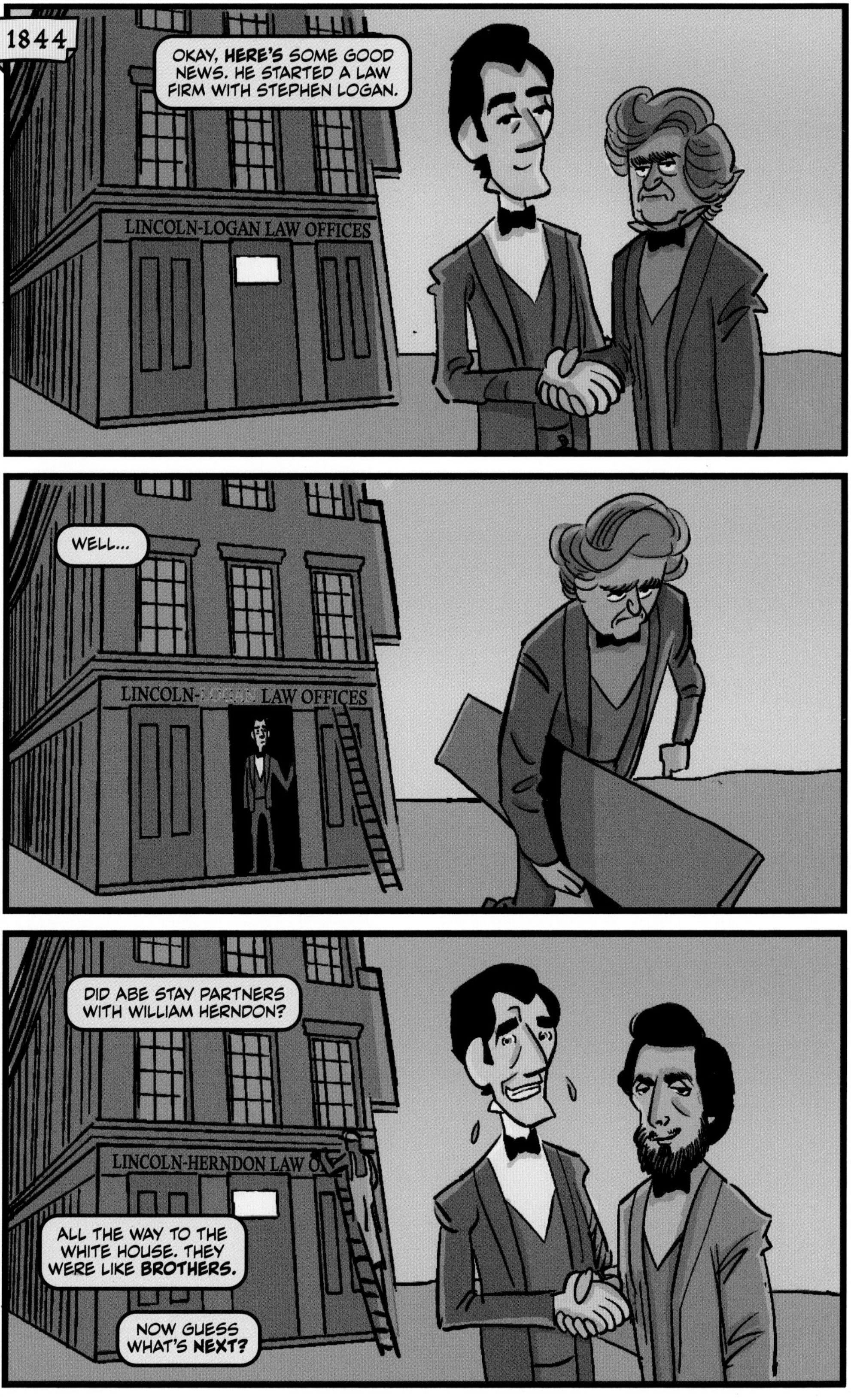
1844
OKAY, HERE'S SOME GOOD NEWS. HE STARTED A LAW FIRM WITH STEPHEN LOGAN.
LINCOLN-LOGAN LAW OFFICES
WELL...
LINCOLN-LOGAN LAW OFFICES
DID ABE STAY PARTNERS WITH WILLIAM HERNDON?
LINCOLN-HERNDON LAW O
ALL THE WAY TO THE WHITE HOUSE. THEY WERE LIKE BROTHERS.
NOW GUESS WHAT'S NEXT?

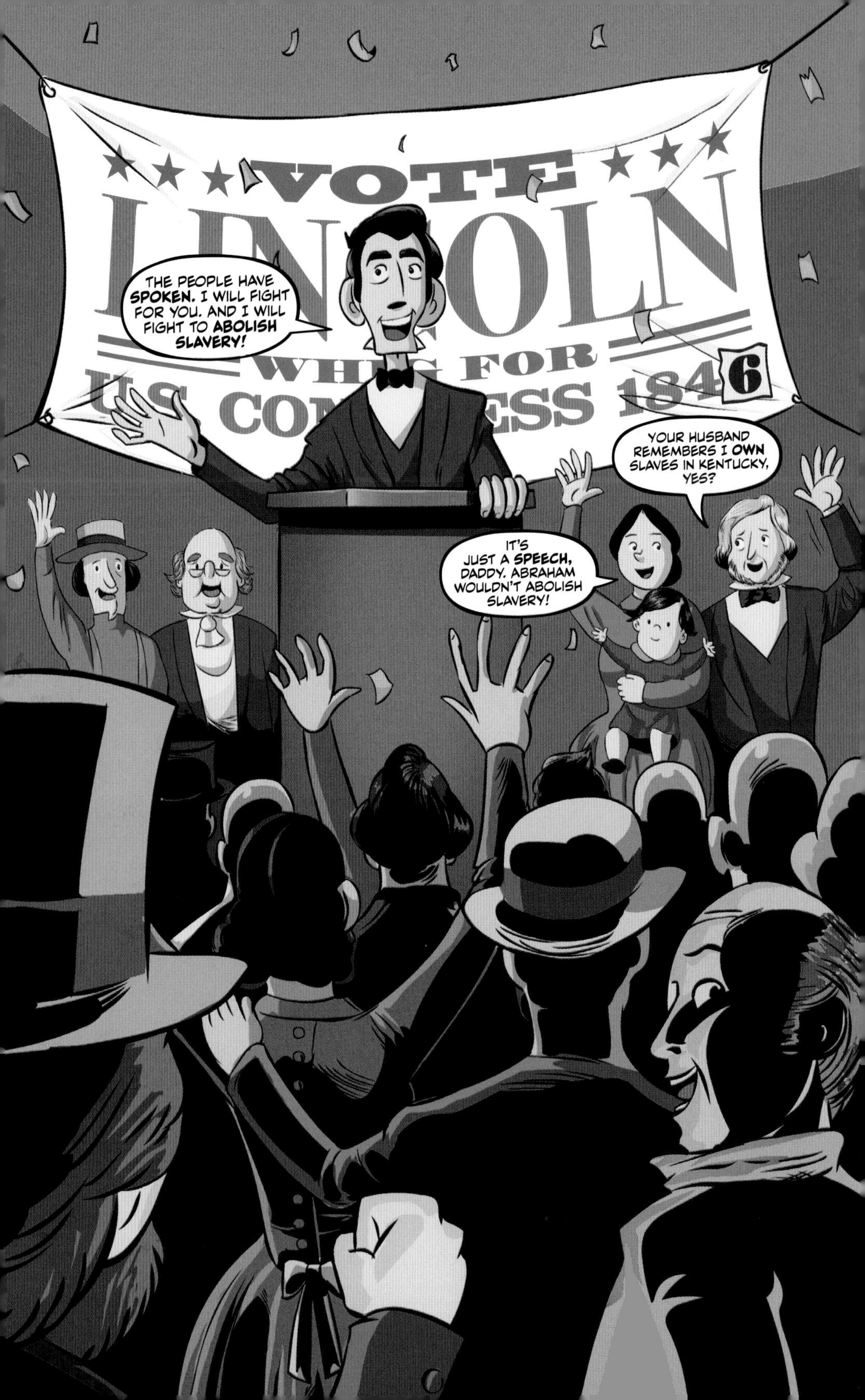
VOTE
THE PEOPLE HAVE **SPOKEN.** I WILL FIGHT FOR YOU. AND I WILL FIGHT TO **ABOLISH SLAVERY!**
YOUR HUSBAND REMEMBERS I **OWN** SLAVES IN KENTUCKY, YES?
IT'S JUST A **SPEECH,** DADDY. ABRAHAM WOULDN'T ABOLISH SLAVERY!

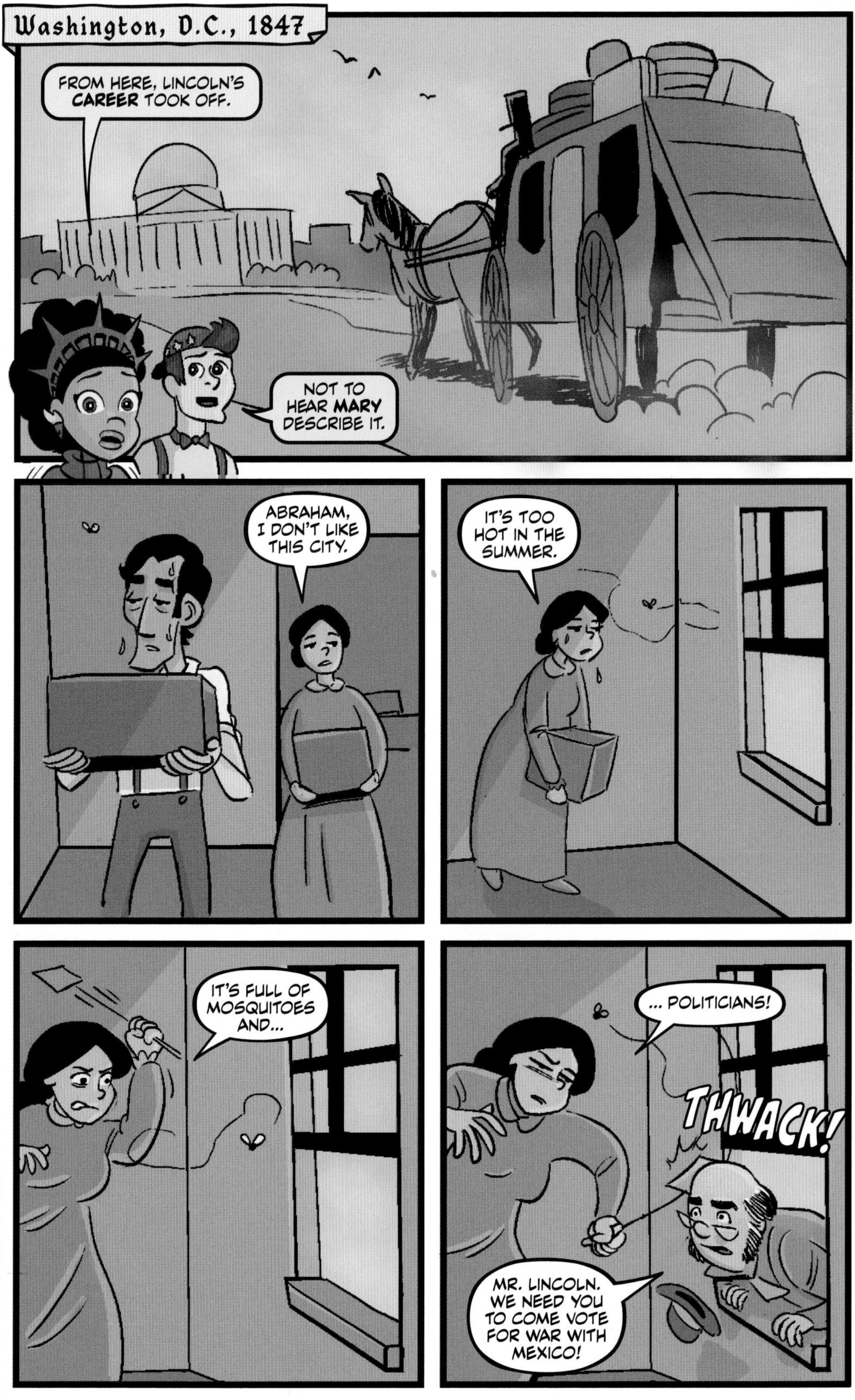
Washington, D.C., 1847
FROM HERE, LINCOLN'S CAREER TOOK OFF.
NOT TO HEAR MARY DESCRIBE IT.
ABRAHAM, I DON'T LIKE THIS CITY.
IT'S TOO HOT IN THE SUMMER.
IT'S FULL OF MOSQUITOES AND...
... POLITICIANS!
THWACK!
MR. LINCOLN. WE NEED YOU TO COME VOTE FOR WAR WITH MEXICO!

PRESIDENT POLK WANTED A WAR WITH **MEXICO**.

BUT LINCOLN DIDN'T **LIKE** POLK'S PLANS.

THERE'S PRESIDENT POLK **NOW**.

MEXICO KILLED AMERICAN SOLDIERS ON **AMERICAN** SOIL!

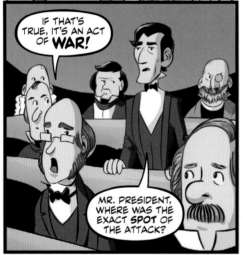

IF THAT'S TRUE, IT'S AN ACT OF **WAR!**

MR. PRESIDENT, WHERE WAS THE EXACT **SPOT** OF THE ATTACK?

WAS THE SPOT IN THE U.S. OR WAS THE SPOT IN MEXICO?

WHO **IS** THAT NOBODY CONGRESSMAN?

LINCOLN. ILLINOIS. WHIG. NEW GUY.

WAS THE SPOT ON LAND THAT MEXICO STOLE FROM SPAIN?

A *WHIG?*

UNTIL WE'RE SURE OF THE SPOT OF THE ATTACK, WE **CANNOT** DECLARE WAR.

HE'S SPOTTY!

HE'S SEEING SPOTS.

WE ACTUALLY CALLED HIM "SPOTTY LINCOLN."

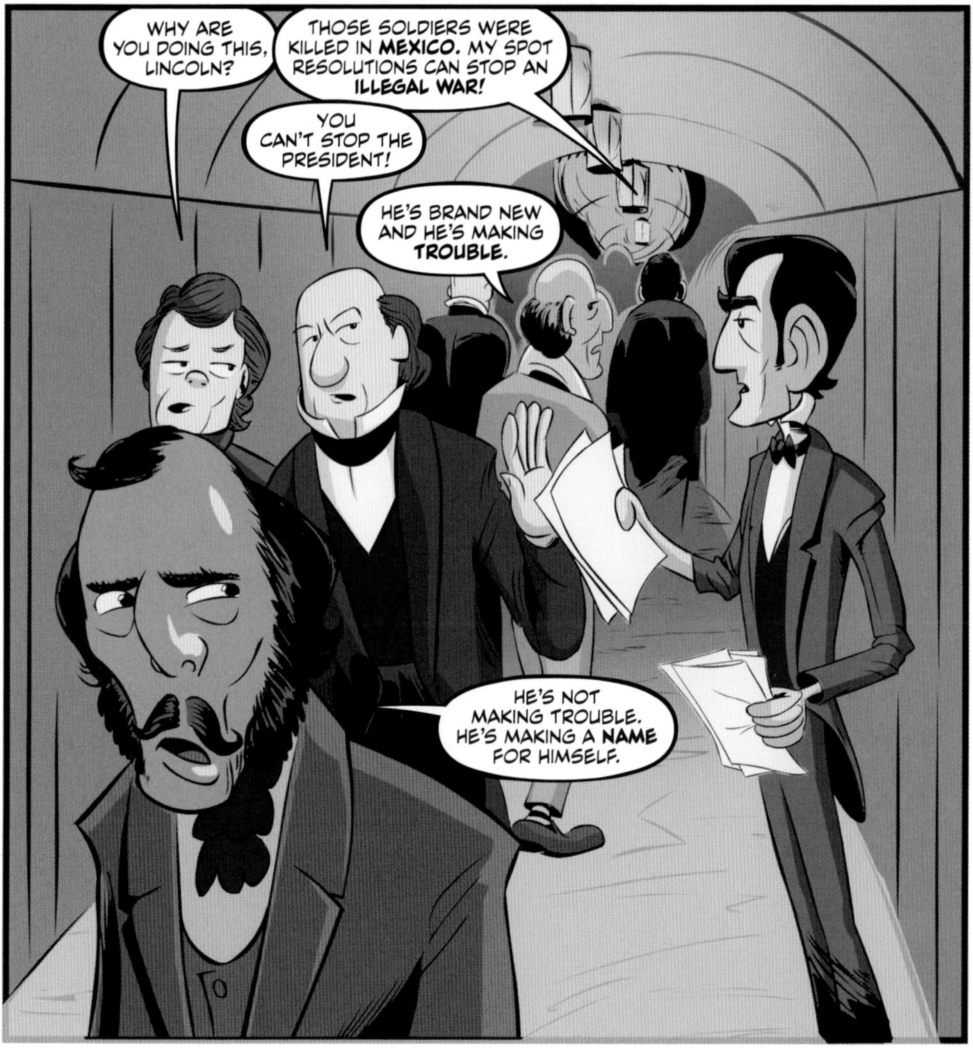
WHY ARE YOU DOING THIS, LINCOLN?
THOSE SOLDIERS WERE KILLED IN **MEXICO.** MY SPOT RESOLUTIONS CAN STOP AN **ILLEGAL WAR!**
YOU CAN'T STOP THE PRESIDENT!
HE'S BRAND NEW AND HE'S MAKING **TROUBLE.**
HE'S NOT MAKING TROUBLE. HE'S MAKING A **NAME** FOR HIMSELF.

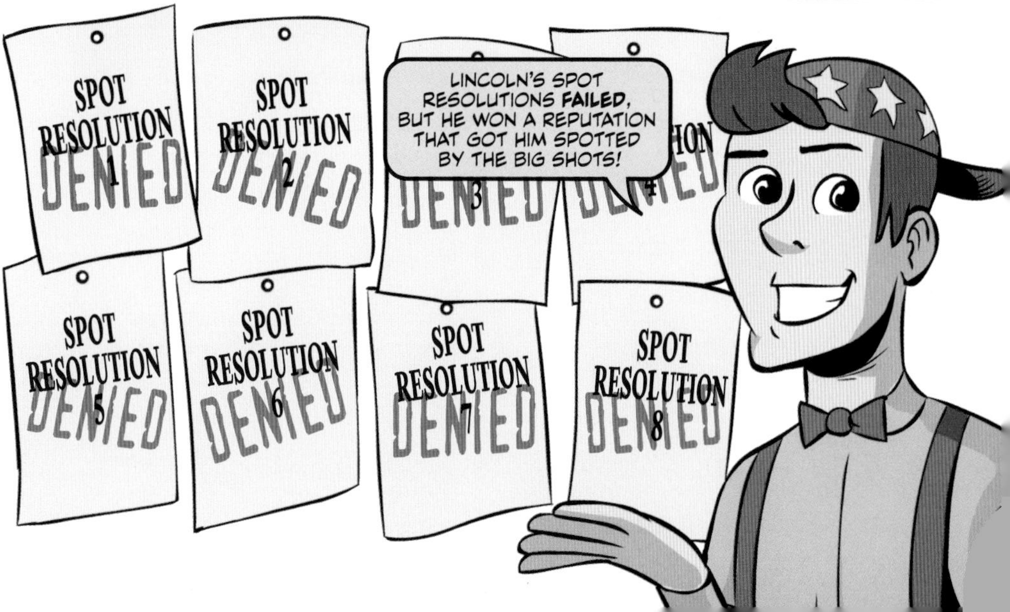
SPOT RESOLUTION 1 DENIED
SPOT RESOLUTION 2 DENIED
LINCOLN'S SPOT RESOLUTIONS **FAILED,** BUT HE WON A REPUTATION THAT GOT HIM SPOTTED BY THE BIG SHOTS!
SPOT RESOLUTION 5 DENIED
SPOT RESOLUTION 6 DENIED
SPOT RESOLUTION 7 DENIED
SPOT RESOLUTION 8 DENIED

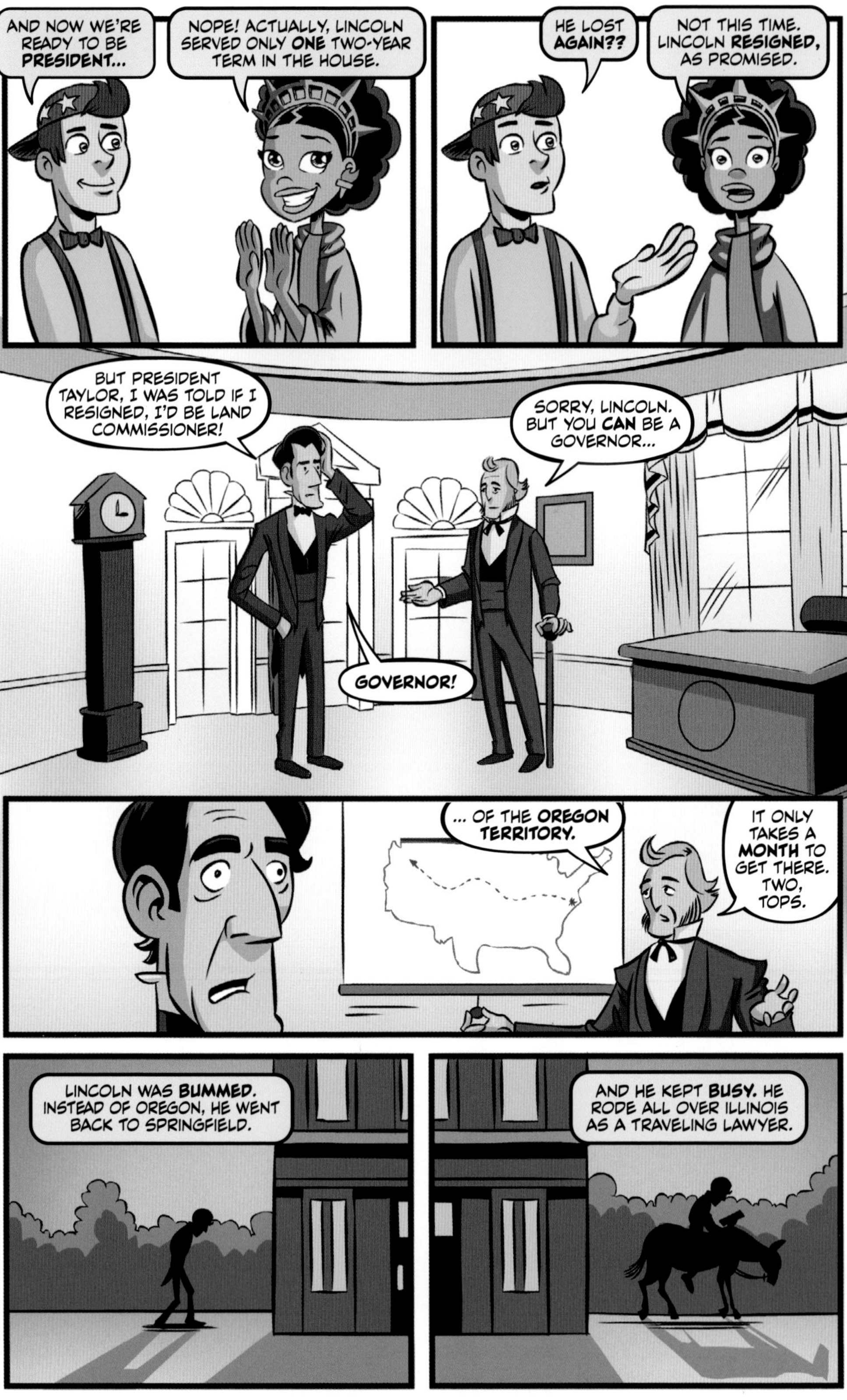
AND NOW WE'RE READY TO BE **PRESIDENT...**
NOPE! ACTUALLY, LINCOLN SERVED ONLY **ONE** TWO-YEAR TERM IN THE HOUSE.
HE LOST **AGAIN??**
NOT THIS TIME. LINCOLN **RESIGNED,** AS PROMISED.
BUT PRESIDENT TAYLOR, I WAS TOLD IF I RESIGNED, I'D BE LAND COMMISSIONER!
SORRY, LINCOLN. BUT YOU **CAN** BE A GOVERNOR...
GOVERNOR!
... OF THE **OREGON TERRITORY.**
IT ONLY TAKES A **MONTH** TO GET THERE. TWO, TOPS.
LINCOLN WAS **BUMMED.** INSTEAD OF OREGON, HE WENT BACK TO SPRINGFIELD.
AND HE KEPT **BUSY.** HE RODE ALL OVER ILLINOIS AS A TRAVELING LAWYER.

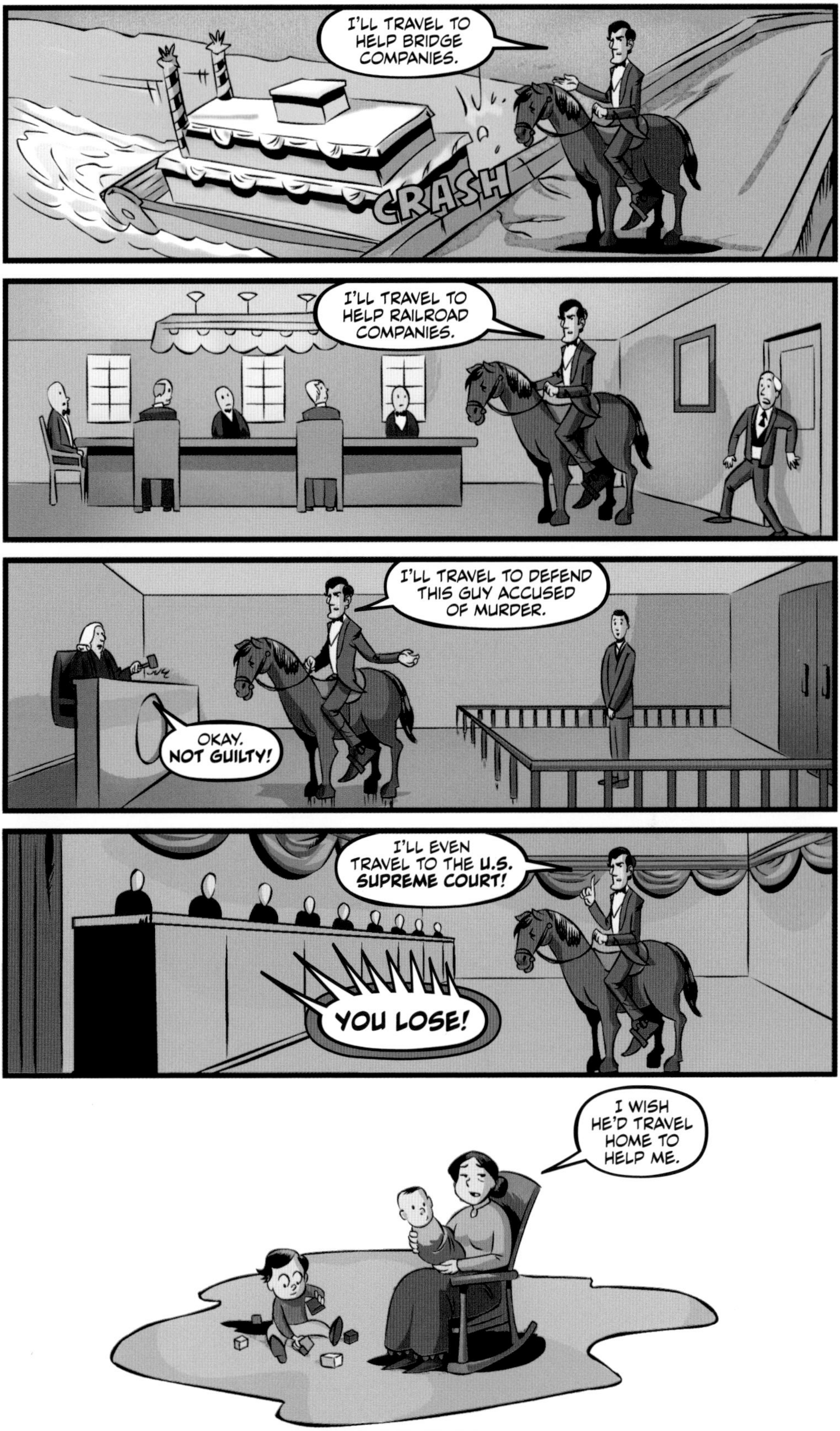

I'LL TRAVEL TO HELP BRIDGE COMPANIES.
CRASH
I'LL TRAVEL TO HELP RAILROAD COMPANIES.
I'LL TRAVEL TO DEFEND THIS GUY ACCUSED OF MURDER.
OKAY. NOT GUILTY!
I'LL EVEN TRAVEL TO THE U.S. SUPREME COURT!
YOU LOSE!
I WISH HE'D TRAVEL HOME TO HELP ME.

ABE SPENT SIX YEARS AS A **CIRCUIT LAWYER.**

THAT MEANS HE TRAVELED FROM TOWN TO TOWN.

AND LINCOLN DID SOMETHING **ELSE** THAT WAS PRETTY COOL.

WHAT'S THAT, LINCOLN? NOTHING TO DO?

PLENTY TO DO, HERNDON.

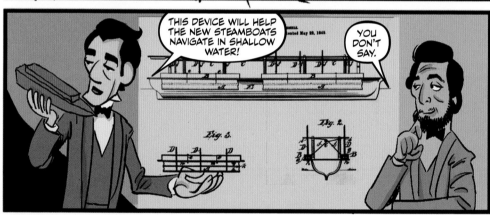

THIS DEVICE WILL HELP THE NEW STEAMBOATS NAVIGATE IN SHALLOW WATER!

YOU DON'T SAY.

HE **DID** SAY. LINCOLN IS THE ONLY PRESIDENT EVER TO GET A **PATENT!**

LOOK OUT, WORLD!

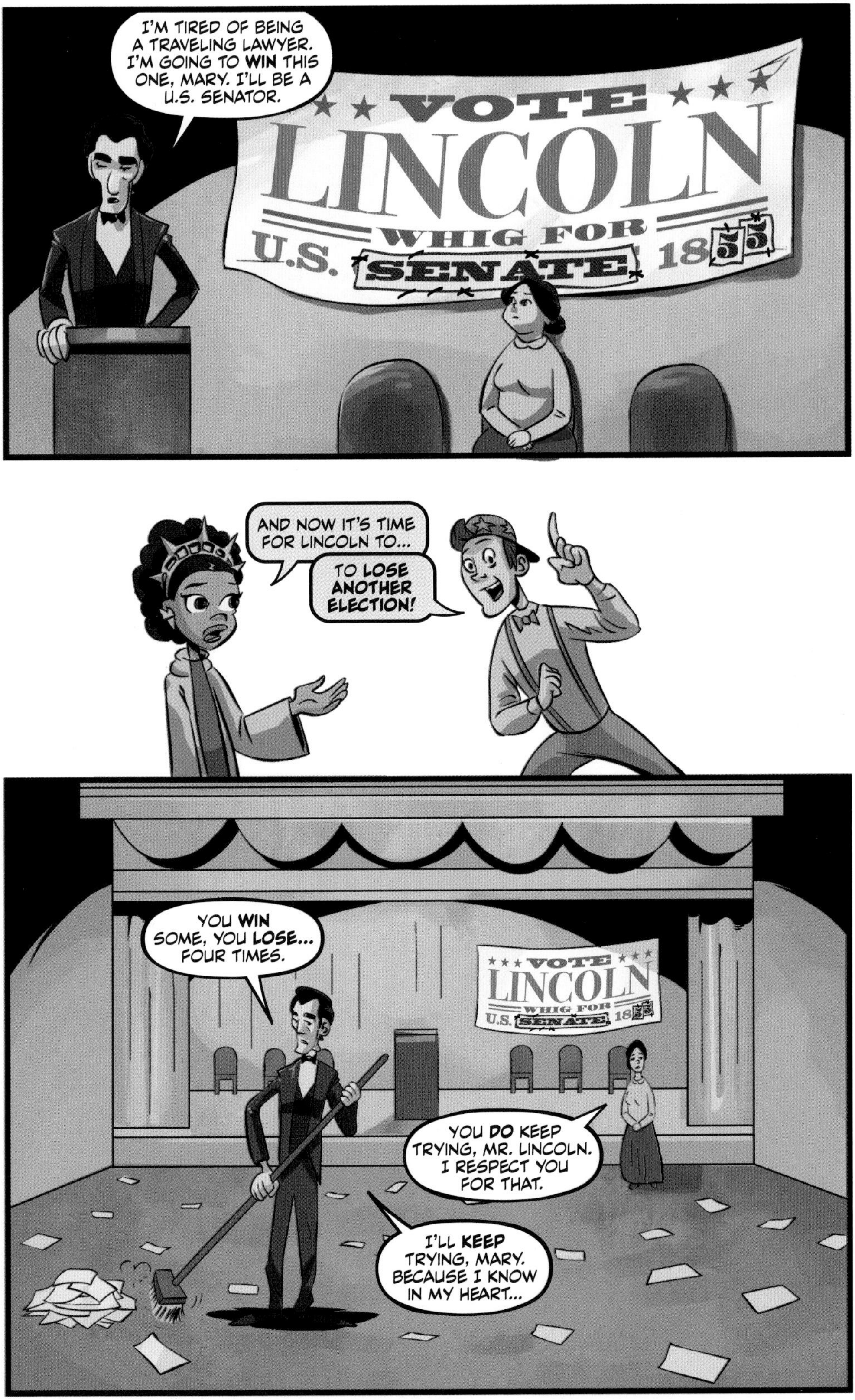

I'M TIRED OF BEING A TRAVELING LAWYER. I'M GOING TO **WIN** THIS ONE, MARY. I'LL BE A U.S. SENATOR.
VOTE LINCOLN
WHIG FOR U.S. SENATE 1855
AND NOW IT'S TIME FOR LINCOLN TO...
TO **LOSE ANOTHER ELECTION!**
YOU **WIN** SOME, YOU **LOSE...** FOUR TIMES.
VOTE LINCOLN
WHIG FOR U.S. SENATE 1855
YOU **DO** KEEP TRYING, MR. LINCOLN. I RESPECT YOU FOR THAT.
I'LL **KEEP** TRYING, MARY. BECAUSE I KNOW IN MY HEART...

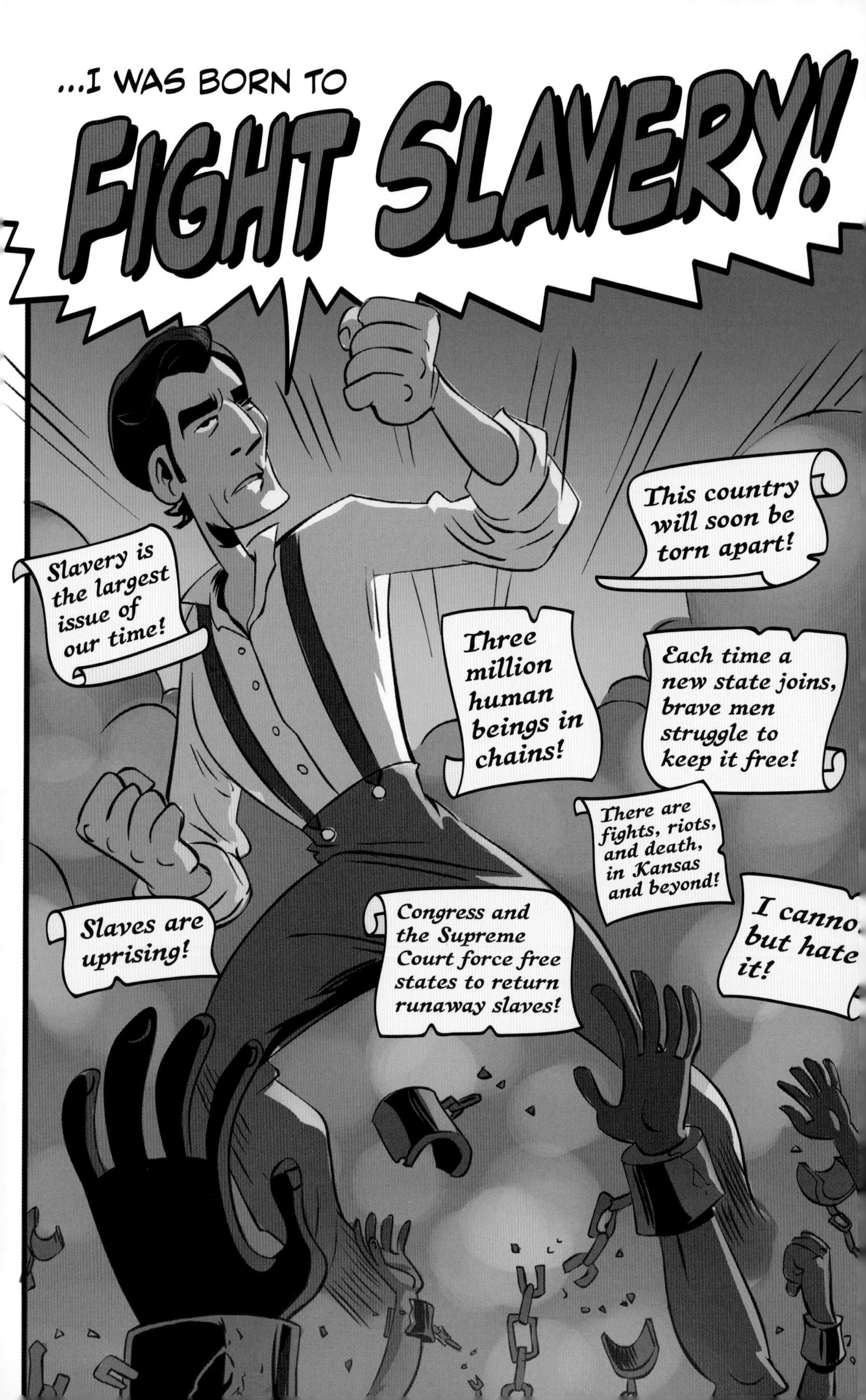
...I WAS BORN TO
FIGHT SLAVERY!
Slavery is the largest issue of our time!
This country will soon be torn apart!
Three million human beings in chains!
Each time a new state joins, brave men struggle to keep it free!
There are fights, riots, and death, in Kansas and beyond!
Slaves are uprising!
Congress and the Supreme Court force free states to return runaway slaves!
I canno but hate it!

EVEN IF WE **HAD** LET LINCOLN RUN FOR VICE PRESIDENT...

JAMES BUCHANAN WOULD HAVE BEAT US.

ILLINOIS LOVES LINCOLN. WHAT A **CAMPAIGNER!**

NOW THAT HE'S A REPUBLICAN LIKE **US**, I HAVE AN IDEA...

WHAT WOULD YOU SAY TO

PROBABLY THE SAME

I'VE GOT AN **IDEA**, MARY.

NOMINATE LINCOLN — REPUBLICAN FOR VICE PRESIDENT, 18??

NOMINATE? REPUBLICAN? VICE PRESIDENT?

YEAH, HE LOST **THAT ONE**, TOO.

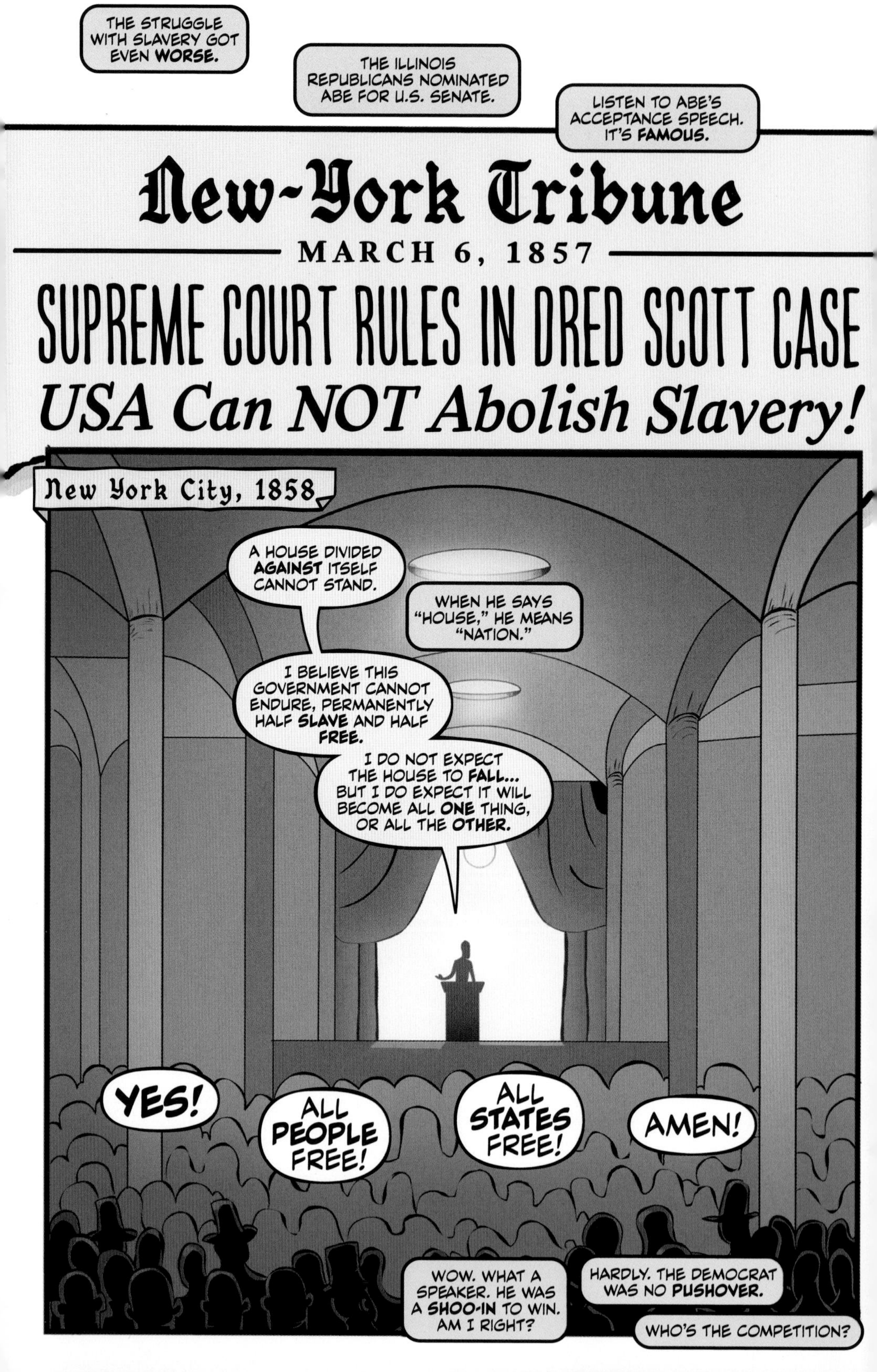
THE STRUGGLE WITH SLAVERY GOT EVEN WORSE.
THE ILLINOIS REPUBLICANS NOMINATED ABE FOR U.S. SENATE.
LISTEN TO ABE'S ACCEPTANCE SPEECH. IT'S FAMOUS.
New-York Tribune
MARCH 6, 1857
SUPREME COURT RULES IN DRED SCOTT CASE
USA Can NOT Abolish Slavery!
New York City, 1858
A HOUSE DIVIDED AGAINST ITSELF CANNOT STAND.
WHEN HE SAYS "HOUSE," HE MEANS "NATION."
I BELIEVE THIS GOVERNMENT CANNOT ENDURE, PERMANENTLY HALF SLAVE AND HALF FREE.
I DO NOT EXPECT THE HOUSE TO FALL... BUT I DO EXPECT IT WILL BECOME ALL ONE THING, OR ALL THE OTHER.
YES!
ALL PEOPLE FREE!
ALL STATES FREE!
AMEN!
WOW. WHAT A SPEAKER. HE WAS A SHOO-IN TO WIN. AM I RIGHT?
HARDLY. THE DEMOCRAT WAS NO PUSHOVER.
WHO'S THE COMPETITION?

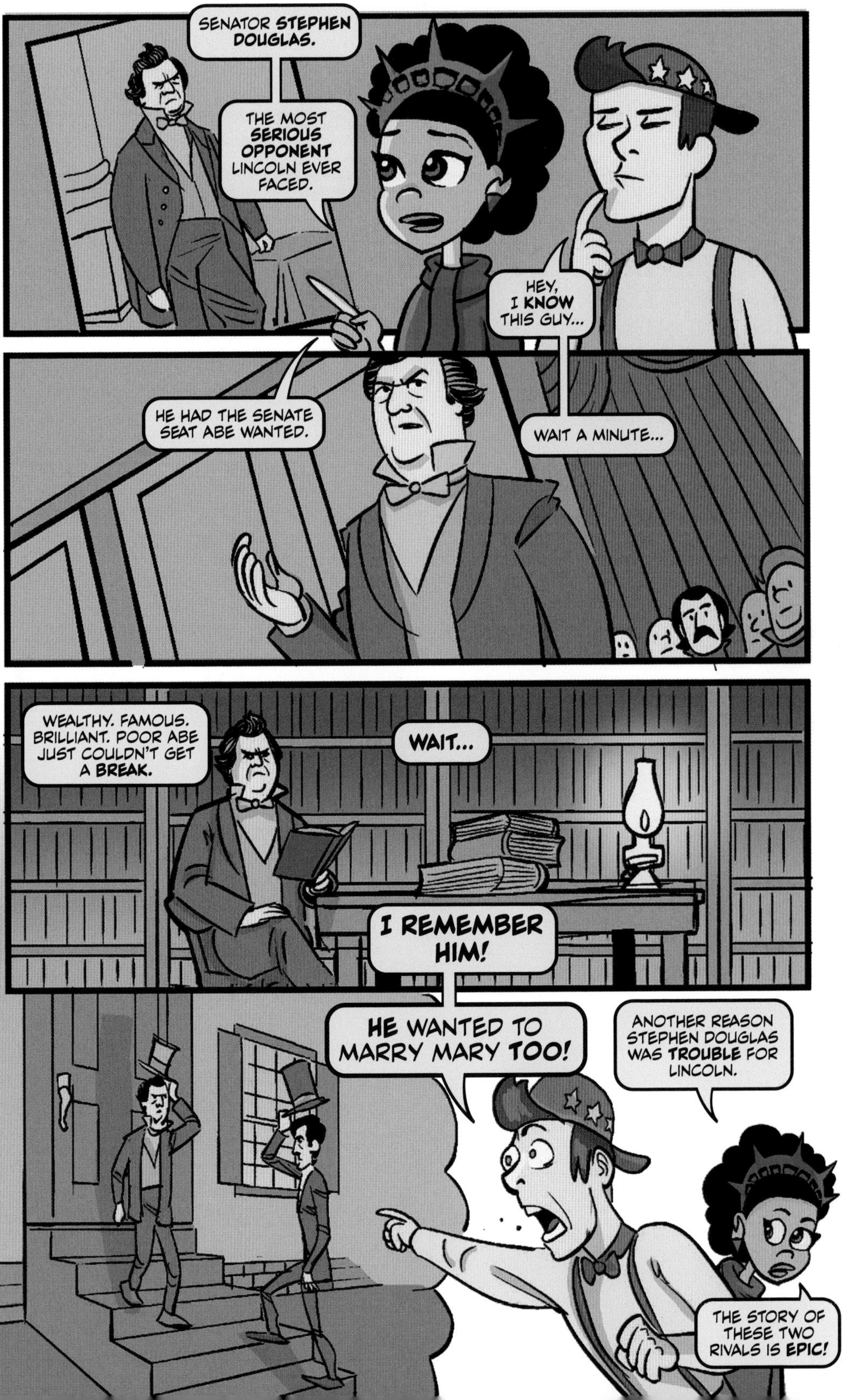
SENATOR STEPHEN DOUGLAS.
THE MOST SERIOUS OPPONENT LINCOLN EVER FACED.
HEY, I KNOW THIS GUY...
HE HAD THE SENATE SEAT ABE WANTED.
WAIT A MINUTE...
WEALTHY. FAMOUS. BRILLIANT. POOR ABE JUST COULDN'T GET A BREAK.
WAIT...
I REMEMBER HIM!
HE WANTED TO MARRY MARY TOO!
ANOTHER REASON STEPHEN DOUGLAS WAS TROUBLE FOR LINCOLN.
THE STORY OF THESE TWO RIVALS IS EPIC!

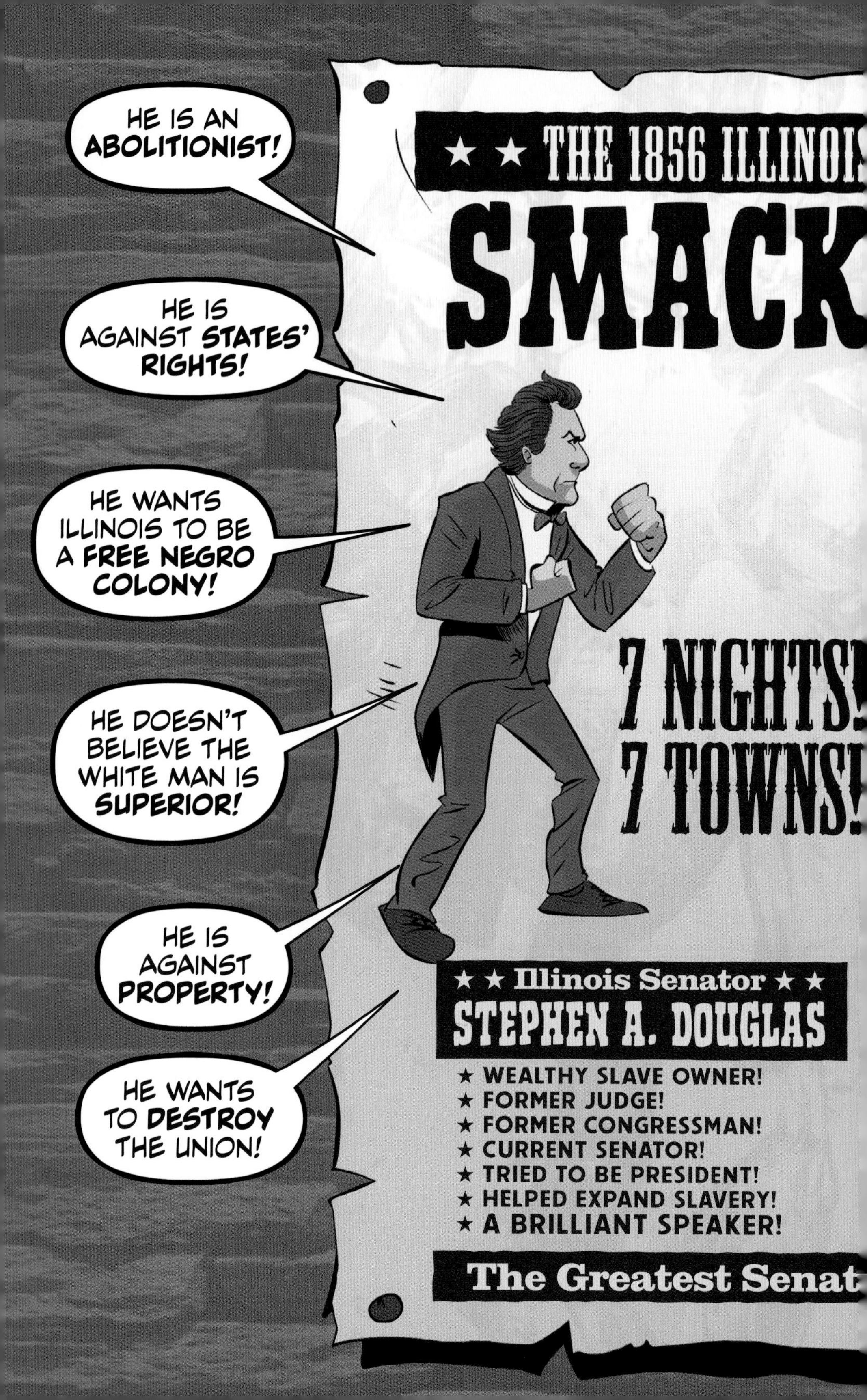

HE IS AN ABOLITIONIST!
HE IS AGAINST STATES' RIGHTS!
HE WANTS ILLINOIS TO BE A FREE NEGRO COLONY!
HE DOESN'T BELIEVE THE WHITE MAN IS SUPERIOR!
HE IS AGAINST PROPERTY!
HE WANTS TO DESTROY THE UNION!
★ ★ THE 1856 ILLINOI
SMACK
7 NIGHTS!
7 TOWNS!
★ ★ Illinois Senator ★ ★
STEPHEN A. DOUGLAS
★ WEALTHY SLAVE OWNER!
★ FORMER JUDGE!
★ FORMER CONGRESSMAN!
★ CURRENT SENATOR!
★ TRIED TO BE PRESIDENT!
★ HELPED EXPAND SLAVERY!
★ A BRILLIANT SPEAKER!
The Greatest Senat

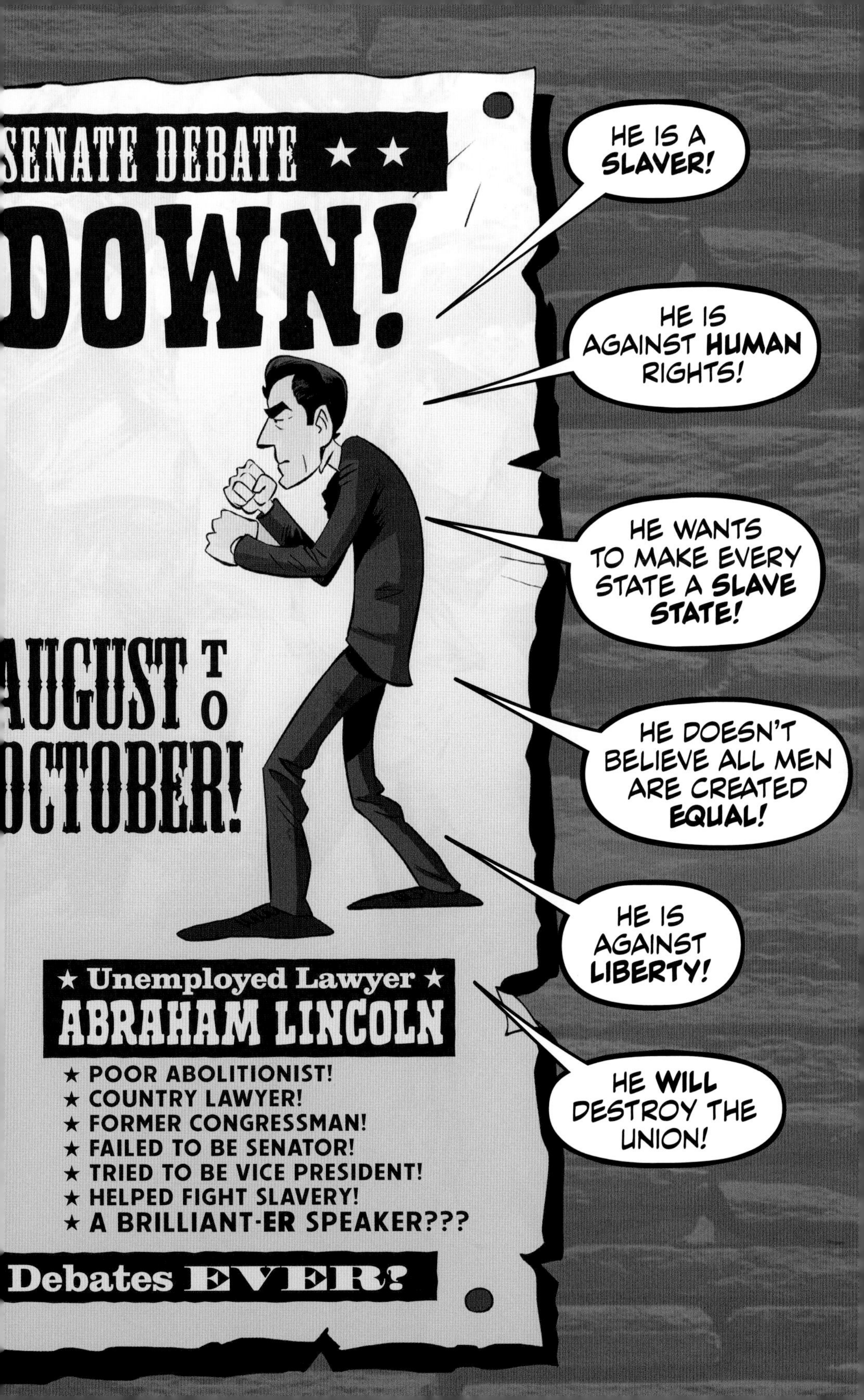
SENATE DEBATE ★ ★
DOWN!
AUGUST TO OCTOBER!
★ Unemployed Lawyer ★
ABRAHAM LINCOLN
★ POOR ABOLITIONIST!
★ COUNTRY LAWYER!
★ FORMER CONGRESSMAN!
★ FAILED TO BE SENATOR!
★ TRIED TO BE VICE PRESIDENT!
★ HELPED FIGHT SLAVERY!
★ A BRILLIANT-ER SPEAKER???
Debates EVER?
HE IS A SLAVER!
HE IS AGAINST HUMAN RIGHTS!
HE WANTS TO MAKE EVERY STATE A SLAVE STATE!
HE DOESN'T BELIEVE ALL MEN ARE CREATED EQUAL!
HE IS AGAINST LIBERTY!
HE WILL DESTROY THE UNION!

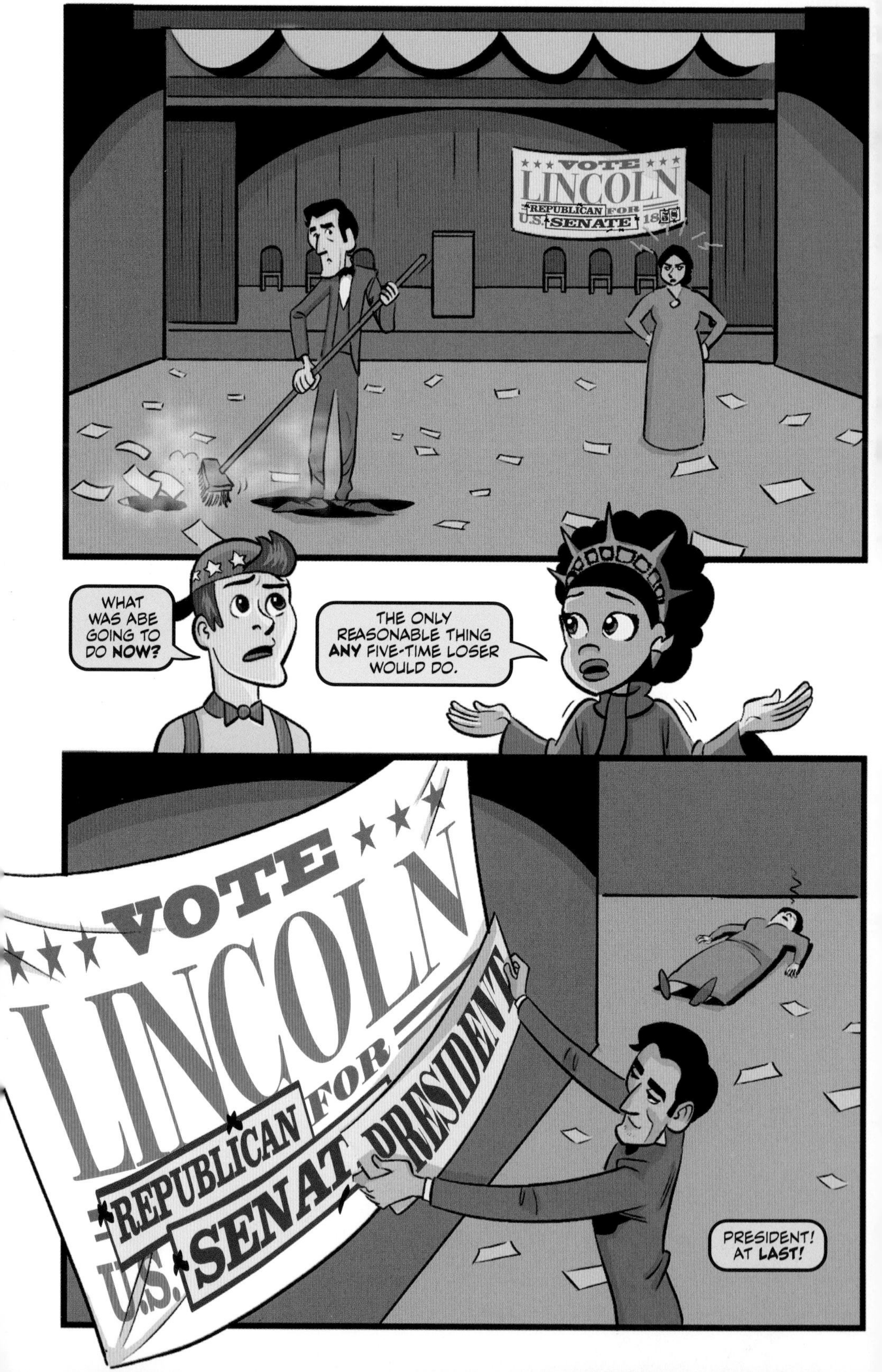
VOTE
LINCOLN
REPUBLICAN FOR
U.S. SENATE 18
WHAT WAS ABE GOING TO DO **NOW?**
THE ONLY REASONABLE THING **ANY** FIVE-TIME LOSER WOULD DO.
VOTE
LINCOLN
REPUBLICAN FOR
U.S. SENAT
PRESIDEN
PRESIDENT! AT **LAST!**

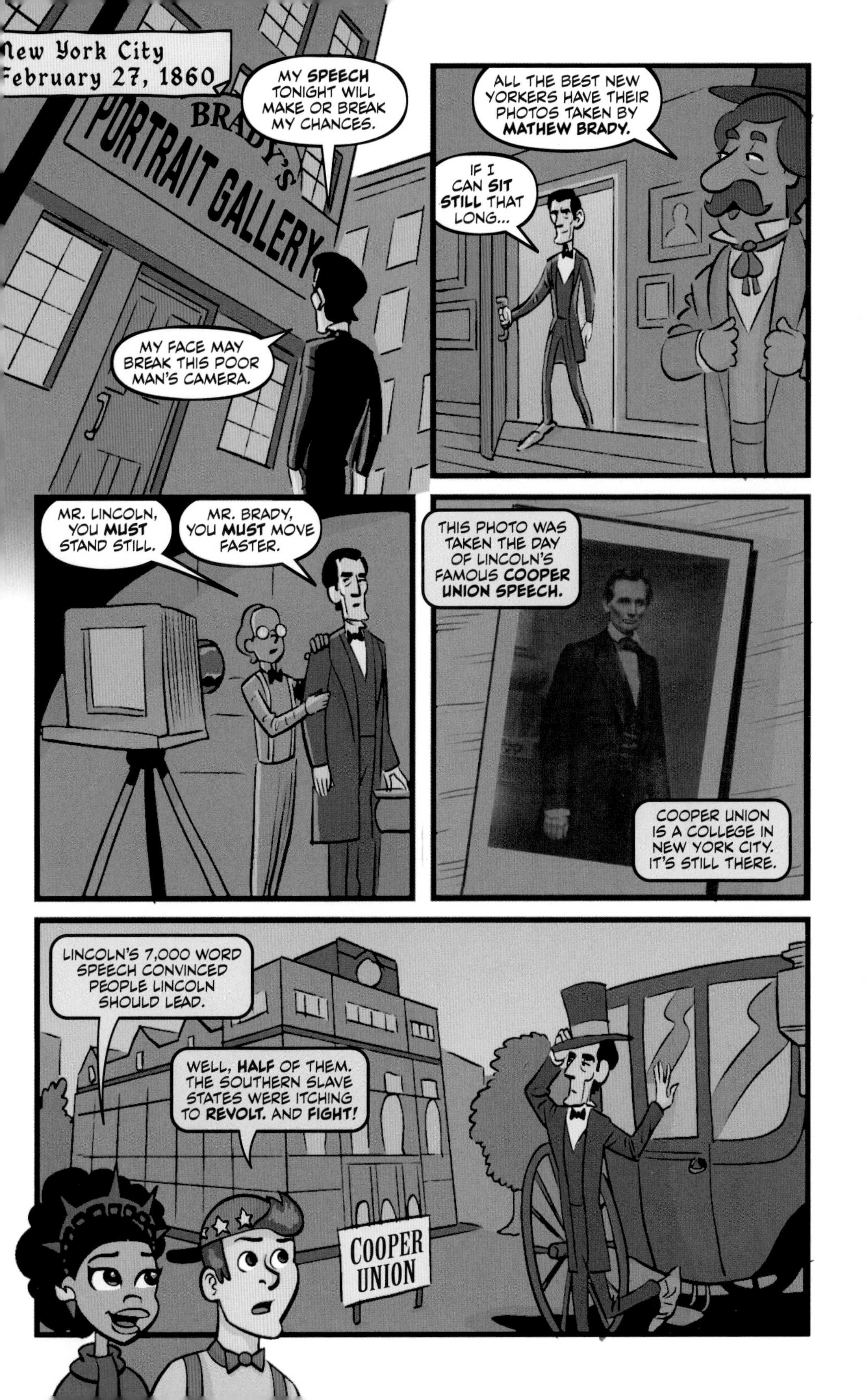
New York City
February 27, 1860
BRADY'S PORTRAIT GALLERY
MY SPEECH TONIGHT WILL MAKE OR BREAK MY CHANCES.
MY FACE MAY BREAK THIS POOR MAN'S CAMERA.
ALL THE BEST NEW YORKERS HAVE THEIR PHOTOS TAKEN BY MATHEW BRADY.
IF I CAN SIT STILL THAT LONG...
MR. LINCOLN, YOU MUST STAND STILL.
MR. BRADY, YOU MUST MOVE FASTER.
THIS PHOTO WAS TAKEN THE DAY OF LINCOLN'S FAMOUS COOPER UNION SPEECH.
COOPER UNION IS A COLLEGE IN NEW YORK CITY. IT'S STILL THERE.
LINCOLN'S 7,000 WORD SPEECH CONVINCED PEOPLE LINCOLN SHOULD LEAD.
WELL, HALF OF THEM. THE SOUTHERN SLAVE STATES WERE ITCHING TO REVOLT. AND FIGHT!
COOPER UNION

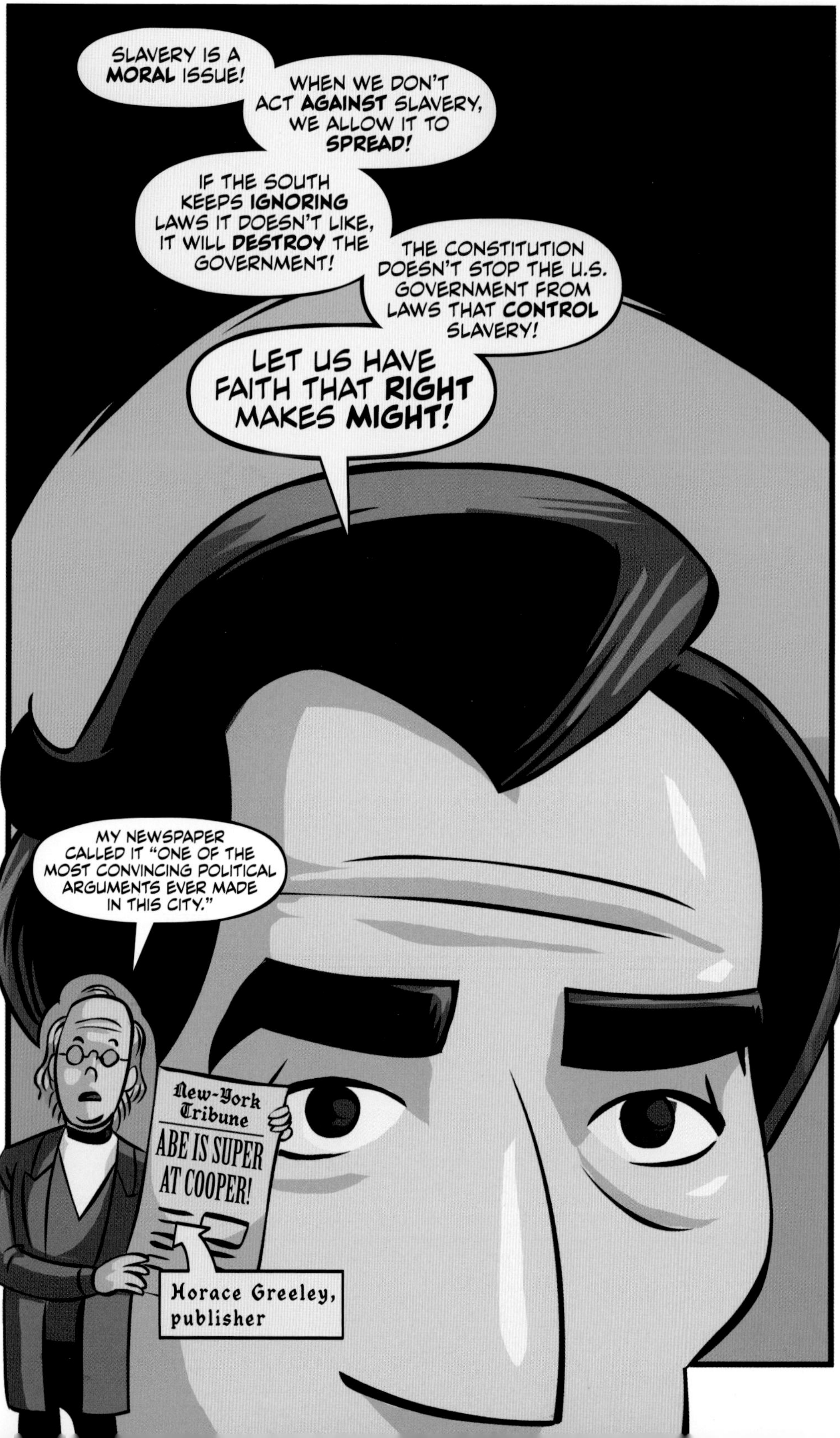
SLAVERY IS A MORAL ISSUE!
WHEN WE DON'T ACT AGAINST SLAVERY, WE ALLOW IT TO SPREAD!
IF THE SOUTH KEEPS IGNORING LAWS IT DOESN'T LIKE, IT WILL DESTROY THE GOVERNMENT!
THE CONSTITUTION DOESN'T STOP THE U.S. GOVERNMENT FROM LAWS THAT CONTROL SLAVERY!
LET US HAVE FAITH THAT RIGHT MAKES MIGHT!
MY NEWSPAPER CALLED IT "ONE OF THE MOST CONVINCING POLITICAL ARGUMENTS EVER MADE IN THIS CITY."
New-York Tribune
ABE IS SUPER AT COOPER!
Horace Greeley, publisher

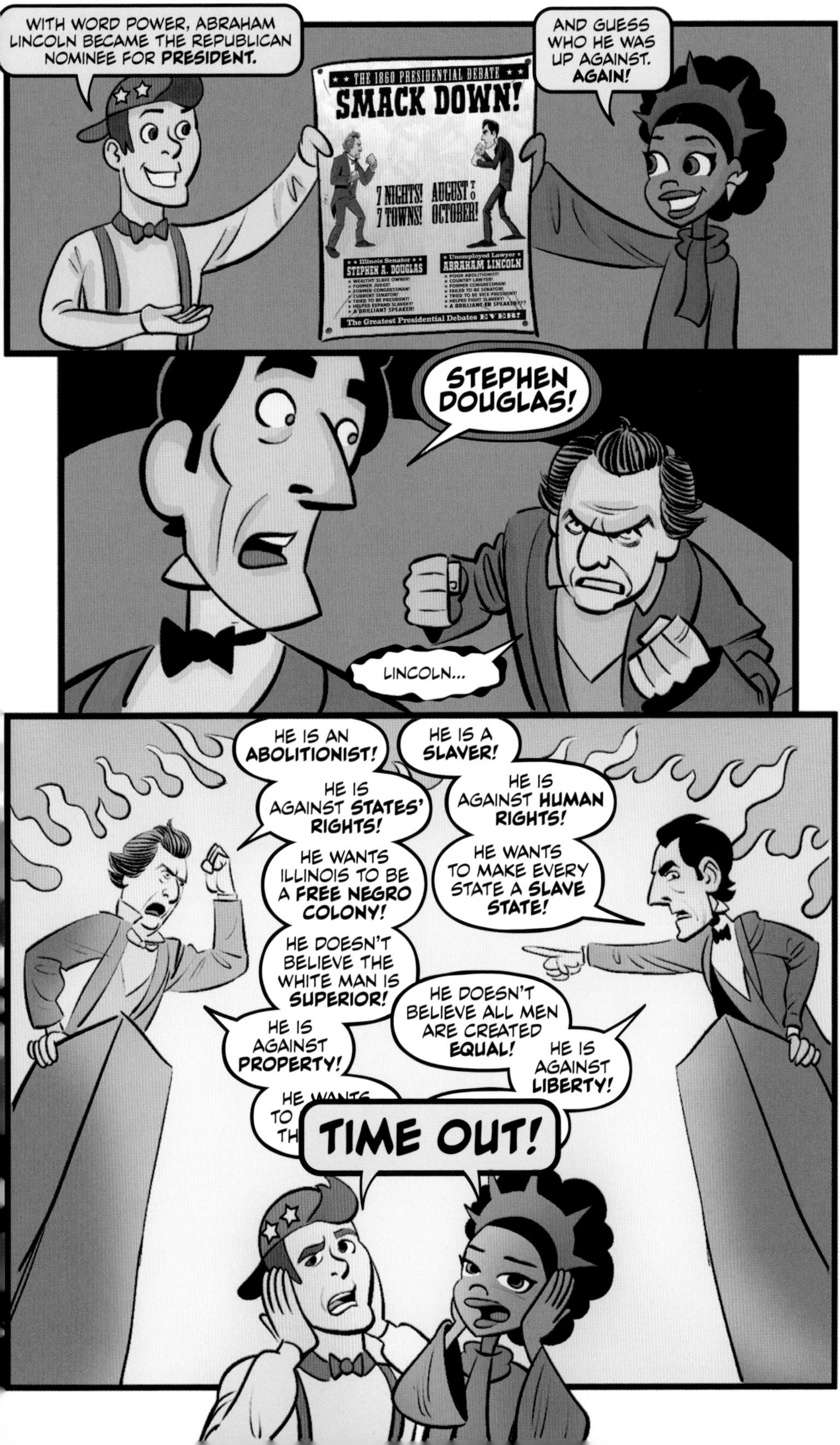
WITH WORD POWER, ABRAHAM LINCOLN BECAME THE REPUBLICAN NOMINEE FOR **PRESIDENT.**
THE 1860 PRESIDENTIAL DEBATE
SMACK DOWN!
7 NIGHTS! 7 TOWNS!
AUGUST TO OCTOBER!
Illinois Senator
STEPHEN A. DOUGLAS
WEALTHY SLAVE OWNER!
FORMER JUDGE!
FORMER CONGRESSMAN!
CURRENT SENATOR!
TRIED TO BE PRESIDENT!
HELPED EXPAND SLAVERY!
A BRILLIANT SPEAKER!
Unemployed Lawyer
ABRAHAM LINCOLN
POOR ABOLITIONIST!
COUNTRY LAWYER!
FORMER CONGRESSMAN!
FAILED TO BE SENATOR!
TRIED TO BE VICE PRESIDENT!
HELPED FIGHT SLAVERY!
A BRILLIANT-ER SPEAKER???
The Greatest Presidential Debates EVER!
AND GUESS WHO HE WAS UP AGAINST. **AGAIN!**
STEPHEN DOUGLAS!
LINCOLN...
HE IS AN **ABOLITIONIST!**
HE IS A **SLAVER!**
HE IS AGAINST **STATES' RIGHTS!**
HE IS AGAINST **HUMAN RIGHTS!**
HE WANTS ILLINOIS TO BE A **FREE NEGRO COLONY!**
HE WANTS TO MAKE EVERY STATE A **SLAVE STATE!**
HE DOESN'T BELIEVE THE WHITE MAN IS **SUPERIOR!**
HE DOESN'T BELIEVE ALL MEN ARE CREATED **EQUAL!**
HE IS AGAINST **PROPERTY!**
HE IS AGAINST **LIBERTY!**
TIME OUT!

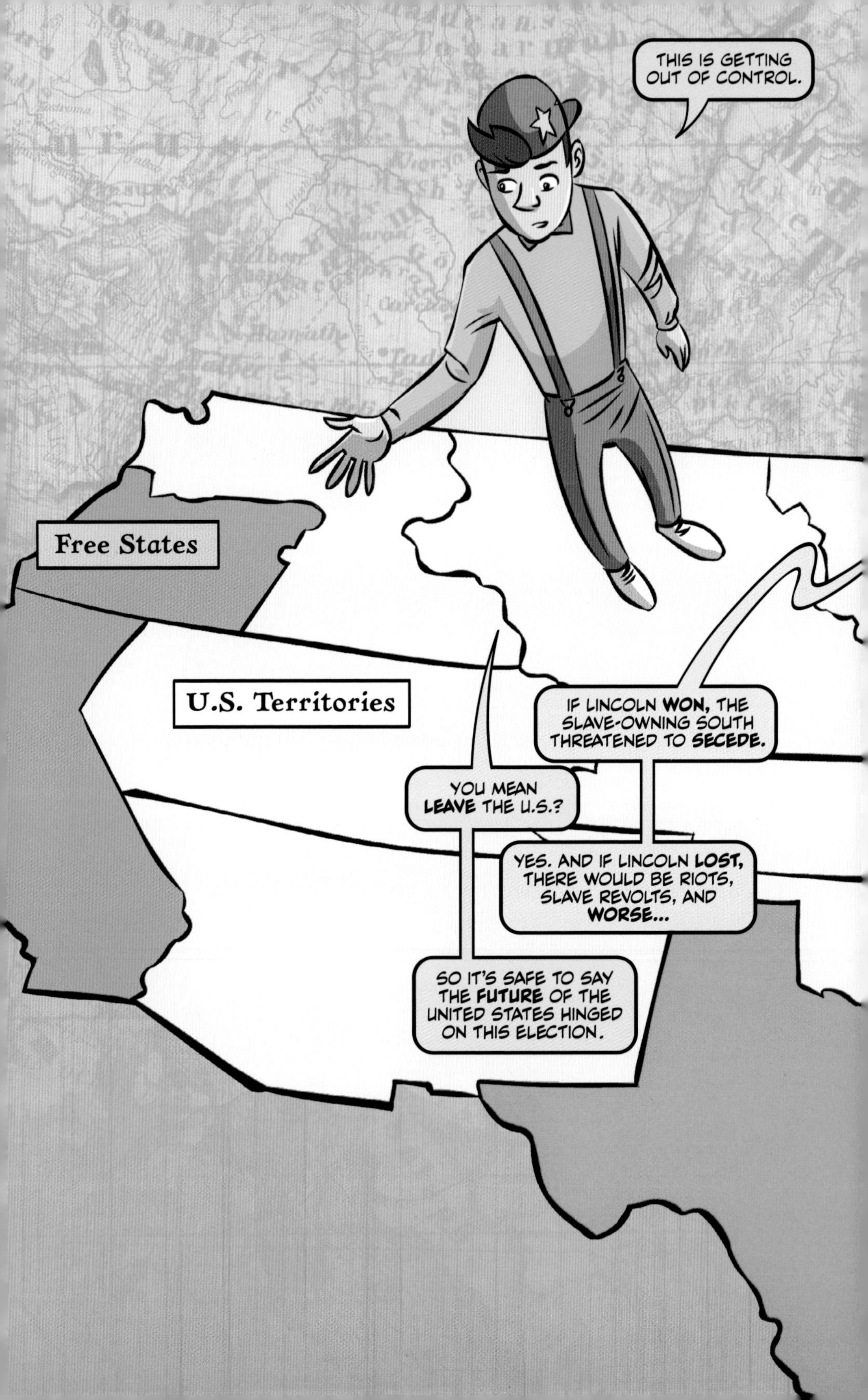
THIS IS GETTING OUT OF CONTROL.
Free States
U.S. Territories
IF LINCOLN WON, THE SLAVE-OWNING SOUTH THREATENED TO SECEDE.
YOU MEAN LEAVE THE U.S.?
YES. AND IF LINCOLN LOST, THERE WOULD BE RIOTS, SLAVE REVOLTS, AND WORSE...
SO IT'S SAFE TO SAY THE FUTURE OF THE UNITED STATES HINGED ON THIS ELECTION.

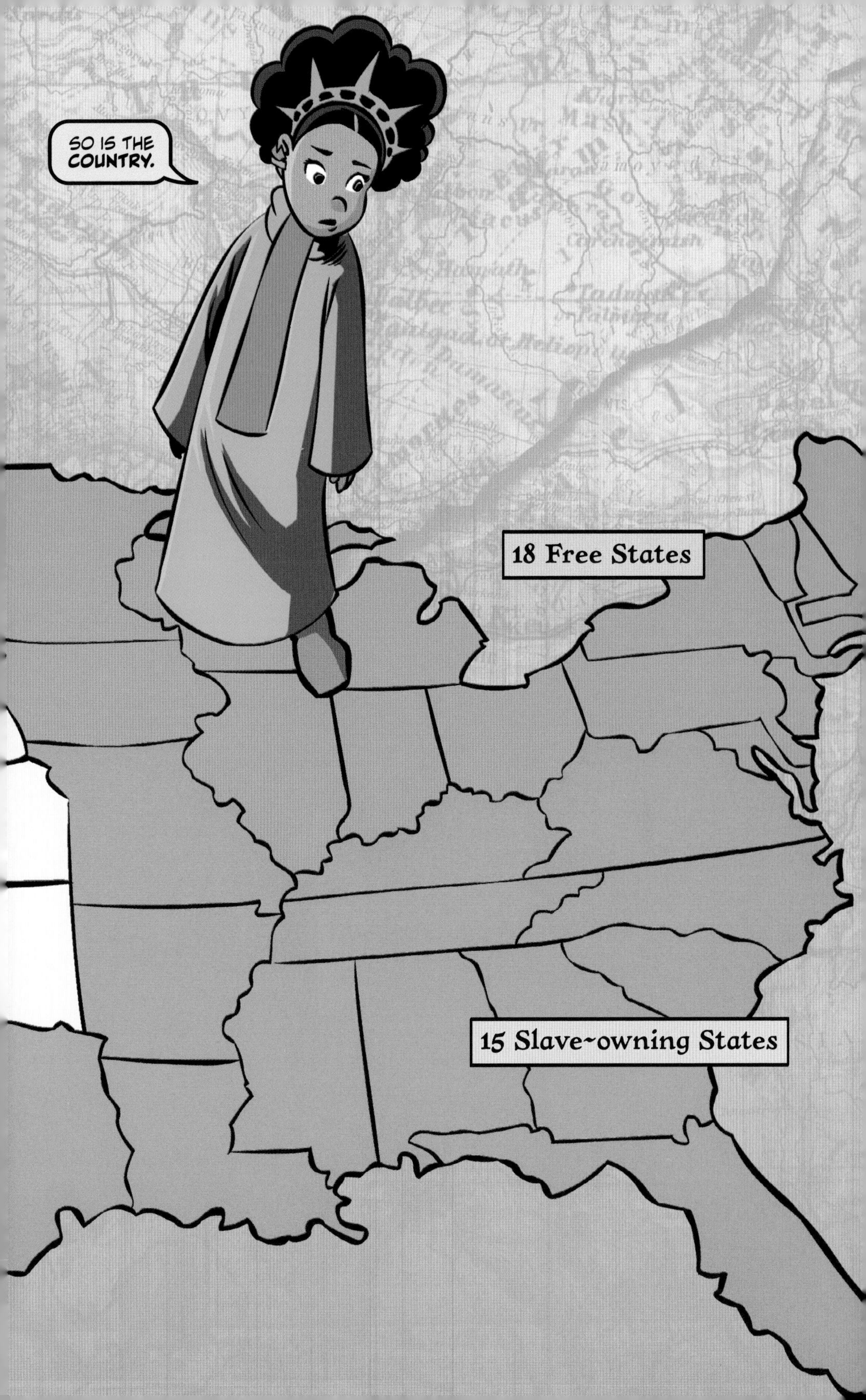
SO IS THE COUNTRY.
18 Free States
15 Slave~owning States

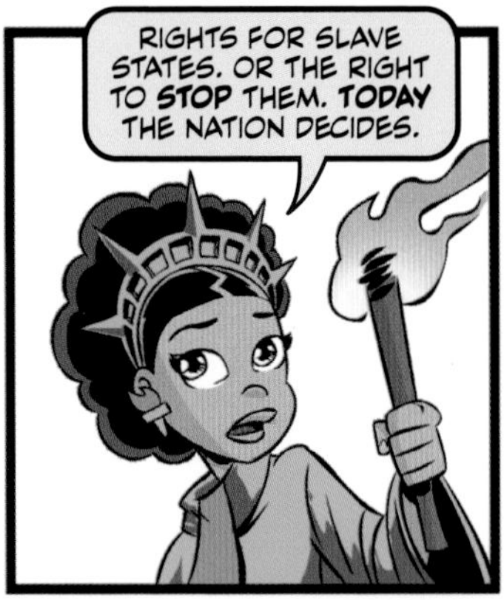
RIGHTS FOR SLAVE STATES. OR THE RIGHT TO **STOP** THEM. **TODAY** THE NATION DECIDES.

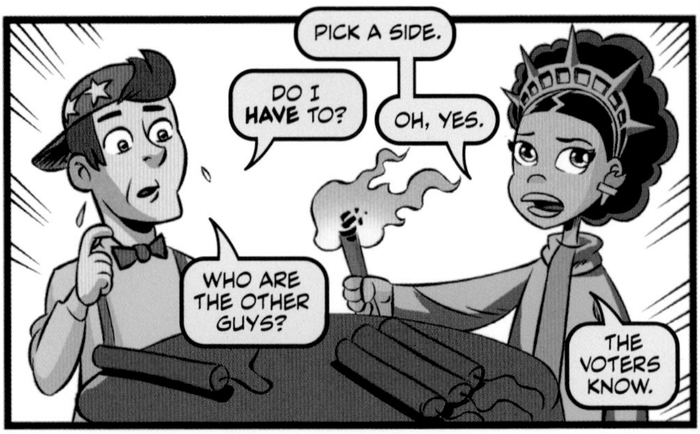
DO I **HAVE** TO?
PICK A SIDE.
OH, YES.
WHO ARE THE OTHER GUYS?
THE VOTERS KNOW.

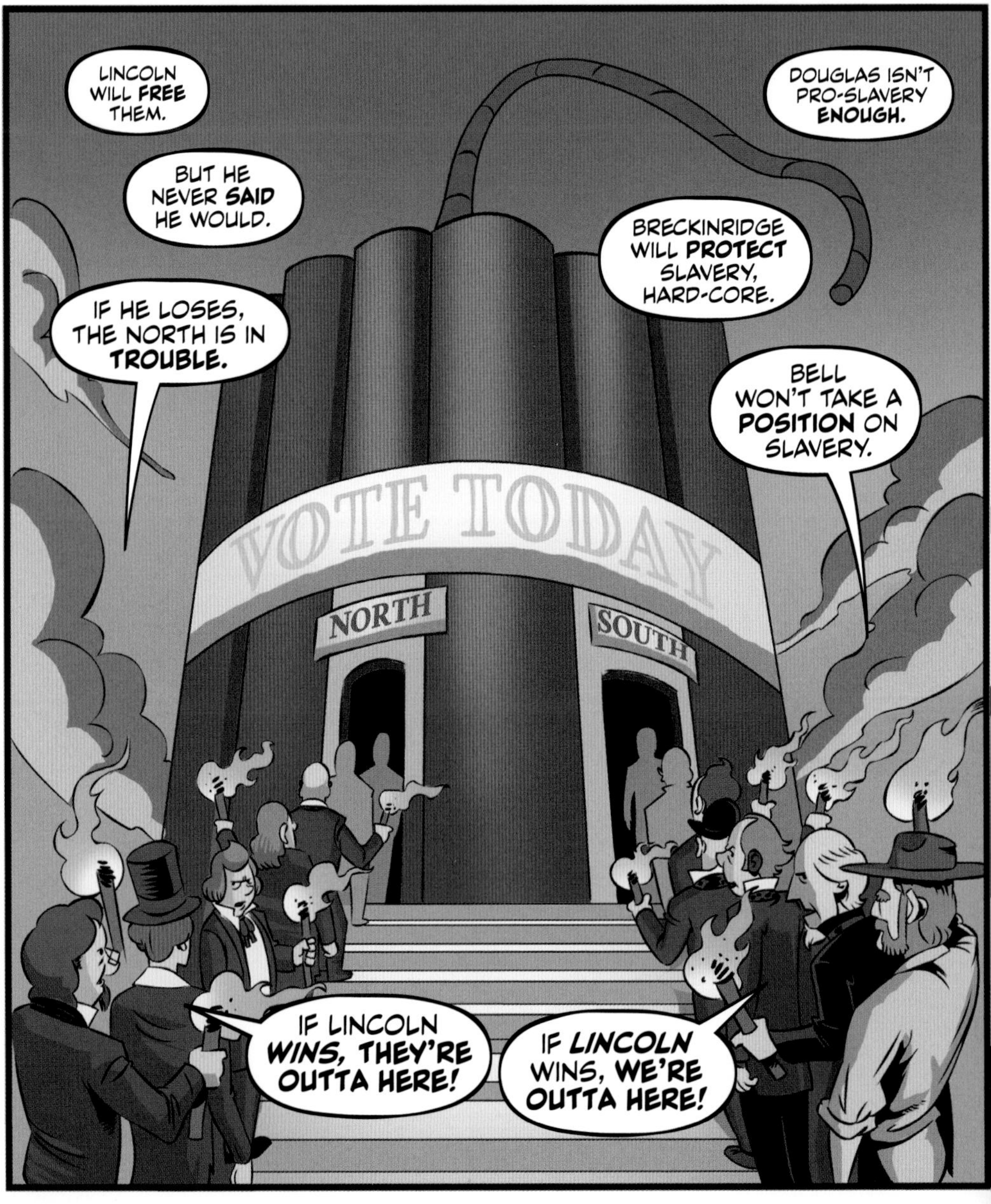
LINCOLN WILL **FREE** THEM.
BUT HE NEVER **SAID** HE WOULD.
IF HE LOSES, THE NORTH IS IN **TROUBLE.**
DOUGLAS ISN'T PRO-SLAVERY **ENOUGH.**
BRECKINRIDGE WILL **PROTECT** SLAVERY, HARD-CORE.
BELL WON'T TAKE A **POSITION** ON SLAVERY.
VOTE TODAY
NORTH
SOUTH
IF LINCOLN ***WINS,* THEY'RE OUTTA HERE!**
IF ***LINCOLN*** WINS, **WE'RE OUTTA HERE!**

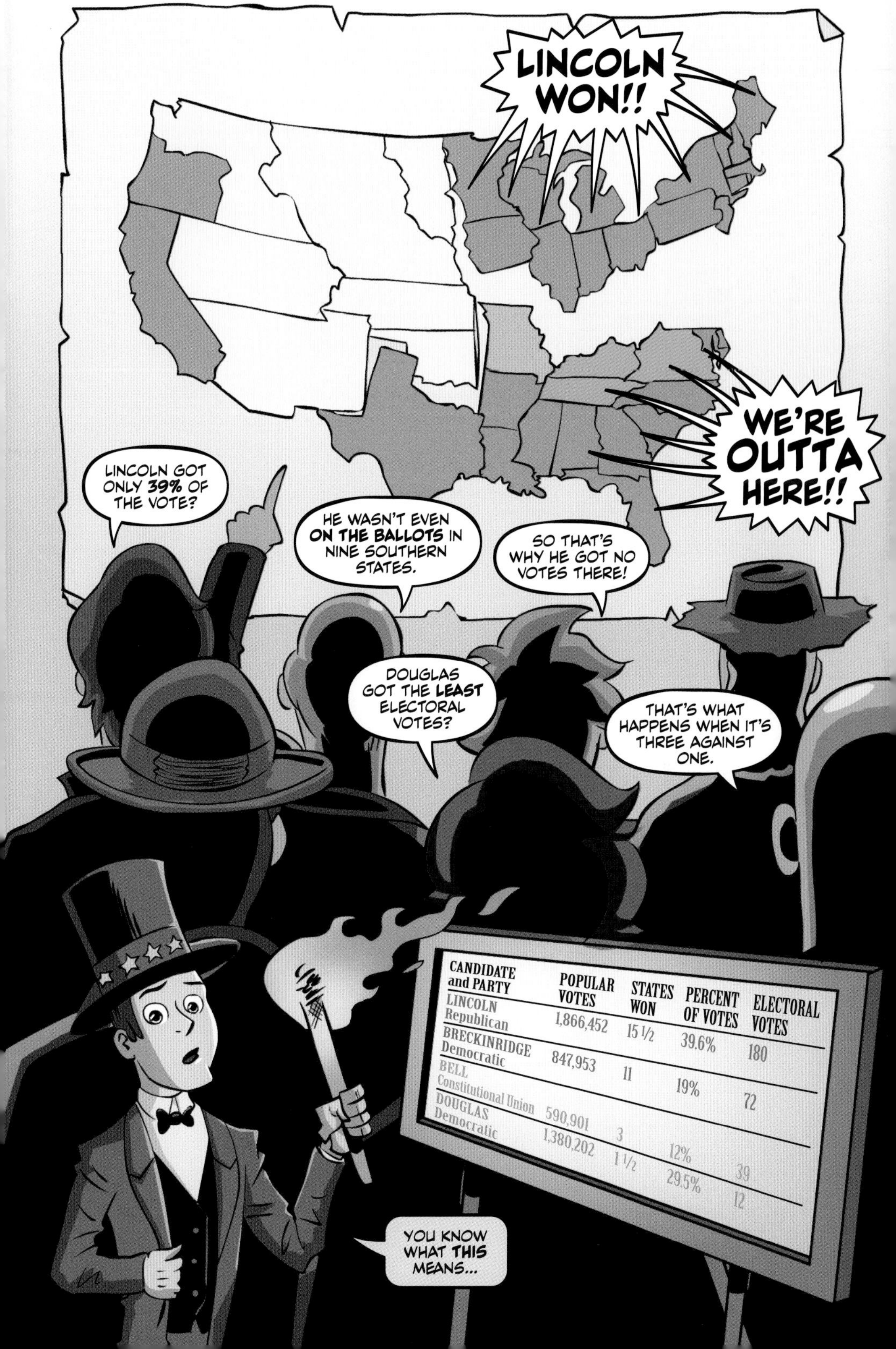
LINCOLN WON!!
WE'RE OUTTA HERE!!
LINCOLN GOT ONLY 39% OF THE VOTE?
HE WASN'T EVEN ON THE BALLOTS IN NINE SOUTHERN STATES.
SO THAT'S WHY HE GOT NO VOTES THERE!
DOUGLAS GOT THE LEAST ELECTORAL VOTES?
THAT'S WHAT HAPPENS WHEN IT'S THREE AGAINST ONE.
CANDIDATE and PARTY
POPULAR VOTES
STATES WON
PERCENT OF VOTES
ELECTORAL VOTES
LINCOLN Republican 1,866,452 15 1/2 39.6% 180
BRECKINRIDGE Democratic 847,953 11 19% 72
BELL Constitutional Union 590,901 3 12% 39
DOUGLAS Democratic 1,380,202 1 1/2 29.5% 12
YOU KNOW WHAT THIS MEANS...

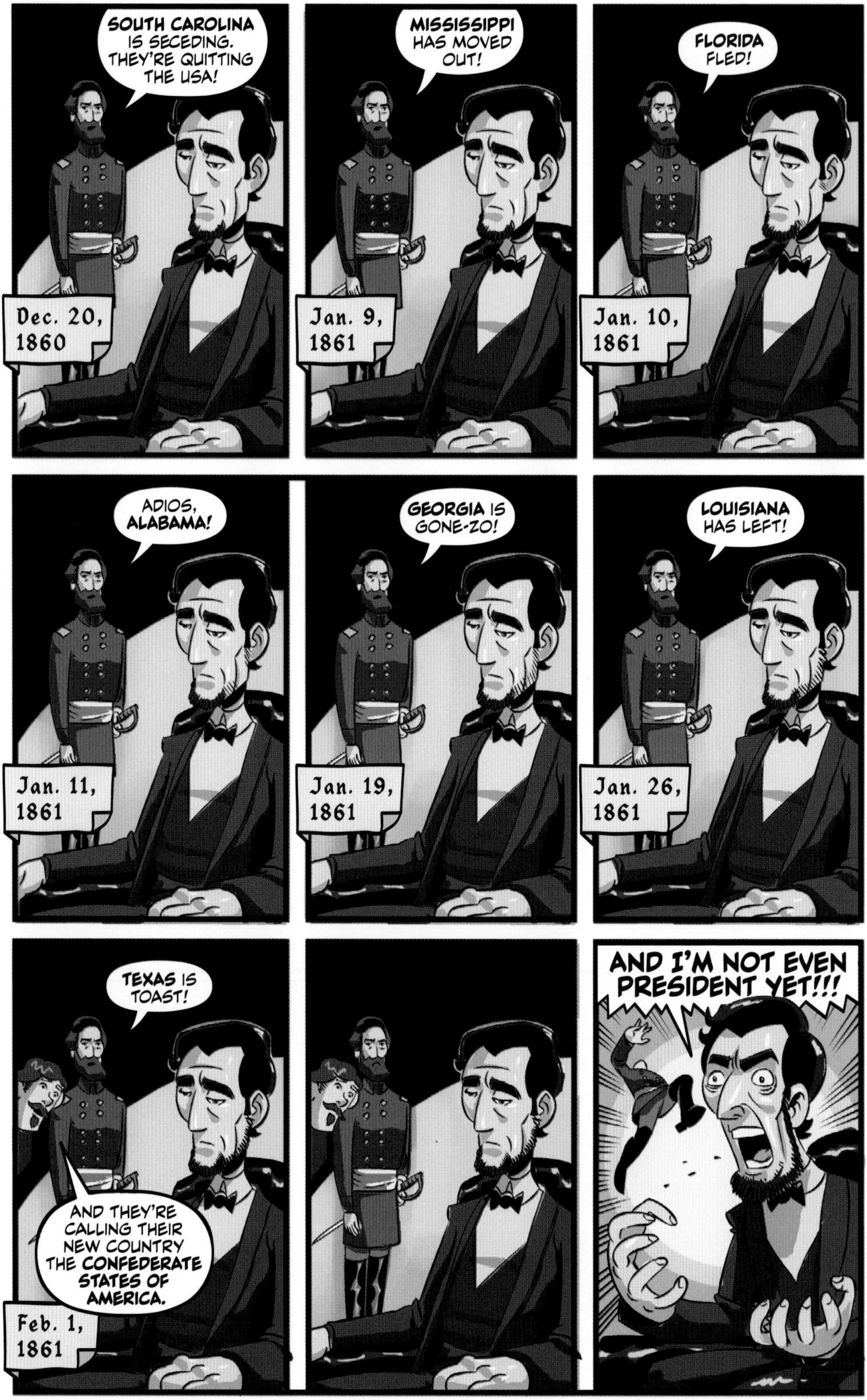
SOUTH CAROLINA IS SECEDING. THEY'RE QUITTING THE USA!
Dec. 20, 1860
MISSISSIPPI HAS MOVED OUT!
Jan. 9, 1861
FLORIDA FLED!
Jan. 10, 1861
ADIOS, ALABAMA!
Jan. 11, 1861
GEORGIA IS GONE-ZO!
Jan. 19, 1861
LOUISIANA HAS LEFT!
Jan. 26, 1861
TEXAS IS TOAST!
AND THEY'RE CALLING THEIR NEW COUNTRY THE CONFEDERATE STATES OF AMERICA.
Feb. 1, 1861
AND I'M NOT EVEN PRESIDENT YET!!!

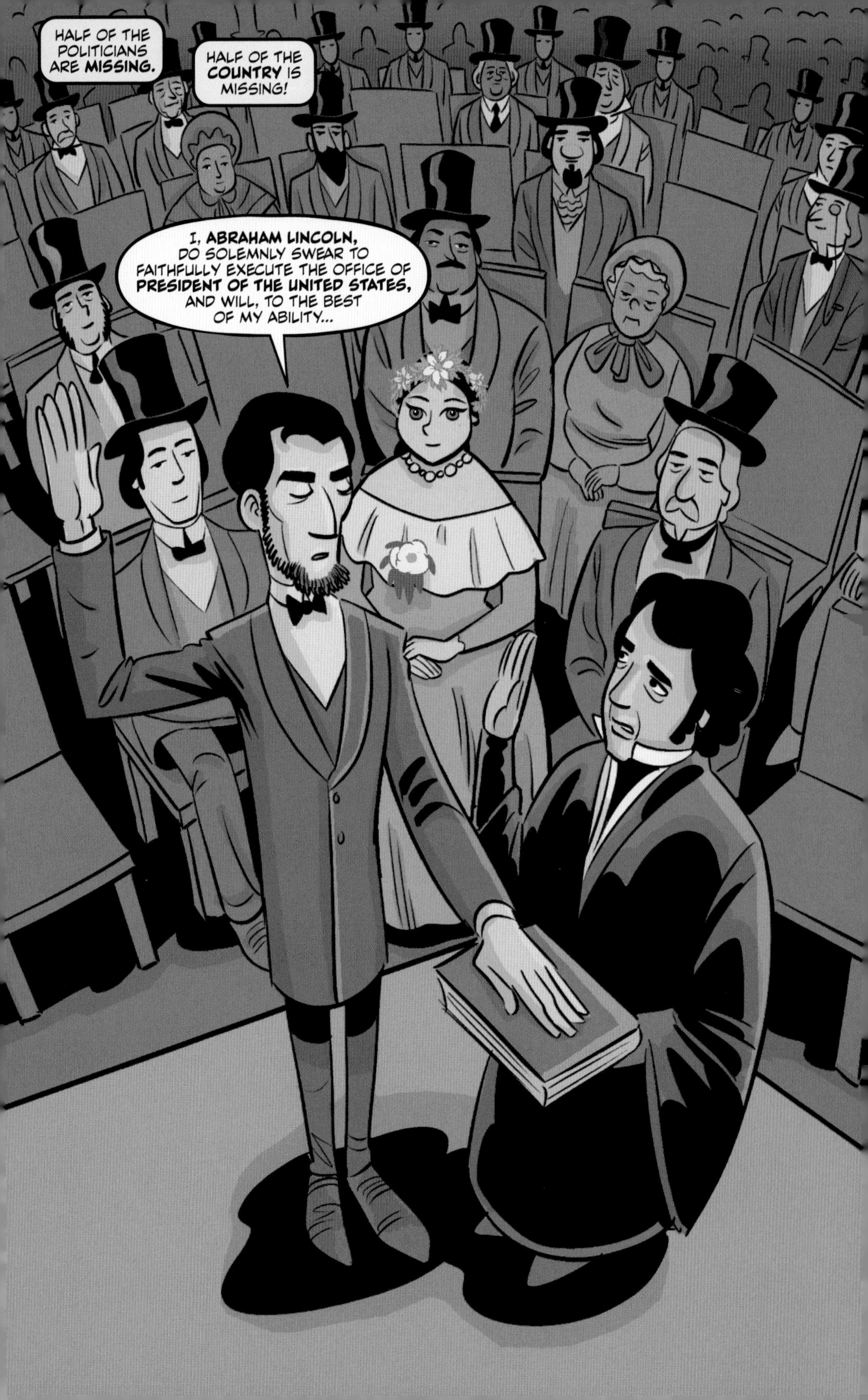
HALF OF THE POLITICIANS ARE **MISSING.**
HALF OF THE **COUNTRY** IS MISSING!
I, **ABRAHAM LINCOLN,** DO SOLEMNLY SWEAR TO FAITHFULLY EXECUTE THE OFFICE OF **PRESIDENT OF THE UNITED STATES,** AND WILL, TO THE BEST OF MY ABILITY...

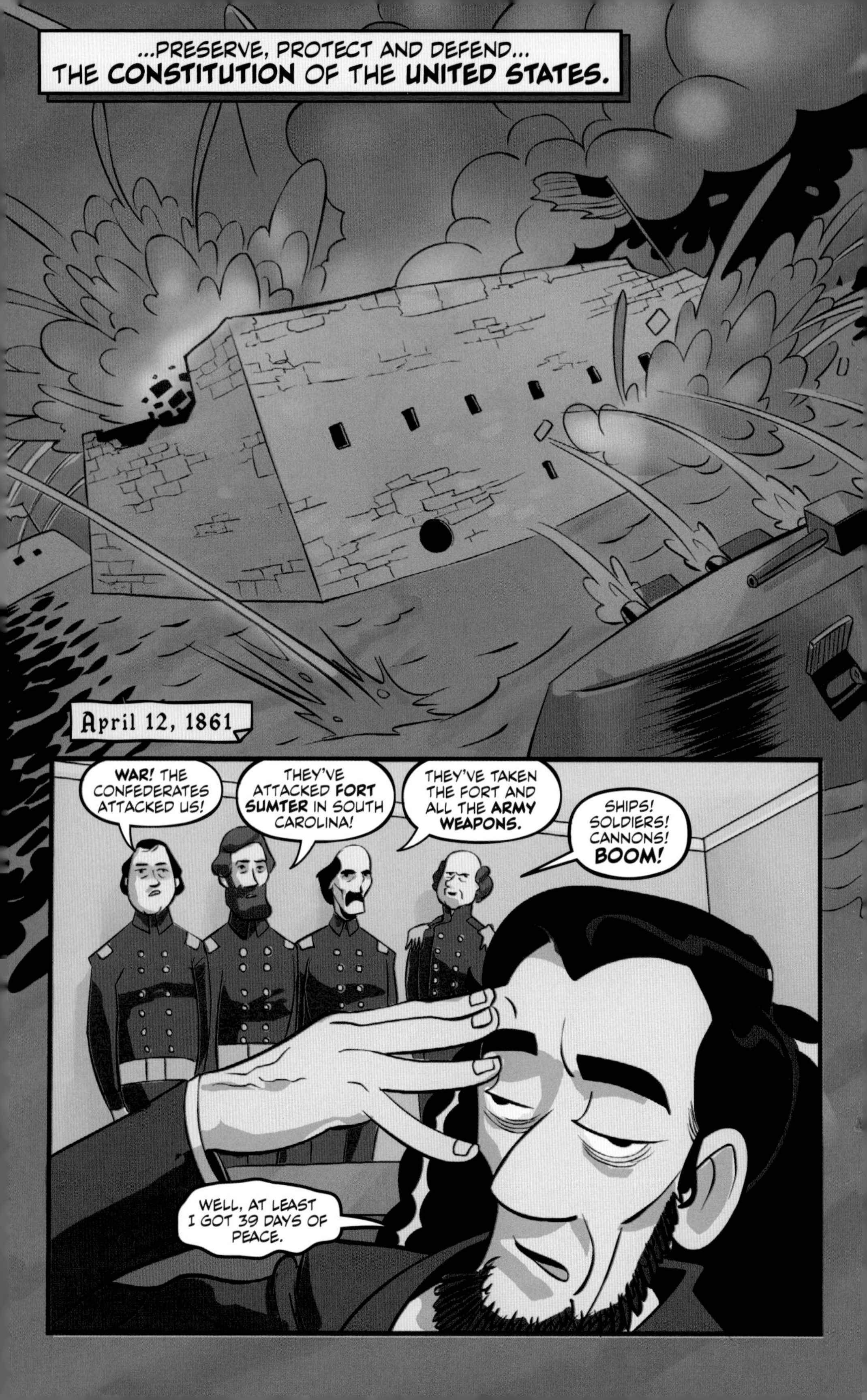
...PRESERVE, PROTECT AND DEFEND...
THE CONSTITUTION OF THE UNITED STATES.
April 12, 1861
WAR! THE CONFEDERATES ATTACKED US!
THEY'VE ATTACKED FORT SUMTER IN SOUTH CAROLINA!
THEY'VE TAKEN THE FORT AND ALL THE ARMY WEAPONS.
SHIPS! SOLDIERS! CANNONS! BOOM!
WELL, AT LEAST I GOT 39 DAYS OF PEACE.

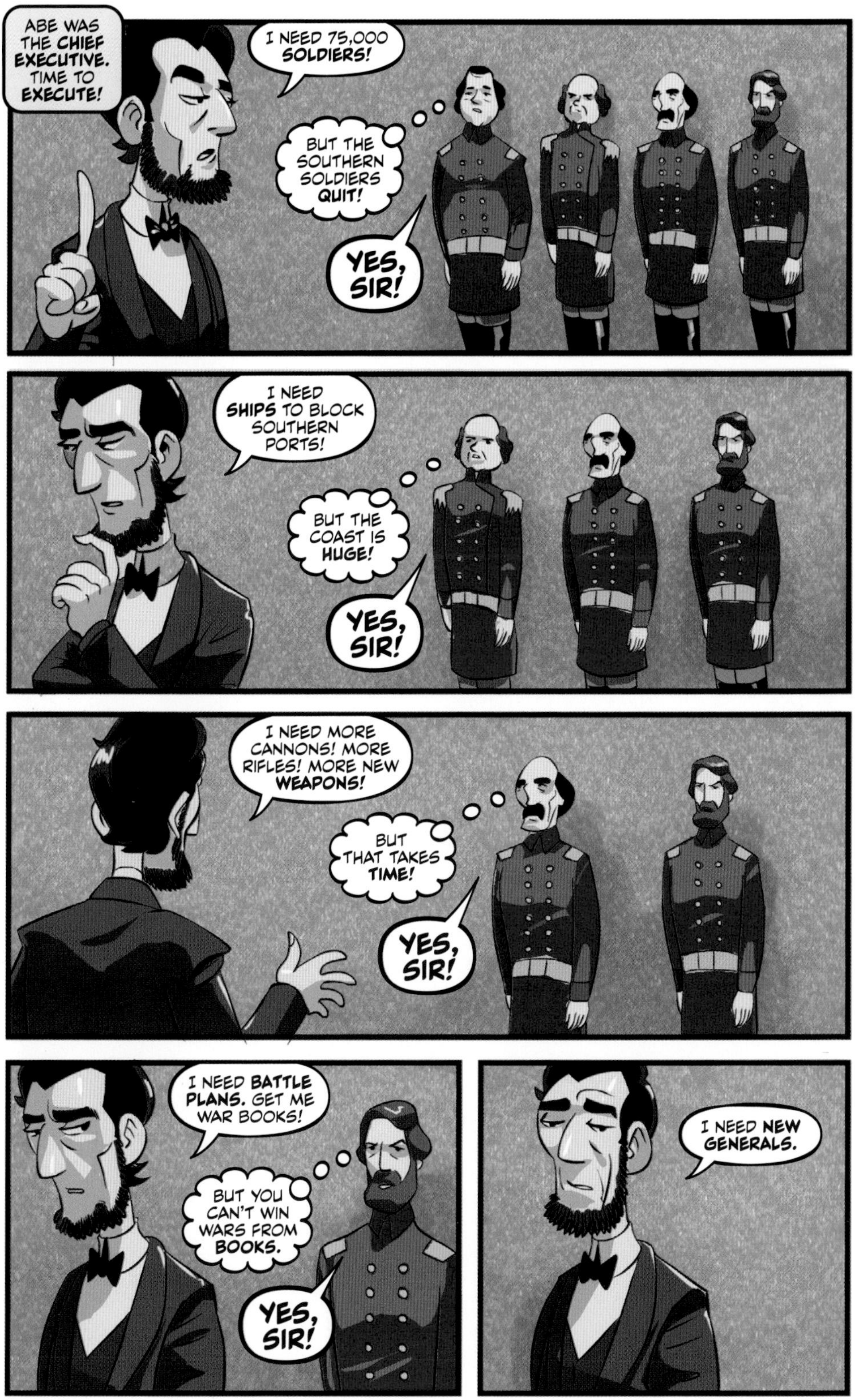
ABE WAS THE CHIEF EXECUTIVE. TIME TO EXECUTE!
I NEED 75,000 SOLDIERS!
BUT THE SOUTHERN SOLDIERS QUIT!
YES, SIR!
I NEED SHIPS TO BLOCK SOUTHERN PORTS!
BUT THE COAST IS HUGE!
YES, SIR!
I NEED MORE CANNONS! MORE RIFLES! MORE NEW WEAPONS!
BUT THAT TAKES TIME!
YES, SIR!
I NEED BATTLE PLANS. GET ME WAR BOOKS!
BUT YOU CAN'T WIN WARS FROM BOOKS.
YES, SIR!
I NEED NEW GENERALS.

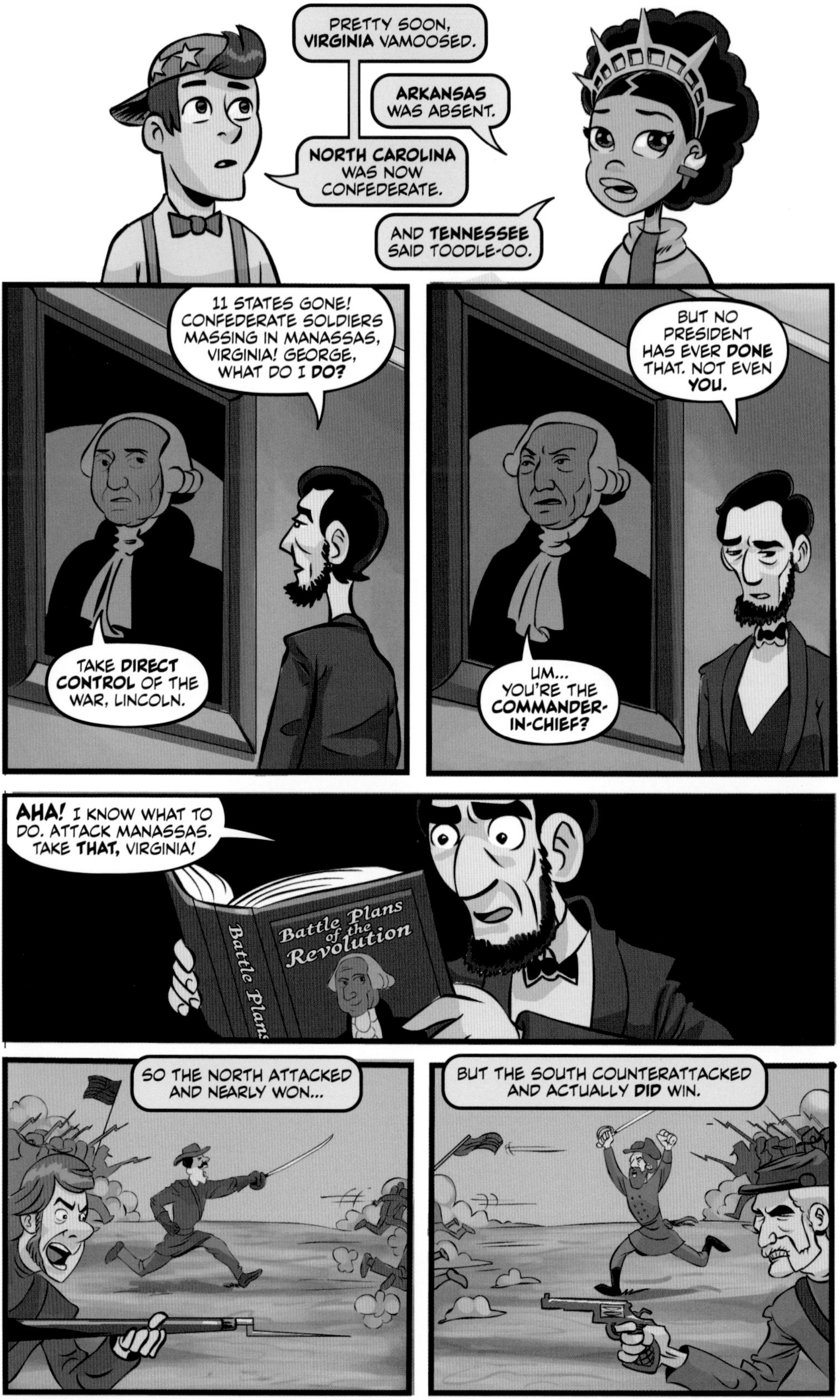
PRETTY SOON, VIRGINIA VAMOOSED.
ARKANSAS WAS ABSENT.
NORTH CAROLINA WAS NOW CONFEDERATE.
AND TENNESSEE SAID TOODLE-OO.
11 STATES GONE! CONFEDERATE SOLDIERS MASSING IN MANASSAS, VIRGINIA! GEORGE, WHAT DO I DO?
TAKE DIRECT CONTROL OF THE WAR, LINCOLN.
BUT NO PRESIDENT HAS EVER DONE THAT. NOT EVEN YOU.
UM... YOU'RE THE COMMANDER-IN-CHIEF?
AHA! I KNOW WHAT TO DO. ATTACK MANASSAS. TAKE THAT, VIRGINIA!
Battle Plans of the Revolution
Battle Plans
SO THE NORTH ATTACKED AND NEARLY WON...
BUT THE SOUTH COUNTERATTACKED AND ACTUALLY DID WIN.

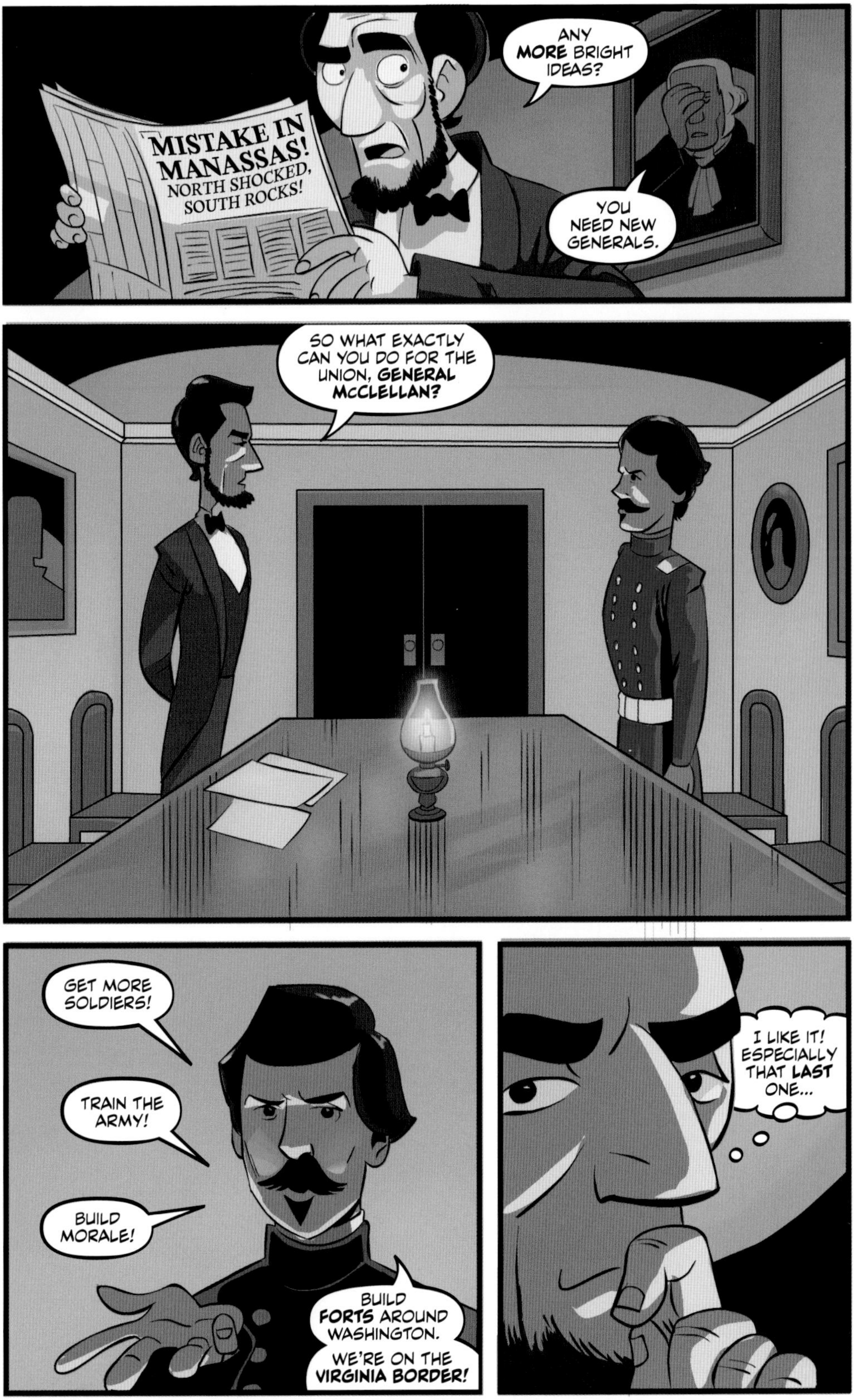
MISTAKE IN MANASSAS! NORTH SHOCKED, SOUTH ROCKS!
ANY MORE BRIGHT IDEAS?
YOU NEED NEW GENERALS.
SO WHAT EXACTLY CAN YOU DO FOR THE UNION, GENERAL McCLELLAN?
GET MORE SOLDIERS!
TRAIN THE ARMY!
BUILD MORALE!
BUILD FORTS AROUND WASHINGTON.
WE'RE ON THE VIRGINIA BORDER!
I LIKE IT! ESPECIALLY THAT LAST ONE...

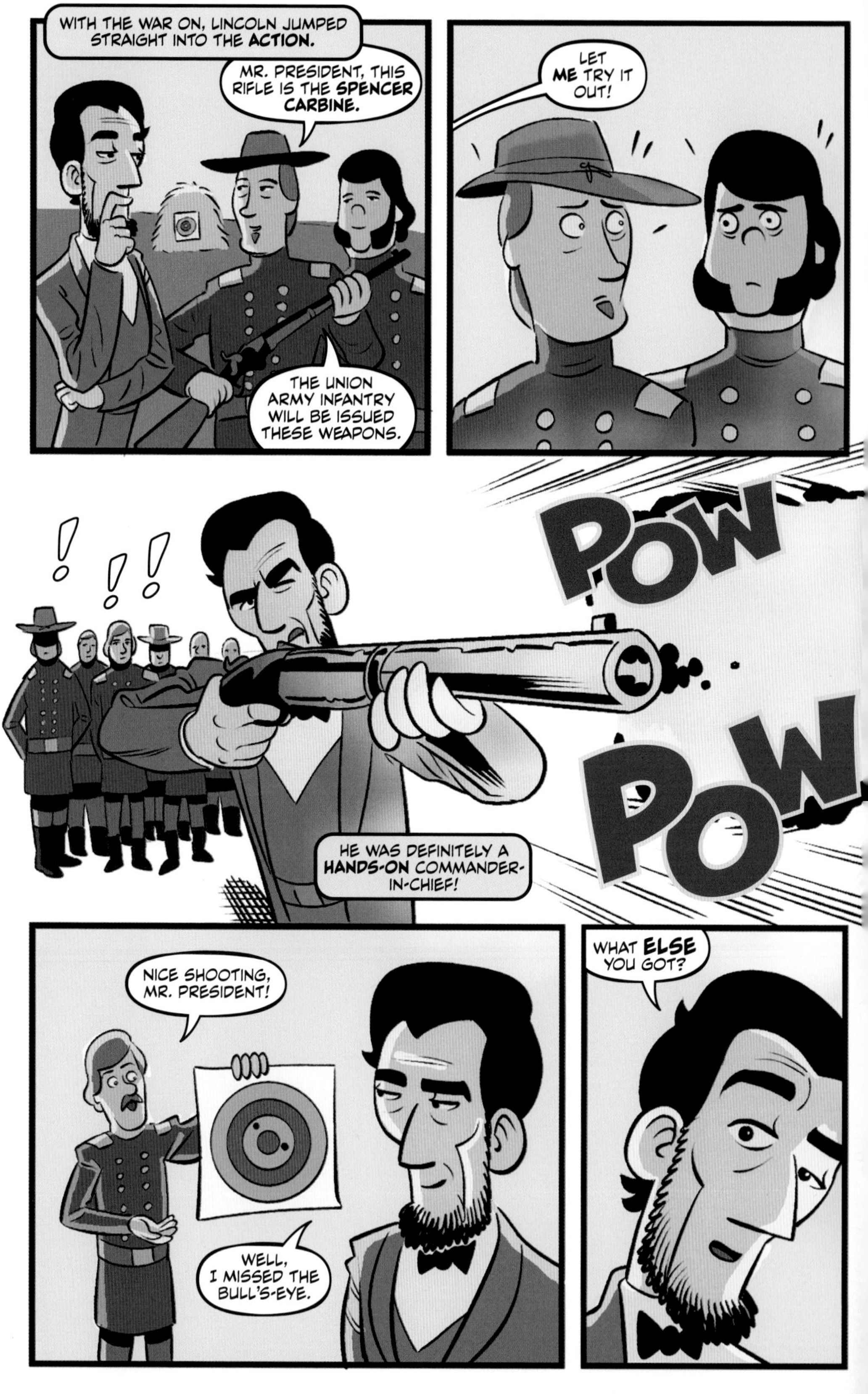
WITH THE WAR ON, LINCOLN JUMPED STRAIGHT INTO THE **ACTION.**
MR. PRESIDENT, THIS RIFLE IS THE **SPENCER CARBINE.**
THE UNION ARMY INFANTRY WILL BE ISSUED THESE WEAPONS.
LET **ME** TRY IT OUT!
POW
POW
HE WAS DEFINITELY A **HANDS-ON** COMMANDER-IN-CHIEF!
NICE SHOOTING, MR. PRESIDENT!
WELL, I MISSED THE BULL'S-EYE.
WHAT **ELSE** YOU GOT?

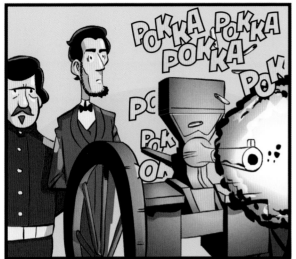

POKKA POKKA POKKA POKKA POK POK POK ON

THAT IS A FEARSOME WEAPON OF WAR. I FEEL SORRY FOR ITS VICTIMS.

WE'LL TAKE A FEW HUNDRED.

LOAD THE "SODA BOTTLE"!

HE MEANS THE DAHLGREN CANNON, SIR.

BWATHOOOOM

BLAMMM

Notice: No cartoon characters were harmed during this naval exercise.

I LIKE IT!

WHAT?

THE **CIVIL WAR** WENT ON... AND **ON**... AND IT WAS **BLOODY**.

AND **EXPENSIVE**.

TREASURY SECRETARY **SALMON P. CHASE**, SIR.

SHOW HIM IN.

IT'S A BAD PLAN. CUT TO THE CHASE, CHASE.

YES, SIR.

USING **PAPER MONEY** WILL SAVE THE UNION, MR. PRESIDENT.

THE TREASURY HASN'T ENOUGH GOLD OR SILVER TO **PAY** THE SOLDIERS. OR ANYONE ELSE.

AND WHY SHOULD PEOPLE **TRUST** PAPER MONEY?

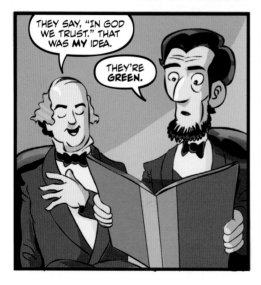

THEY SAY, "IN GOD WE TRUST." THAT WAS **MY** IDEA.

THEY'RE **GREEN**.

AND THESE PICTURES... WERE **THEY** YOUR IDEA, TOO?

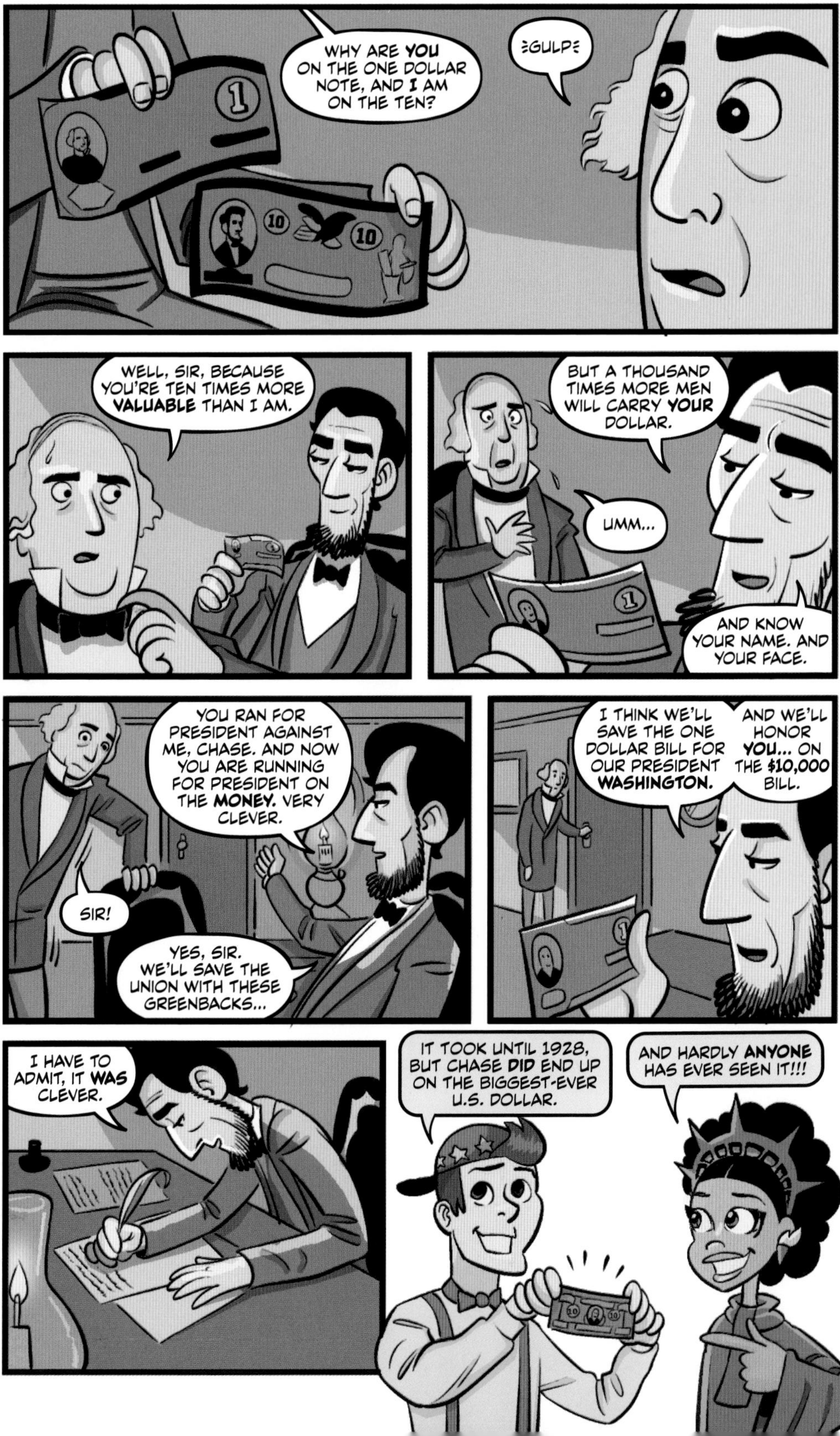
WHY ARE **YOU** ON THE ONE DOLLAR NOTE, AND **I** AM ON THE TEN?
GULP
WELL, SIR, BECAUSE YOU'RE TEN TIMES MORE **VALUABLE** THAN I AM.
BUT A THOUSAND TIMES MORE MEN WILL CARRY **YOUR** DOLLAR.
UMM...
AND KNOW YOUR NAME. AND YOUR FACE.
YOU RAN FOR PRESIDENT AGAINST ME, CHASE. AND NOW YOU ARE RUNNING FOR PRESIDENT ON THE **MONEY.** VERY CLEVER.
SIR!
YES, SIR. WE'LL SAVE THE UNION WITH THESE GREENBACKS...
I THINK WE'LL SAVE THE ONE DOLLAR BILL FOR OUR PRESIDENT **WASHINGTON.**
AND WE'LL HONOR **YOU...** ON THE **$10,000** BILL.
I HAVE TO ADMIT, IT **WAS** CLEVER.
IT TOOK UNTIL 1928, BUT CHASE **DID** END UP ON THE BIGGEST-EVER U.S. DOLLAR.
AND HARDLY **ANYONE** HAS EVER SEEN IT!!!

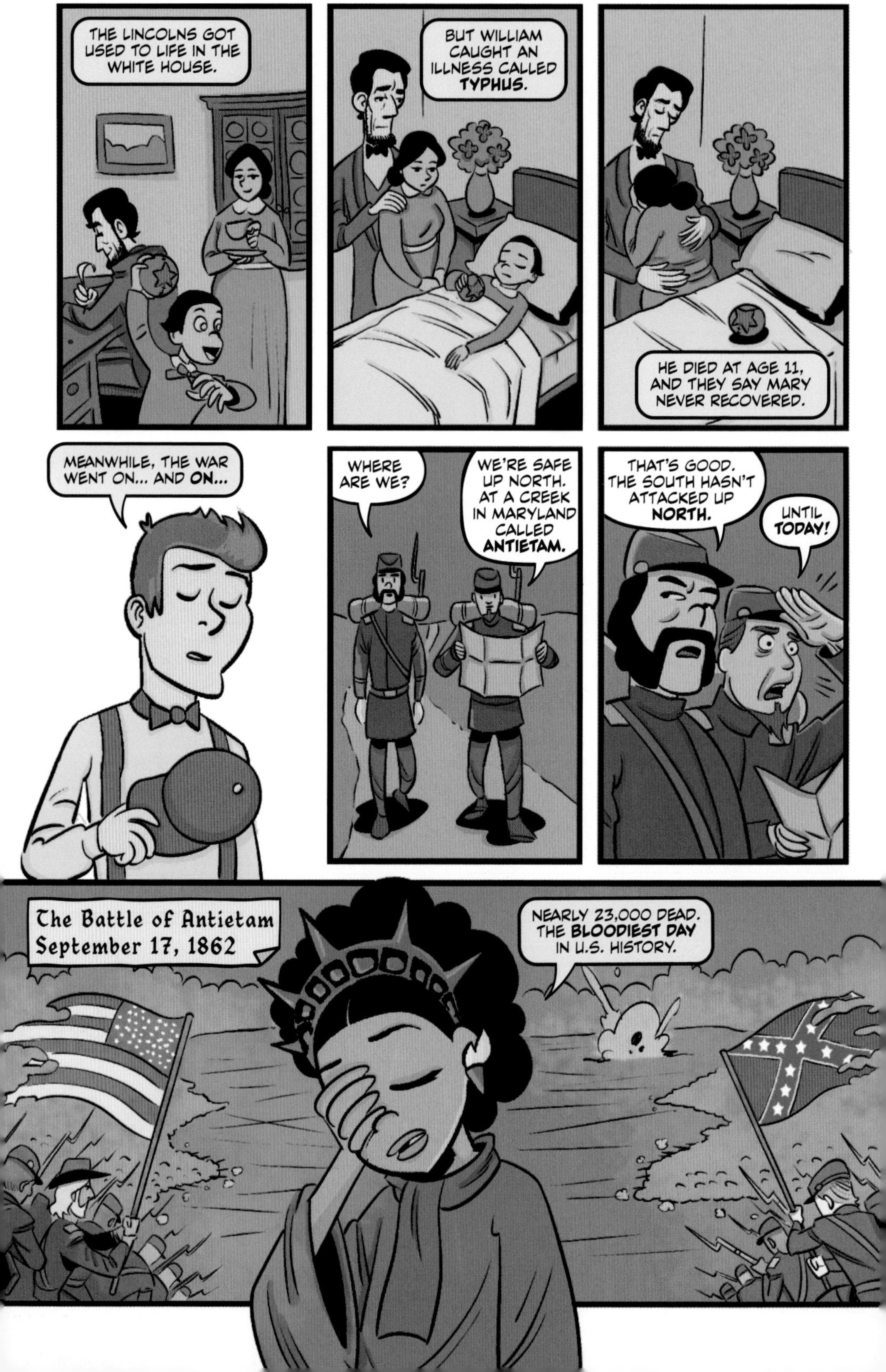
THE LINCOLNS GOT USED TO LIFE IN THE WHITE HOUSE.
BUT WILLIAM CAUGHT AN ILLNESS CALLED TYPHUS.
HE DIED AT AGE 11, AND THEY SAY MARY NEVER RECOVERED.
MEANWHILE, THE WAR WENT ON... AND ON...
WHERE ARE WE?
WE'RE SAFE UP NORTH. AT A CREEK IN MARYLAND CALLED ANTIETAM.
THAT'S GOOD. THE SOUTH HASN'T ATTACKED UP NORTH.
UNTIL TODAY!
The Battle of Antietam September 17, 1862
NEARLY 23,000 DEAD. THE BLOODIEST DAY IN U.S. HISTORY.

GENERAL McCLELLAN LOST ANTIETAM.
WE COULD HAVE WON, GENERAL GRANT.
McClellan
WE STOPPED THEM FROM GOING NORTH, SIR.
GENERAL McCLELLAN DIDN'T PUSH HARD ENOUGH.
HE THOUGHT THEY HAD MORE MEN.
THE SOUTH DID RETREAT BACK TO VIRGINIA, SIR.
GENERAL McCLELLAN LOST 25% OF OUR SOLDIERS.
Battle Losses
25%
31%
North
South
THE SOUTH LOST 31% OF THEIRS, SIR.
GENERAL McCLELLAN CAN'T GET MORE SOLDIERS TO SERVE.
WE'LL DRAFT MEN. MAKE IT A LAW TO SERVE, SIR.
GENERAL ULYSSES GRANT, I'M GOING TO FIRE McCLELLAN.
25%
HERE'S MY APPLICATION FOR THE JOB, SIR.
PEOPLE ARE LOSING FAITH IN THE WAR. SAVING THE UNION MAY NOT BE ENOUGH.
YOU MEAN...
YES, GENERAL GRANT.
IT'S TIME.

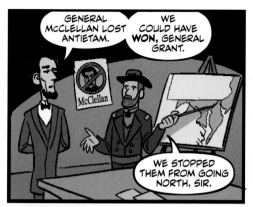

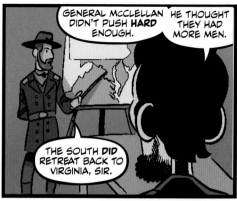

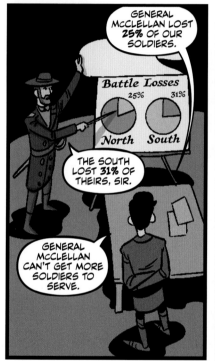

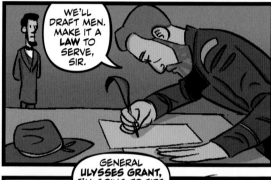

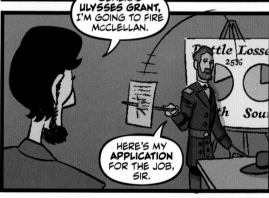

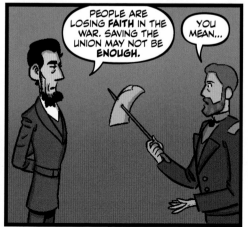

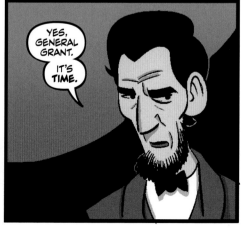

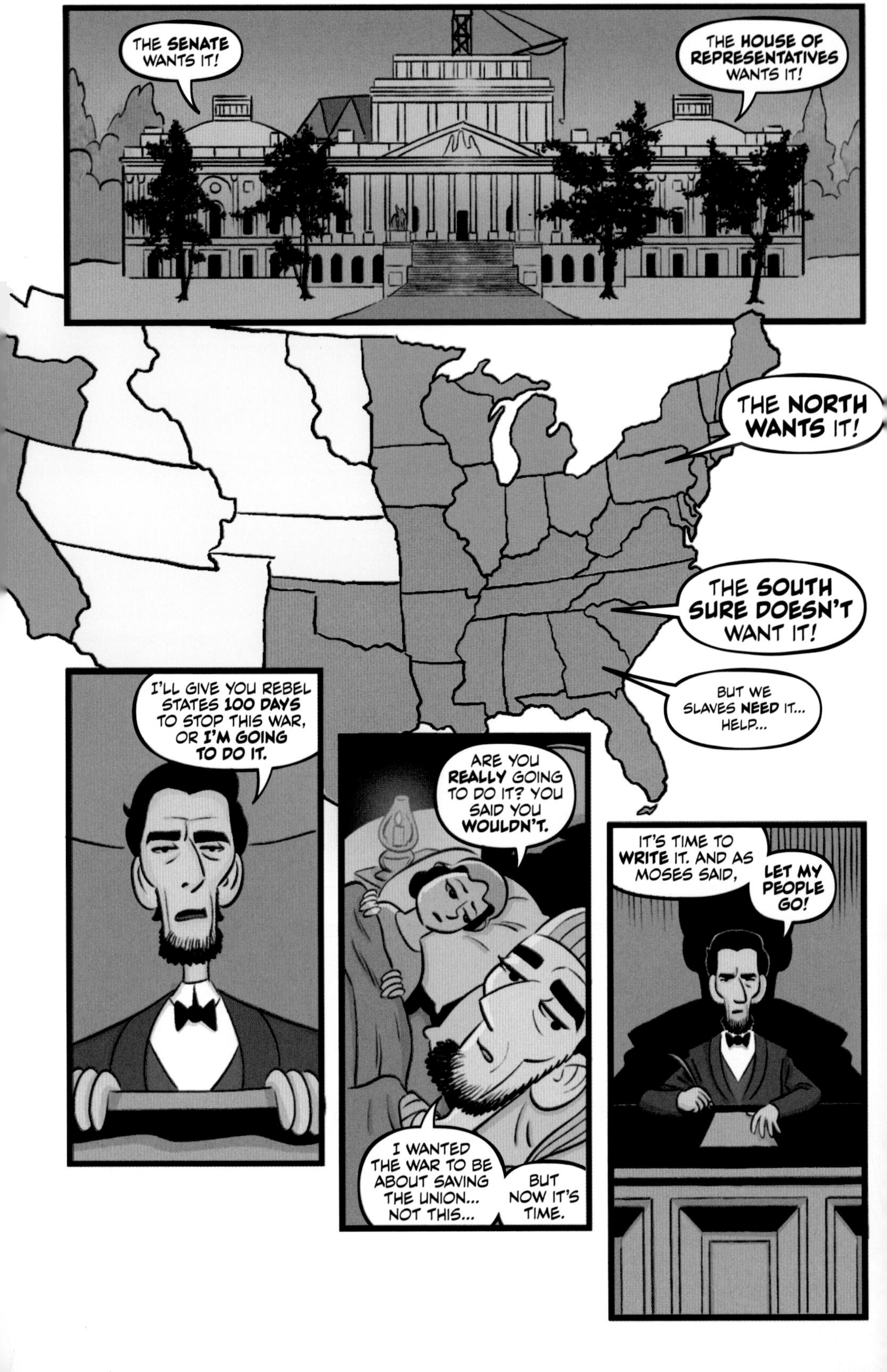

THE **SENATE** WANTS IT!
THE **HOUSE OF REPRESENTATIVES** WANTS IT!
THE **NORTH WANTS** IT!
THE **SOUTH SURE DOESN'T** WANT IT!
BUT WE SLAVES **NEED** IT... HELP...
I'LL GIVE YOU REBEL STATES **100 DAYS** TO STOP THIS WAR, OR **I'M GOING TO DO IT.**
ARE YOU **REALLY** GOING TO DO IT? YOU SAID YOU **WOULDN'T.**
I WANTED THE WAR TO BE ABOUT SAVING THE UNION... NOT THIS...
BUT NOW IT'S TIME.
IT'S TIME TO **WRITE** IT. AND AS MOSES SAID,
LET MY PEOPLE GO!

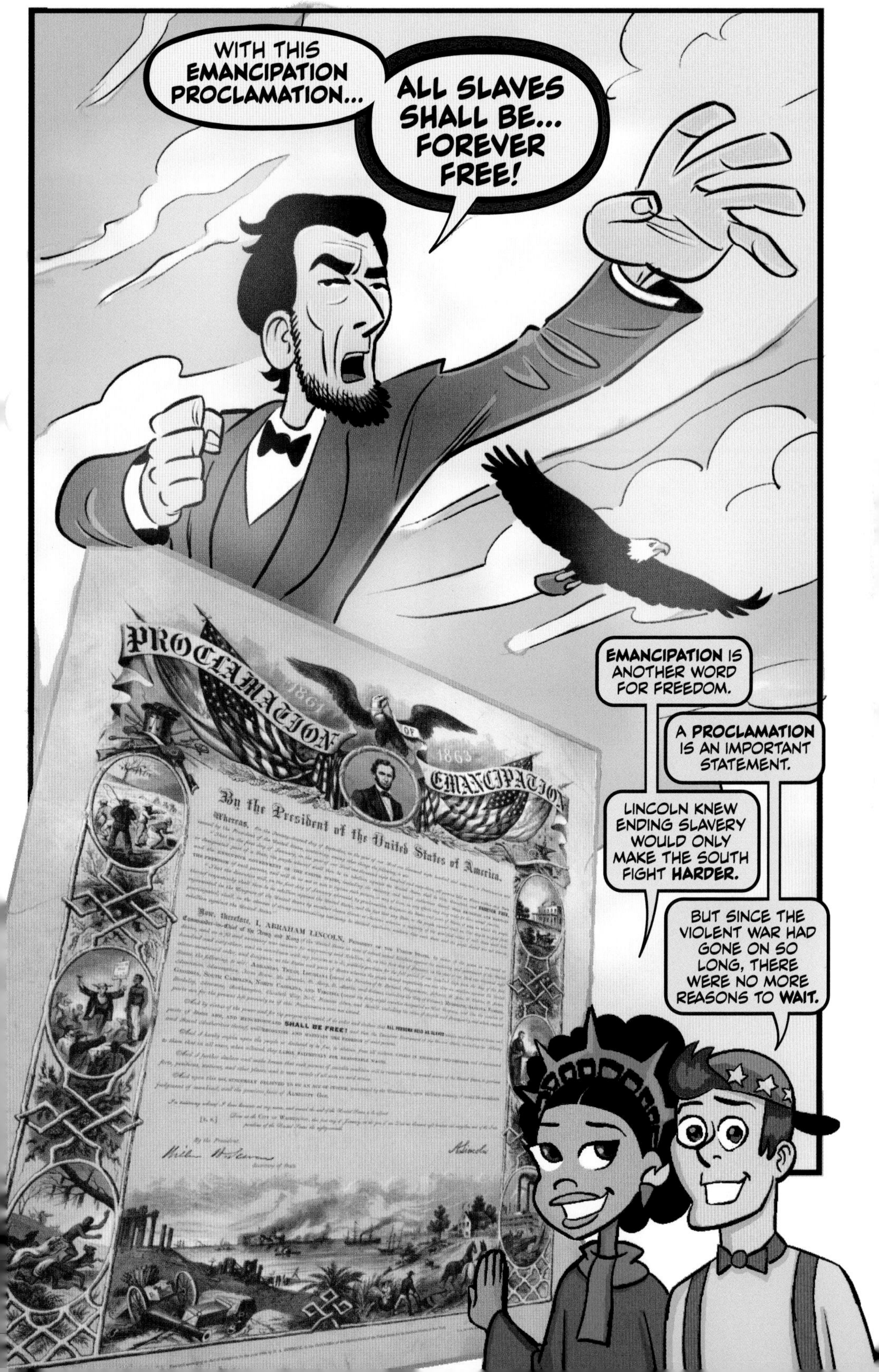
WITH THIS EMANCIPATION PROCLAMATION...
ALL SLAVES SHALL BE... FOREVER FREE!
PROCLAMATION OF EMANCIPATION
1861
1863
By the President of the United States of America.
SHALL BE FREE!
EMANCIPATION IS ANOTHER WORD FOR FREEDOM.
A PROCLAMATION IS AN IMPORTANT STATEMENT.
LINCOLN KNEW ENDING SLAVERY WOULD ONLY MAKE THE SOUTH FIGHT HARDER.
BUT SINCE THE VIOLENT WAR HAD GONE ON SO LONG, THERE WERE NO MORE REASONS TO WAIT.

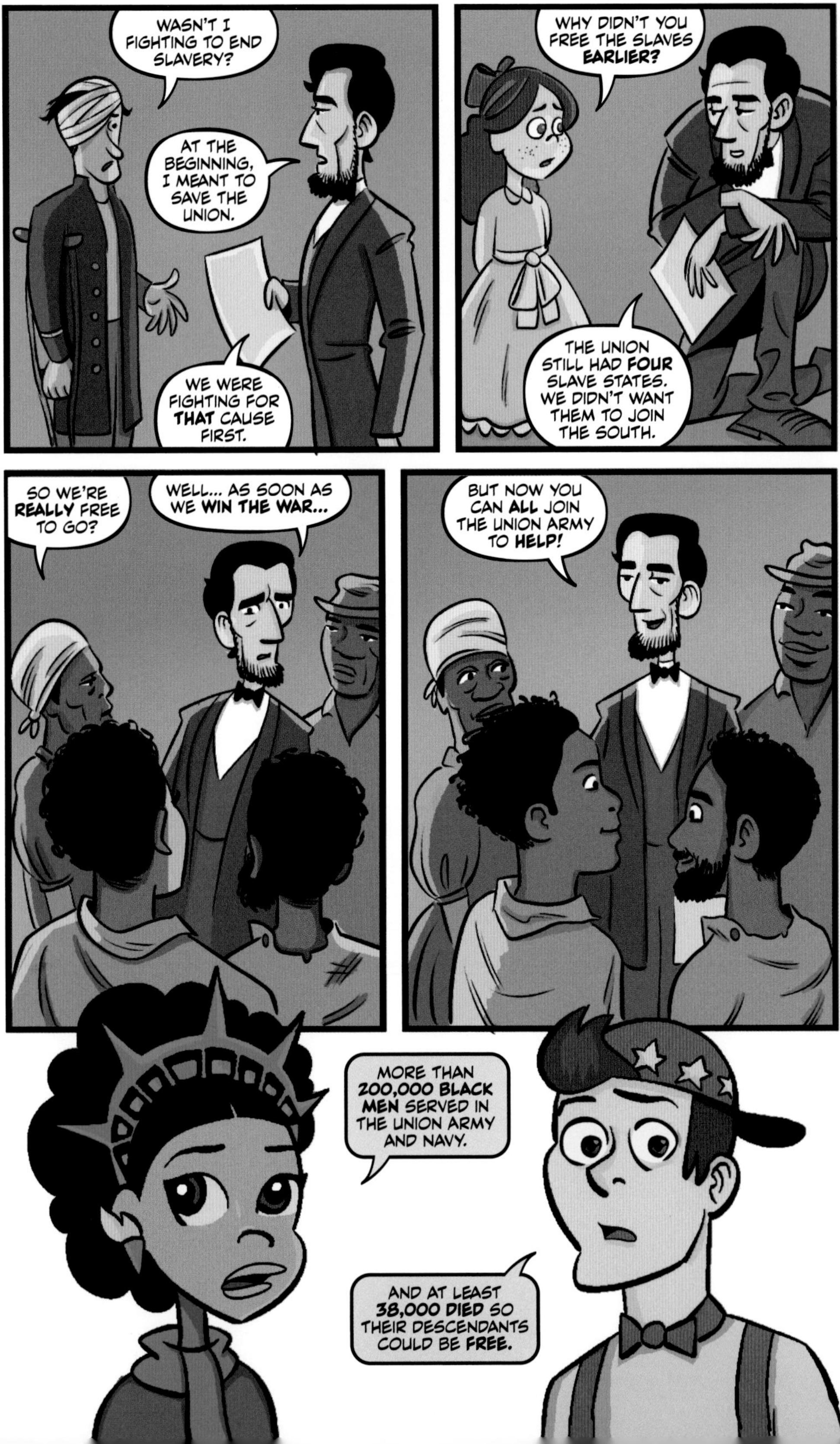
WASN'T I FIGHTING TO END SLAVERY?
AT THE BEGINNING, I MEANT TO SAVE THE UNION.
WE WERE FIGHTING FOR **THAT** CAUSE FIRST.
WHY DIDN'T YOU FREE THE SLAVES **EARLIER?**
THE UNION STILL HAD **FOUR** SLAVE STATES. WE DIDN'T WANT THEM TO JOIN THE SOUTH.
SO WE'RE **REALLY** FREE TO GO?
WELL... AS SOON AS WE **WIN THE WAR...**
BUT NOW YOU CAN **ALL** JOIN THE UNION ARMY TO **HELP!**
MORE THAN **200,000 BLACK MEN** SERVED IN THE UNION ARMY AND NAVY.
AND AT LEAST **38,000 DIED** SO THEIR DESCENDANTS COULD BE **FREE.**

SPEAKING OF THE WAR...

YOU KNOW, HOOKER, MCCLELLAN GOT FIRED FOR BEING **SLOW AND TIMID.**

ISN'T THAT GOOD NEWS FOR **YOU,** GRANT?

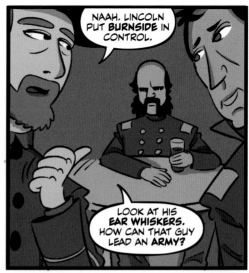

NAAH. LINCOLN PUT **BURNSIDE** IN CONTROL.

LOOK AT HIS **EAR WHISKERS.** HOW CAN THAT GUY LEAD AN **ARMY?**

HEY! LOOK AT THOSE **SIDEBURNS** ON BURNSIDE!

UM, SAM, THAT'S ACTUALLY WHERE THE WORD **"SIDEBURNS"** COMES FROM.

One month later

YOU KNOW, MEADE, LINCOLN FIRED BURNSIDE FOR LOSING **A LOT** OF MEN IN BATTLE.

MAYBE THIS IS **YOUR TURN,** GRANT?

NAAH. HE PUT **HOOKER** IN CONTROL. LOOK AT HIS **HAIRCUT.** HOW CAN THAT GUY LEAD AN ARMY?

FIRST MCCLELLAN. THEN BURNSIDE. THEN HOOKER. I NEED A **REAL** LEADER.

AT YOUR SERVICE, MR. PRESIDENT.

GENERAL **MEADE,** IT'S YOUR ARMY NOW.

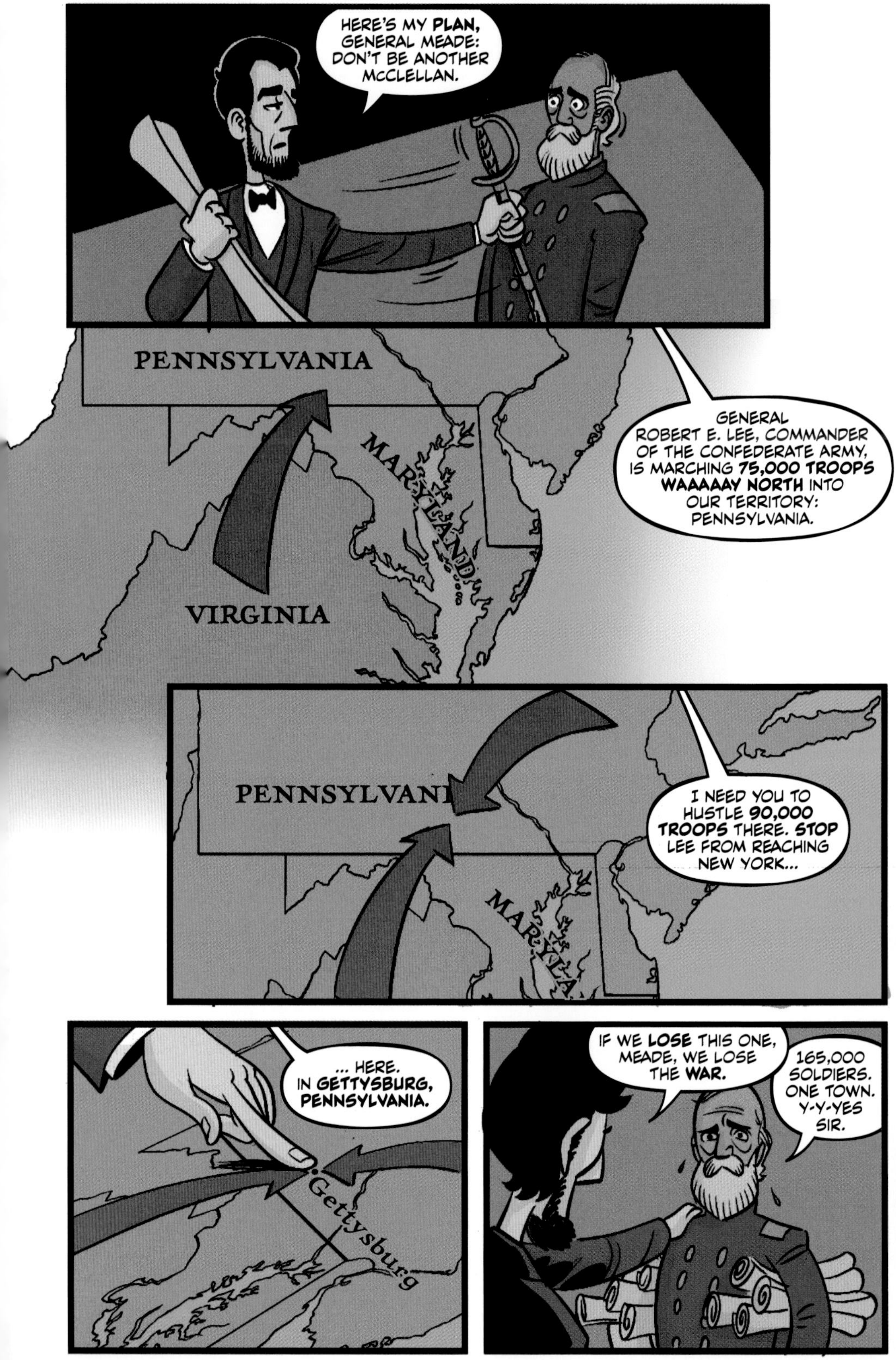
HERE'S MY **PLAN**, GENERAL MEADE: DON'T BE ANOTHER McCLELLAN.
PENNSYLVANIA
MARYLAND
VIRGINIA
GENERAL ROBERT E. LEE, COMMANDER OF THE CONFEDERATE ARMY, IS MARCHING **75,000 TROOPS WAAAAAY NORTH** INTO OUR TERRITORY: PENNSYLVANIA.
I NEED YOU TO HUSTLE **90,000 TROOPS** THERE. **STOP** LEE FROM REACHING NEW YORK...
... HERE. IN **GETTYSBURG, PENNSYLVANIA.**
Gettysburg
IF WE **LOSE** THIS ONE, MEADE, WE LOSE THE **WAR.**
165,000 SOLDIERS. ONE TOWN. Y-Y-YES SIR.

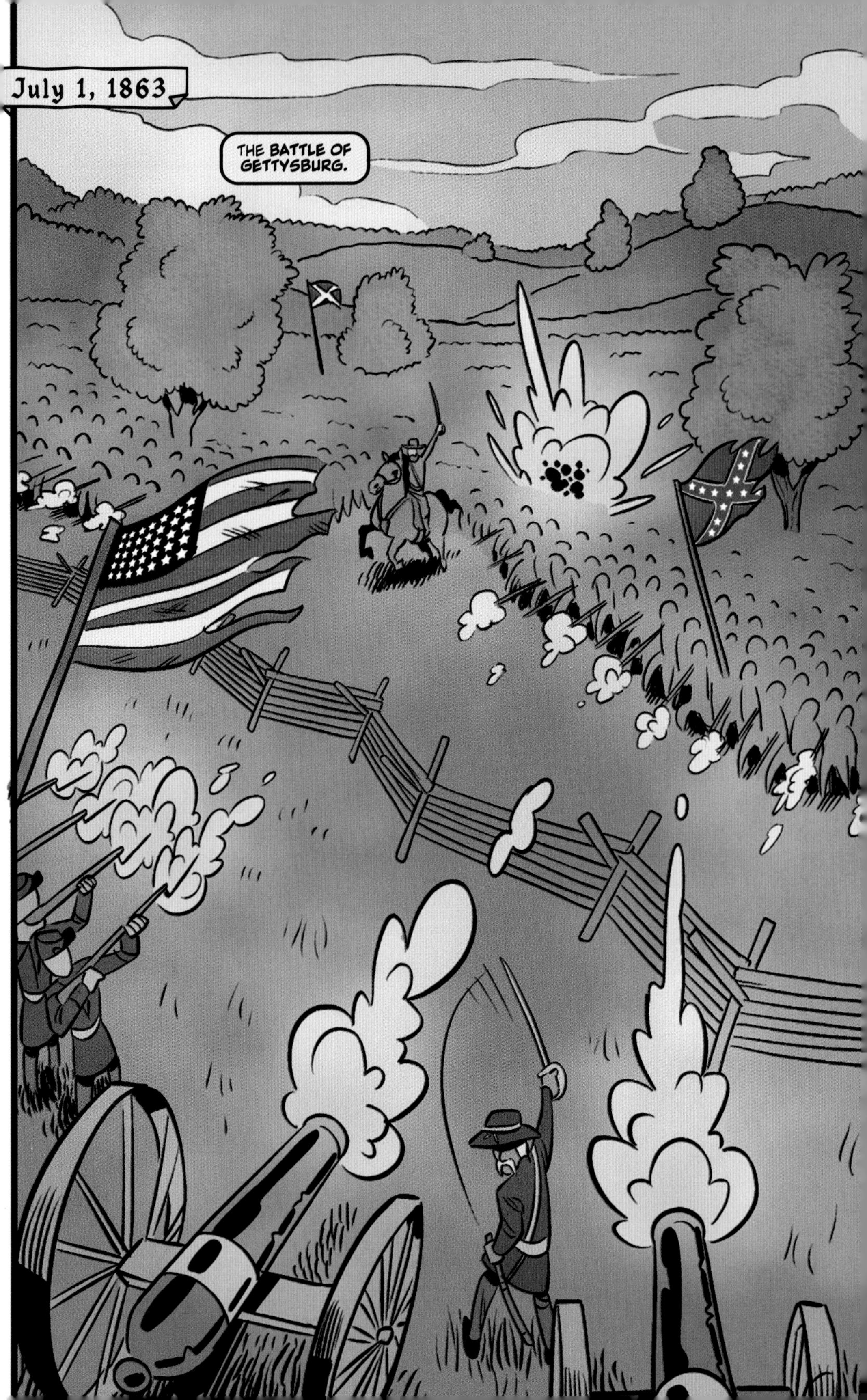
July 1, 1863
THE BATTLE OF GETTYSBURG.

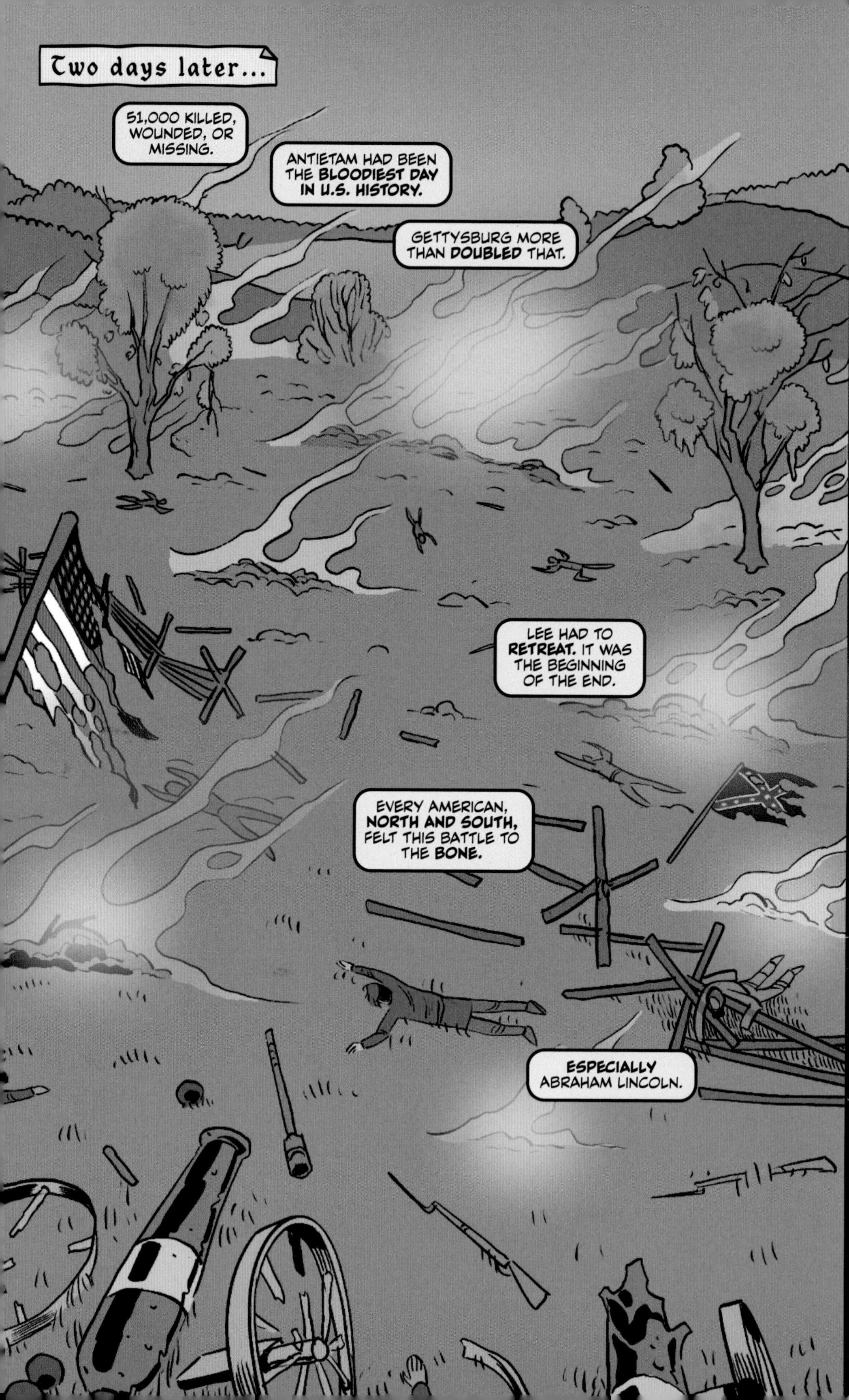

Two days later...
51,000 KILLED, WOUNDED, OR MISSING.
ANTIETAM HAD BEEN THE BLOODIEST DAY IN U.S. HISTORY.
GETTYSBURG MORE THAN DOUBLED THAT.
LEE HAD TO RETREAT. IT WAS THE BEGINNING OF THE END.
EVERY AMERICAN, NORTH AND SOUTH, FELT THIS BATTLE TO THE BONE.
ESPECIALLY ABRAHAM LINCOLN.

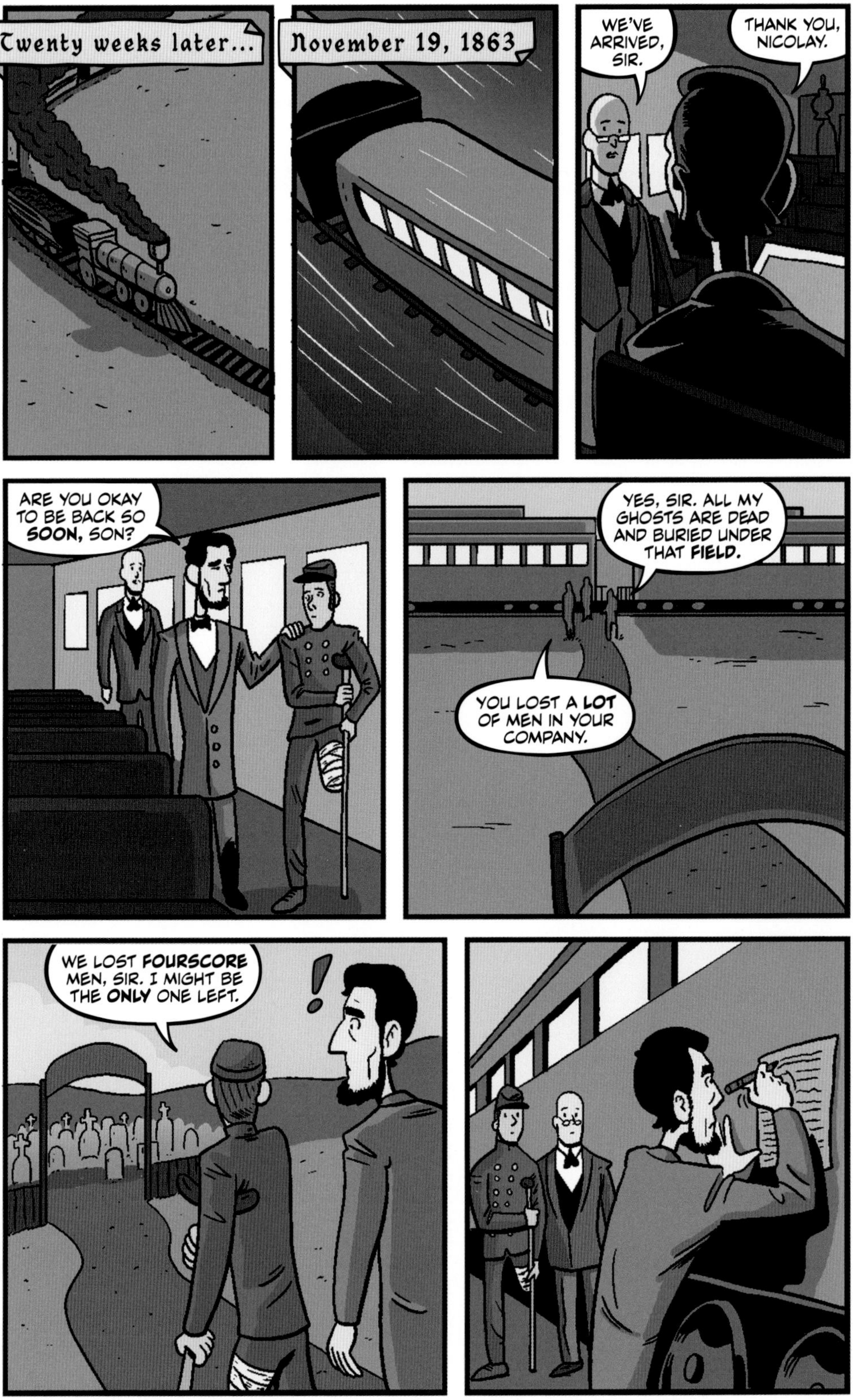
Twenty weeks later...
November 19, 1863
WE'VE ARRIVED, SIR.
THANK YOU, NICOLAY.
ARE YOU OKAY TO BE BACK SO SOON, SON?
YES, SIR. ALL MY GHOSTS ARE DEAD AND BURIED UNDER THAT FIELD.
YOU LOST A LOT OF MEN IN YOUR COMPANY.
WE LOST FOURSCORE MEN, SIR. I MIGHT BE THE ONLY ONE LEFT.
!

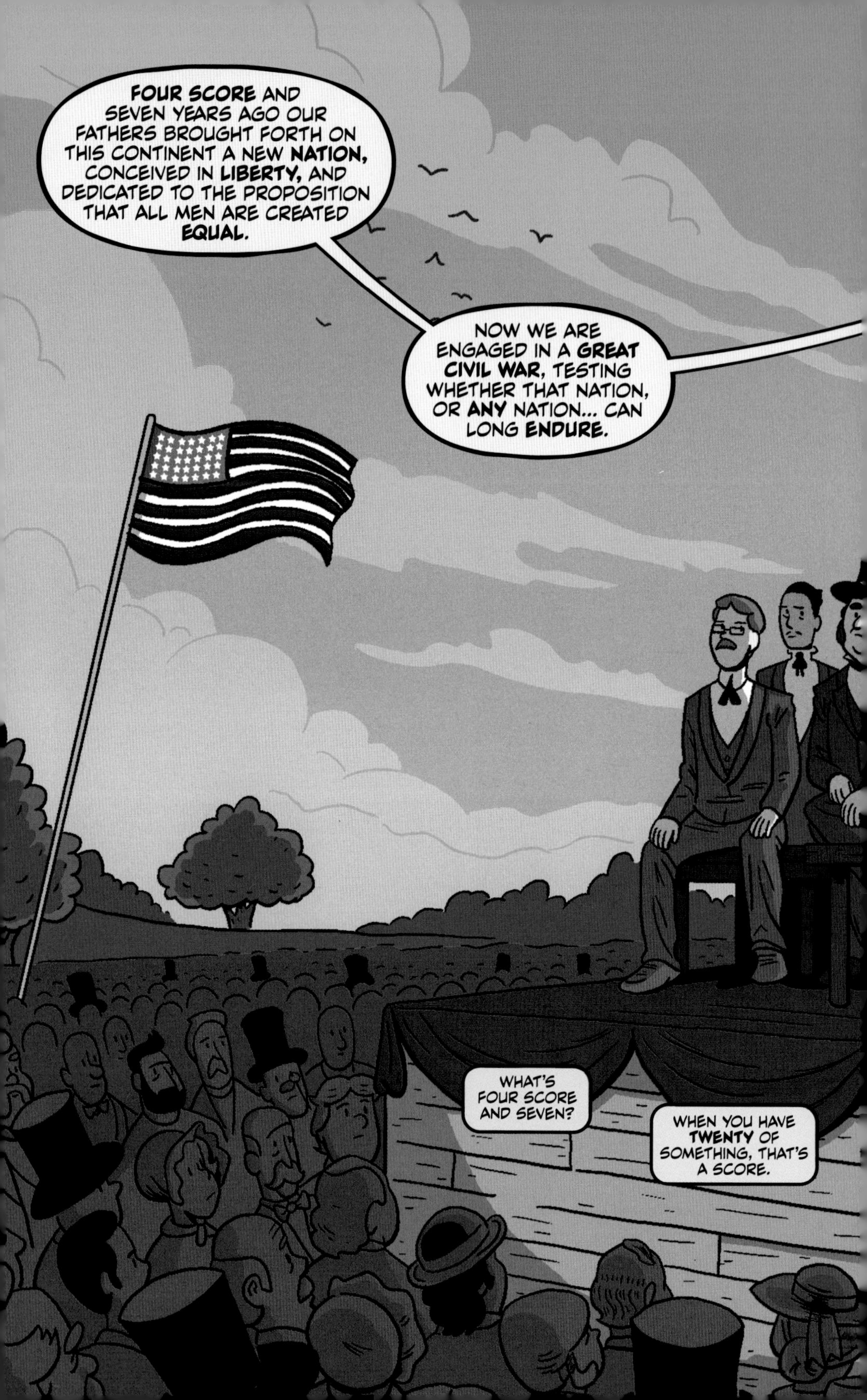
FOUR SCORE AND SEVEN YEARS AGO OUR FATHERS BROUGHT FORTH ON THIS CONTINENT A NEW NATION, CONCEIVED IN LIBERTY, AND DEDICATED TO THE PROPOSITION THAT ALL MEN ARE CREATED EQUAL.
NOW WE ARE ENGAGED IN A GREAT CIVIL WAR, TESTING WHETHER THAT NATION, OR ANY NATION... CAN LONG ENDURE.
WHAT'S FOUR SCORE AND SEVEN?
WHEN YOU HAVE TWENTY OF SOMETHING, THAT'S A SCORE.

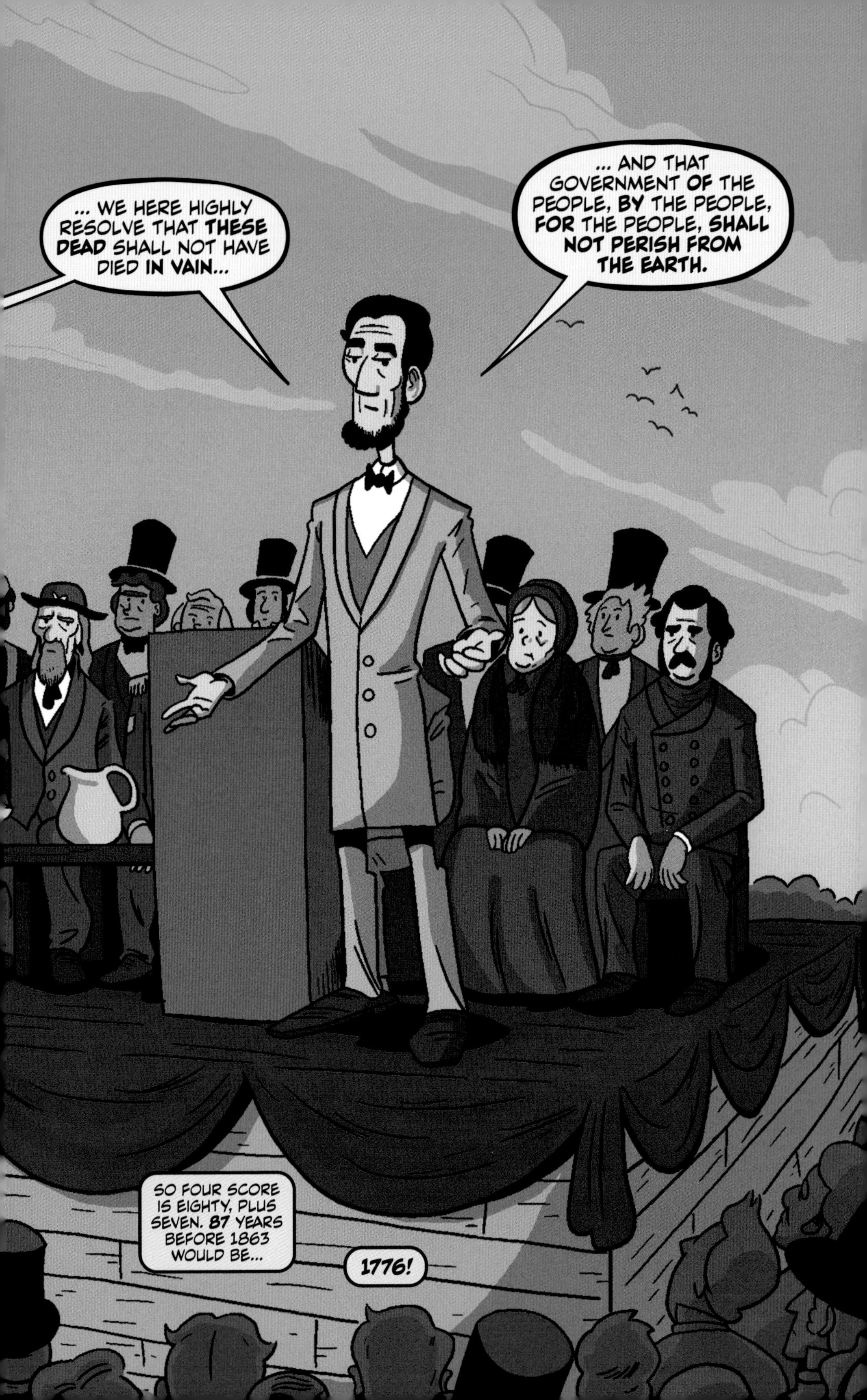
... WE HERE HIGHLY RESOLVE THAT THESE DEAD SHALL NOT HAVE DIED IN VAIN...
... AND THAT GOVERNMENT OF THE PEOPLE, BY THE PEOPLE, FOR THE PEOPLE, SHALL NOT PERISH FROM THE EARTH.
SO FOUR SCORE IS EIGHTY, PLUS SEVEN. 87 YEARS BEFORE 1863 WOULD BE...
1776!

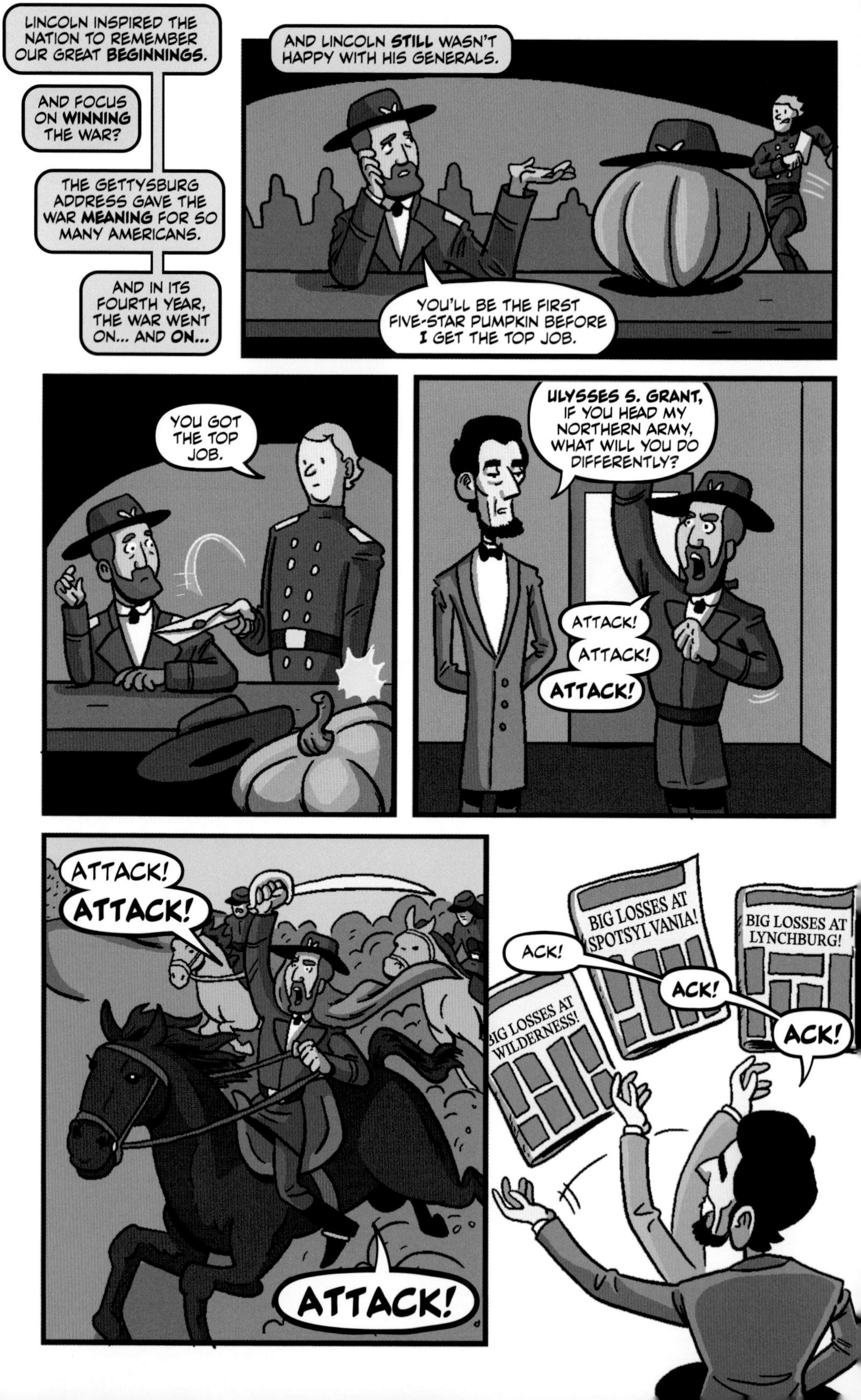
LINCOLN INSPIRED THE NATION TO REMEMBER OUR GREAT BEGINNINGS.
AND FOCUS ON WINNING THE WAR?
THE GETTYSBURG ADDRESS GAVE THE WAR MEANING FOR SO MANY AMERICANS.
AND IN ITS FOURTH YEAR, THE WAR WENT ON... AND ON...
AND LINCOLN STILL WASN'T HAPPY WITH HIS GENERALS.
YOU'LL BE THE FIRST FIVE-STAR PUMPKIN BEFORE I GET THE TOP JOB.
YOU GOT THE TOP JOB.
ULYSSES S. GRANT, IF YOU HEAD MY NORTHERN ARMY, WHAT WILL YOU DO DIFFERENTLY?
ATTACK!
ATTACK!
ATTACK!
ATTACK!
ATTACK!
ATTACK!
BIG LOSSES AT WILDERNESS!
BIG LOSSES AT SPOTSYLVANIA!
BIG LOSSES AT LYNCHBURG!
ACK!
ACK!
ACK!

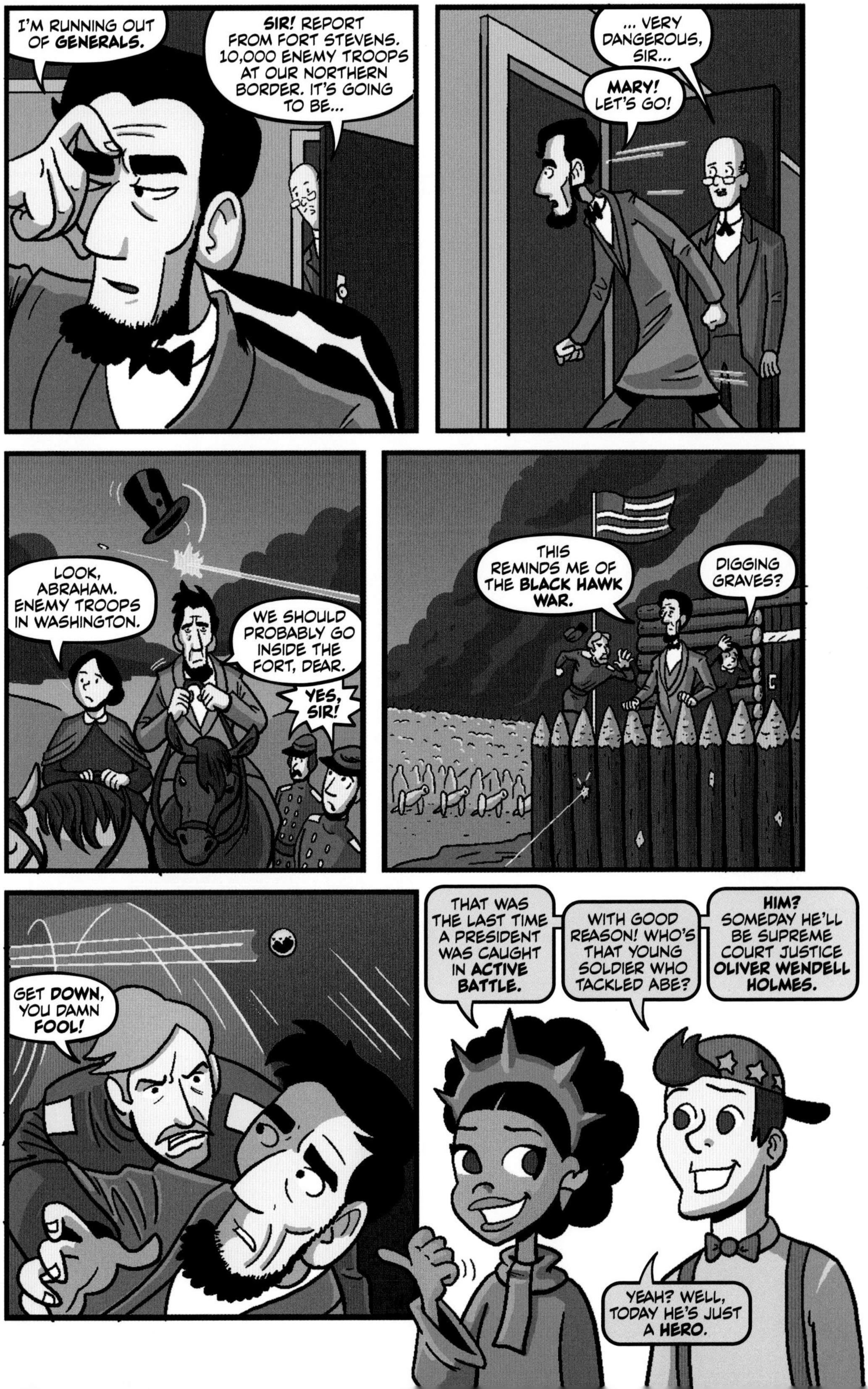
I'M RUNNING OUT OF **GENERALS.**
SIR! REPORT FROM FORT STEVENS. 10,000 ENEMY TROOPS AT OUR NORTHERN BORDER. IT'S GOING TO BE...
... VERY DANGEROUS, SIR...
MARY! LET'S GO!
LOOK, ABRAHAM. ENEMY TROOPS IN WASHINGTON.
WE SHOULD PROBABLY GO INSIDE THE FORT, DEAR.
YES, SIR!
THIS REMINDS ME OF THE **BLACK HAWK WAR.**
DIGGING GRAVES?
GET **DOWN,** YOU DAMN **FOOL!**
THAT WAS THE LAST TIME A PRESIDENT WAS CAUGHT IN **ACTIVE BATTLE.**
WITH GOOD REASON! WHO'S THAT YOUNG SOLDIER WHO TACKLED ABE?
HIM? SOMEDAY HE'LL BE SUPREME COURT JUSTICE **OLIVER WENDELL HOLMES.**
YEAH? WELL, TODAY HE'S JUST A **HERO.**

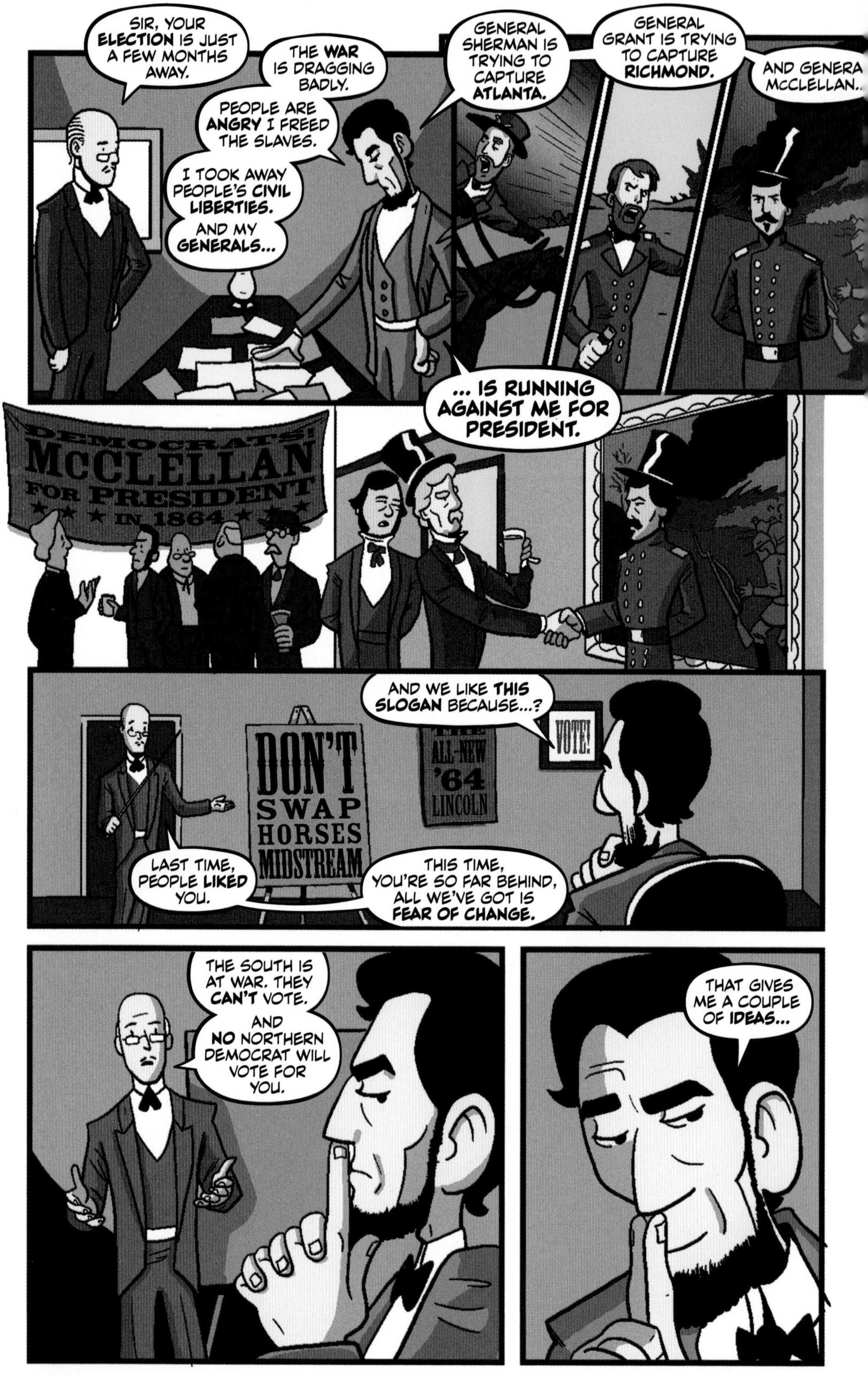
SIR, YOUR ELECTION IS JUST A FEW MONTHS AWAY.
THE WAR IS DRAGGING BADLY.
PEOPLE ARE ANGRY I FREED THE SLAVES.
I TOOK AWAY PEOPLE'S CIVIL LIBERTIES.
AND MY GENERALS...
GENERAL SHERMAN IS TRYING TO CAPTURE ATLANTA.
GENERAL GRANT IS TRYING TO CAPTURE RICHMOND.
AND GENERA McCLELLAN...
... IS RUNNING AGAINST ME FOR PRESIDENT.
DEMOCRATS! McCLELLAN FOR PRESIDENT IN 1864
AND WE LIKE THIS SLOGAN BECAUSE...?
DON'T SWAP HORSES MIDSTREAM
ALL-NEW '64 LINCOLN
VOTE!
LAST TIME, PEOPLE LIKED YOU.
THIS TIME, YOU'RE SO FAR BEHIND, ALL WE'VE GOT IS FEAR OF CHANGE.
THE SOUTH IS AT WAR. THEY CAN'T VOTE.
AND NO NORTHERN DEMOCRAT WILL VOTE FOR YOU.
THAT GIVES ME A COUPLE OF IDEAS...

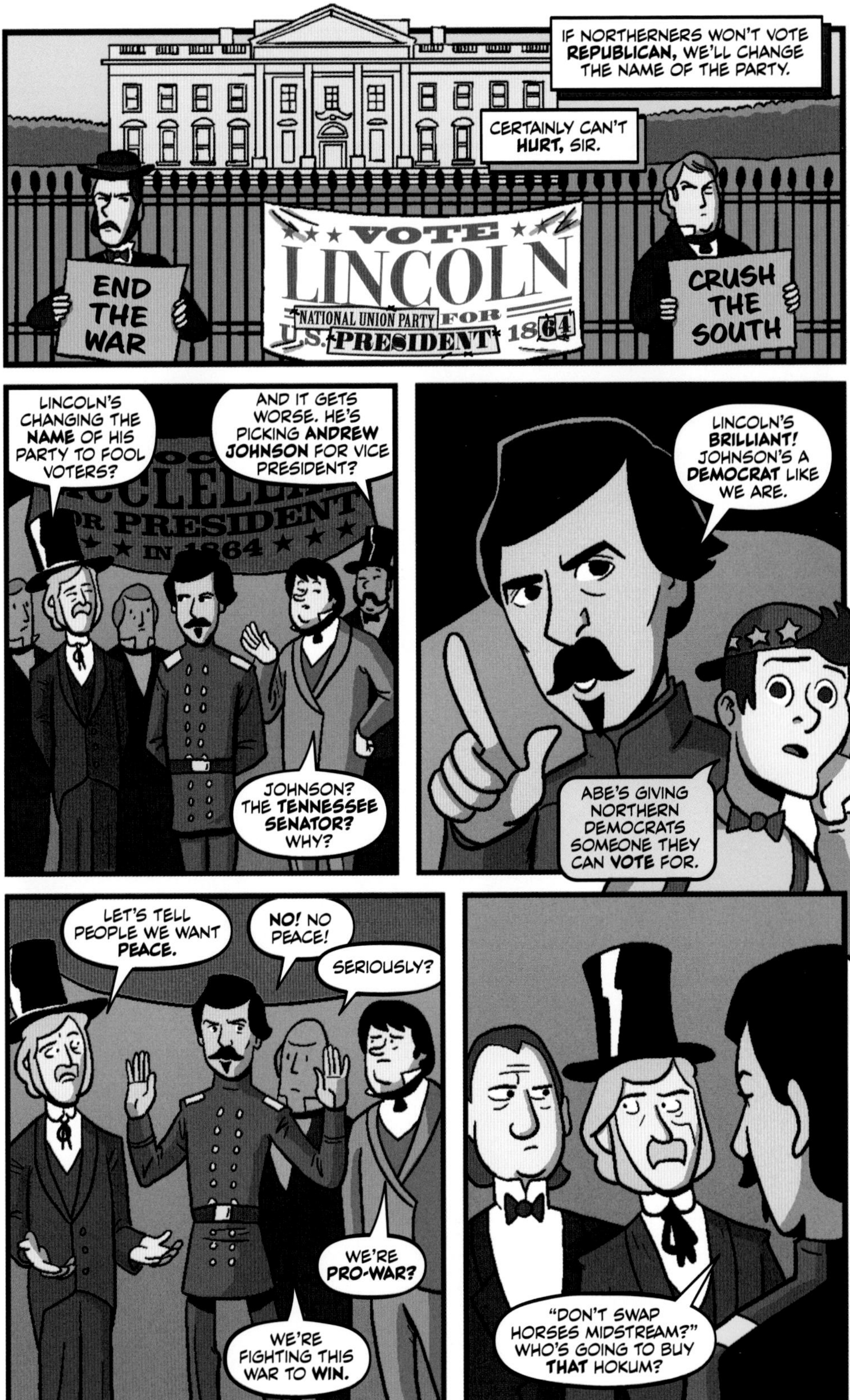
IF NORTHERNERS WON'T VOTE REPUBLICAN, WE'LL CHANGE THE NAME OF THE PARTY.
CERTAINLY CAN'T HURT, SIR.
END THE WAR
VOTE LINCOLN FOR U.S. PRESIDENT NATIONAL UNION PARTY 1864
CRUSH THE SOUTH
LINCOLN'S CHANGING THE NAME OF HIS PARTY TO FOOL VOTERS?
AND IT GETS WORSE. HE'S PICKING ANDREW JOHNSON FOR VICE PRESIDENT?
JOHNSON? THE TENNESSEE SENATOR? WHY?
LINCOLN'S BRILLIANT! JOHNSON'S A DEMOCRAT LIKE WE ARE.
ABE'S GIVING NORTHERN DEMOCRATS SOMEONE THEY CAN VOTE FOR.
LET'S TELL PEOPLE WE WANT PEACE.
NO! NO PEACE!
SERIOUSLY?
WE'RE PRO-WAR?
WE'RE FIGHTING THIS WAR TO WIN.
"DON'T SWAP HORSES MIDSTREAM?" WHO'S GOING TO BUY THAT HOKUM?

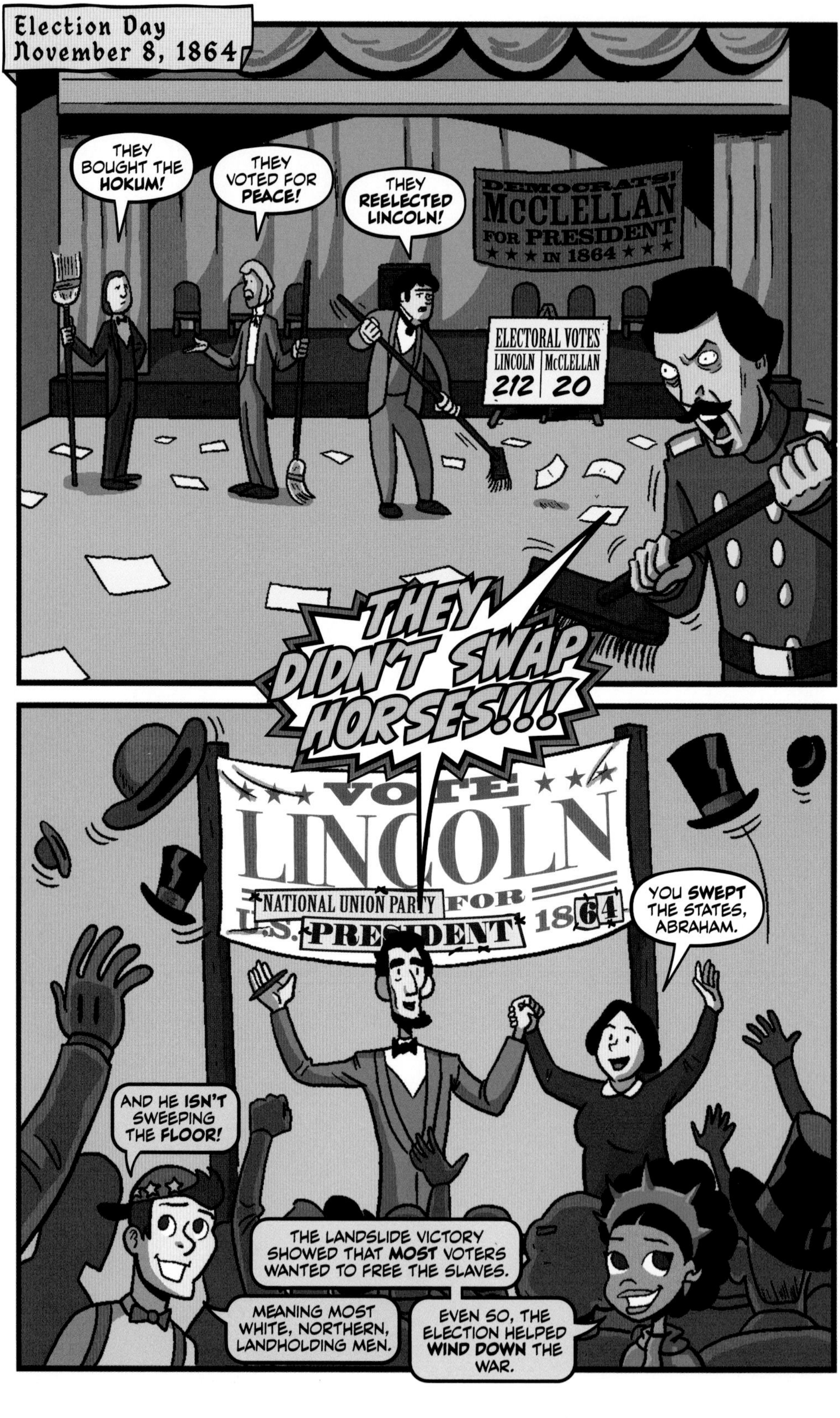
Election Day
November 8, 1864
THEY BOUGHT THE HOKUM!
THEY VOTED FOR PEACE!
THEY REELECTED LINCOLN!
DEMOCRATS! McCLELLAN FOR PRESIDENT IN 1864
ELECTORAL VOTES
LINCOLN 212
McCLELLAN 20
THEY DIDN'T SWAP HORSES!!!
VOTE LINCOLN
NATIONAL UNION PARTY FOR U.S. PRESIDENT 1864
YOU SWEPT THE STATES, ABRAHAM.
AND HE ISN'T SWEEPING THE FLOOR!
THE LANDSLIDE VICTORY SHOWED THAT MOST VOTERS WANTED TO FREE THE SLAVES.
MEANING MOST WHITE, NORTHERN, LANDHOLDING MEN.
EVEN SO, THE ELECTION HELPED WIND DOWN THE WAR.

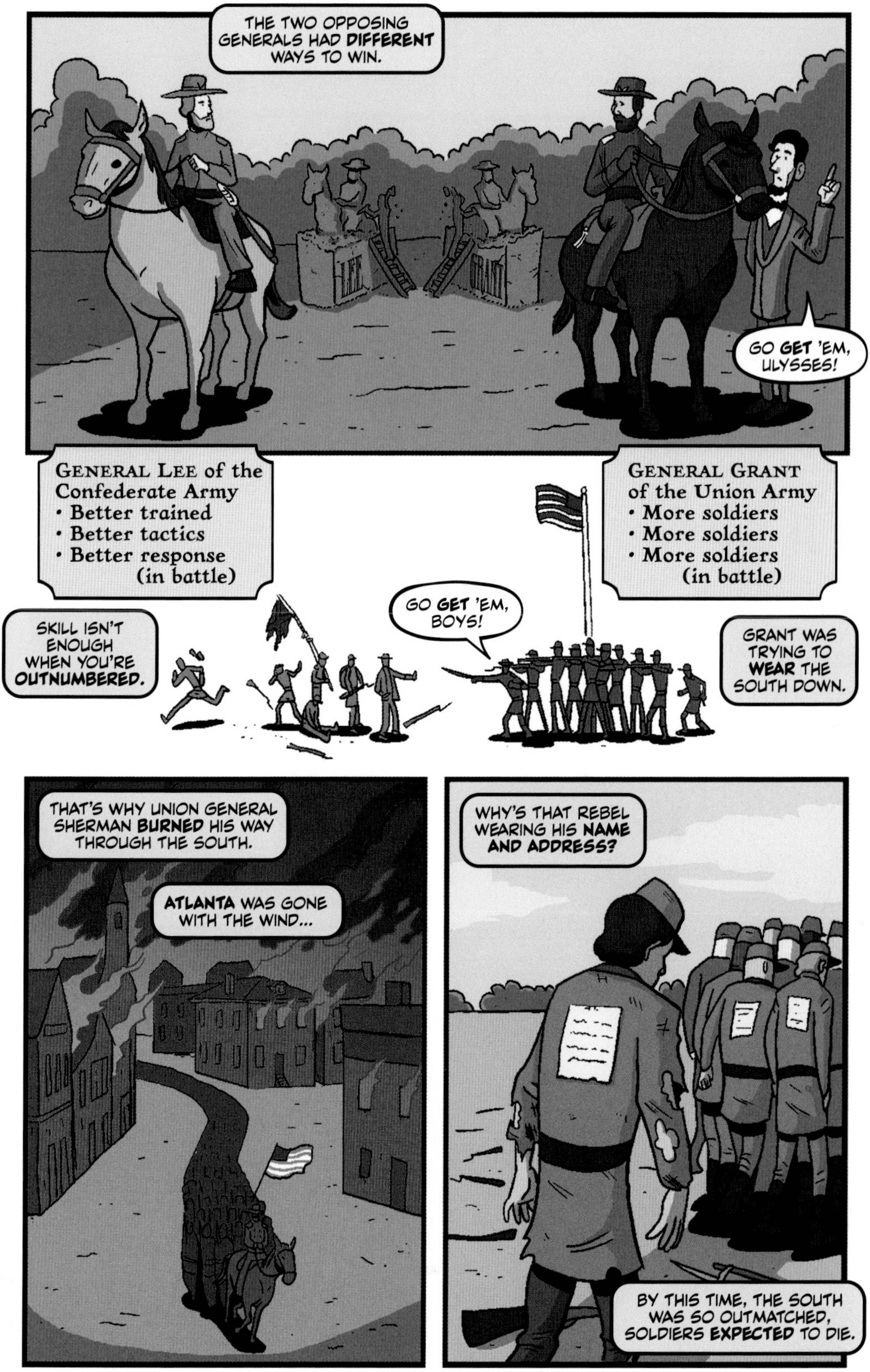
THE TWO OPPOSING GENERALS HAD DIFFERENT WAYS TO WIN.
LEE
GRANT
GO GET 'EM, ULYSSES!
GENERAL LEE of the Confederate Army
• Better trained
• Better tactics
• Better response (in battle)
GENERAL GRANT of the Union Army
• More soldiers
• More soldiers
• More soldiers (in battle)
SKILL ISN'T ENOUGH WHEN YOU'RE OUTNUMBERED.
GO GET 'EM, BOYS!
GRANT WAS TRYING TO WEAR THE SOUTH DOWN.
THAT'S WHY UNION GENERAL SHERMAN BURNED HIS WAY THROUGH THE SOUTH.
ATLANTA WAS GONE WITH THE WIND...
WHY'S THAT REBEL WEARING HIS NAME AND ADDRESS?
BY THIS TIME, THE SOUTH WAS SO OUTMATCHED, SOLDIERS EXPECTED TO DIE.

April 3, 1865
WHERE ARE THESE UNION SOLDIERS GOING?
THE NORTH'S INVADING RICHMOND, CAPITAL OF THE SOUTH.
THE CAPITOL BUILDING. ON FIRE IN THE CAPITAL CITY.
GOOD SPELLING, SAM.
THE CONFEDERATE ARMY SET FIRES AS THEY RETREATED FROM RICHMOND.
THEY BURNED THEIR CAPITAL TO THE GROUND.
IT WAS A SYMBOLIC ENDING TO THE MOST DESTRUCTIVE WAR IN U.S. HISTORY.
April 4, 1865
LINCOLN AND HIS SON, TAD, ARRIVED THE NEXT DAY.
WILL YOU BE HAVING A CONQUEROR'S TOUR, SIR?
SIGH ALL I CARE TO SEE IS THE LOVELY CITY I ONCE LOVED.
WE WON, PA!
WE WON NOTHING, TAD. WE JUST DIDN'T LOSE.
THE SOUTHERN LEADERS HAD ALREADY FLED THE CITY.

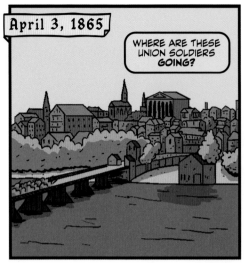

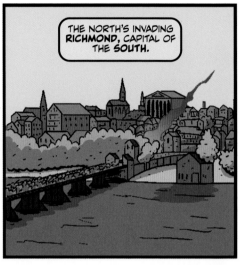

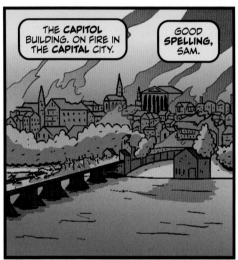

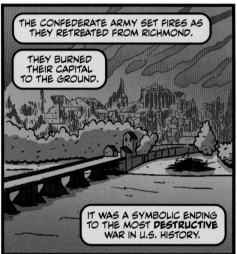

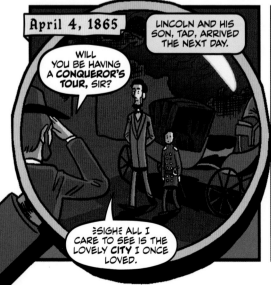

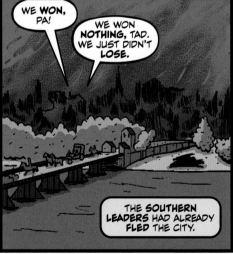

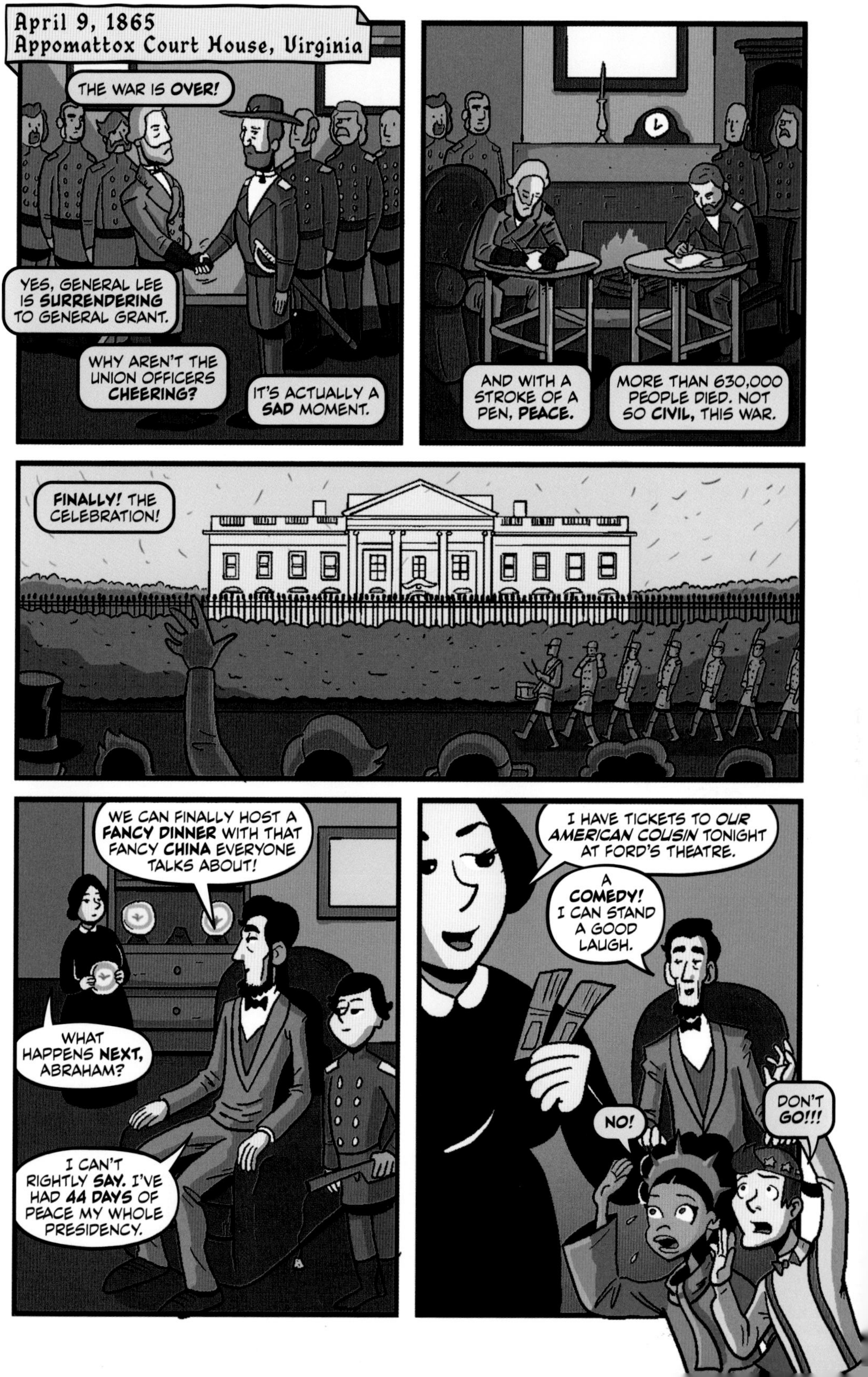

April 9, 1865
Appomattox Court House, Virginia
THE WAR IS OVER!
YES, GENERAL LEE IS SURRENDERING TO GENERAL GRANT.
WHY AREN'T THE UNION OFFICERS CHEERING?
IT'S ACTUALLY A SAD MOMENT.
AND WITH A STROKE OF A PEN, PEACE.
MORE THAN 630,000 PEOPLE DIED. NOT SO CIVIL, THIS WAR.
FINALLY! THE CELEBRATION!
WE CAN FINALLY HOST A FANCY DINNER WITH THAT FANCY CHINA EVERYONE TALKS ABOUT!
WHAT HAPPENS NEXT, ABRAHAM?
I CAN'T RIGHTLY SAY. I'VE HAD 44 DAYS OF PEACE MY WHOLE PRESIDENCY.
I HAVE TICKETS TO OUR AMERICAN COUSIN TONIGHT AT FORD'S THEATRE.
A COMEDY! I CAN STAND A GOOD LAUGH.
NO!
DON'T GO!!!

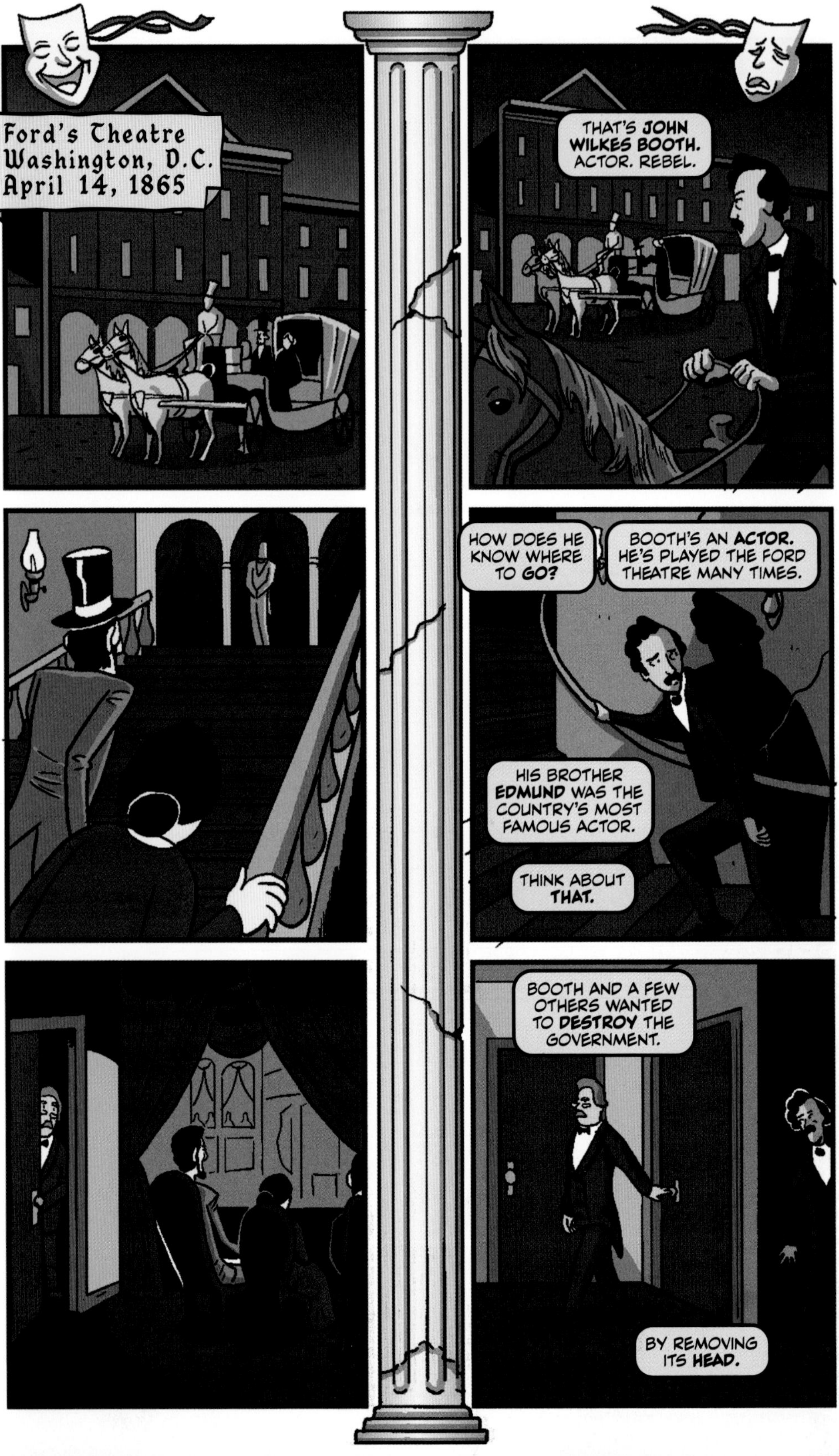
Ford's Theatre
Washington, D.C.
April 14, 1865
THAT'S JOHN WILKES BOOTH. ACTOR. REBEL.
HOW DOES HE KNOW WHERE TO GO?
BOOTH'S AN ACTOR. HE'S PLAYED THE FORD THEATRE MANY TIMES.
HIS BROTHER EDMUND WAS THE COUNTRY'S MOST FAMOUS ACTOR.
THINK ABOUT THAT.
BOOTH AND A FEW OTHERS WANTED TO DESTROY THE GOVERNMENT.
BY REMOVING ITS HEAD.

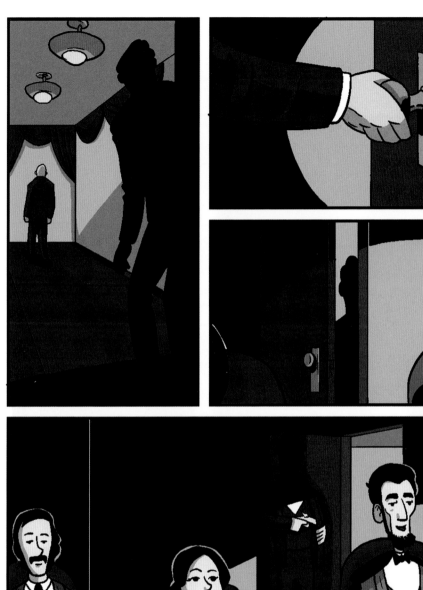

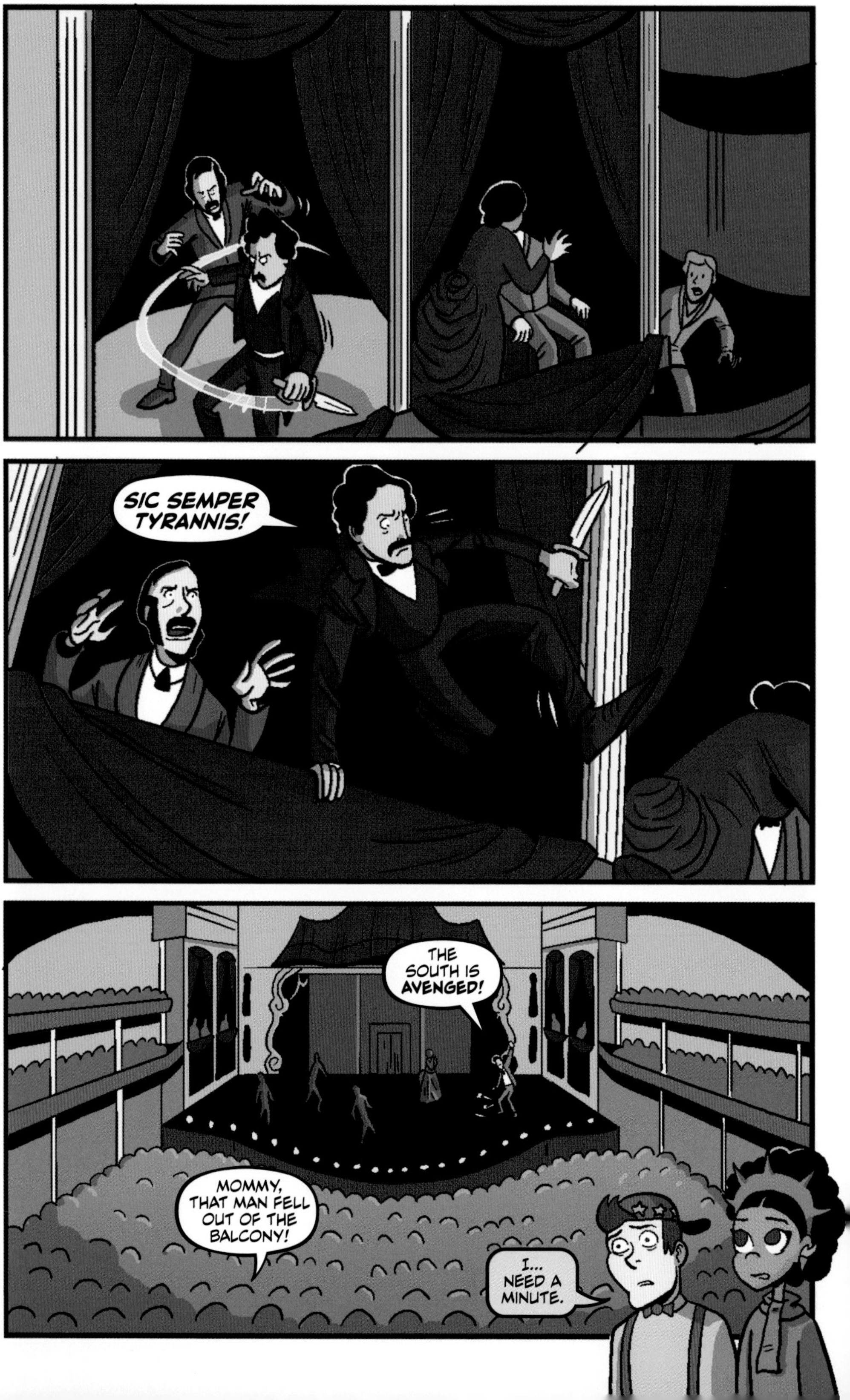
SIC SEMPER TYRANNIS!
THE SOUTH IS AVENGED!
MOMMY, THAT MAN FELL OUT OF THE BALCONY!
I... NEED A MINUTE.

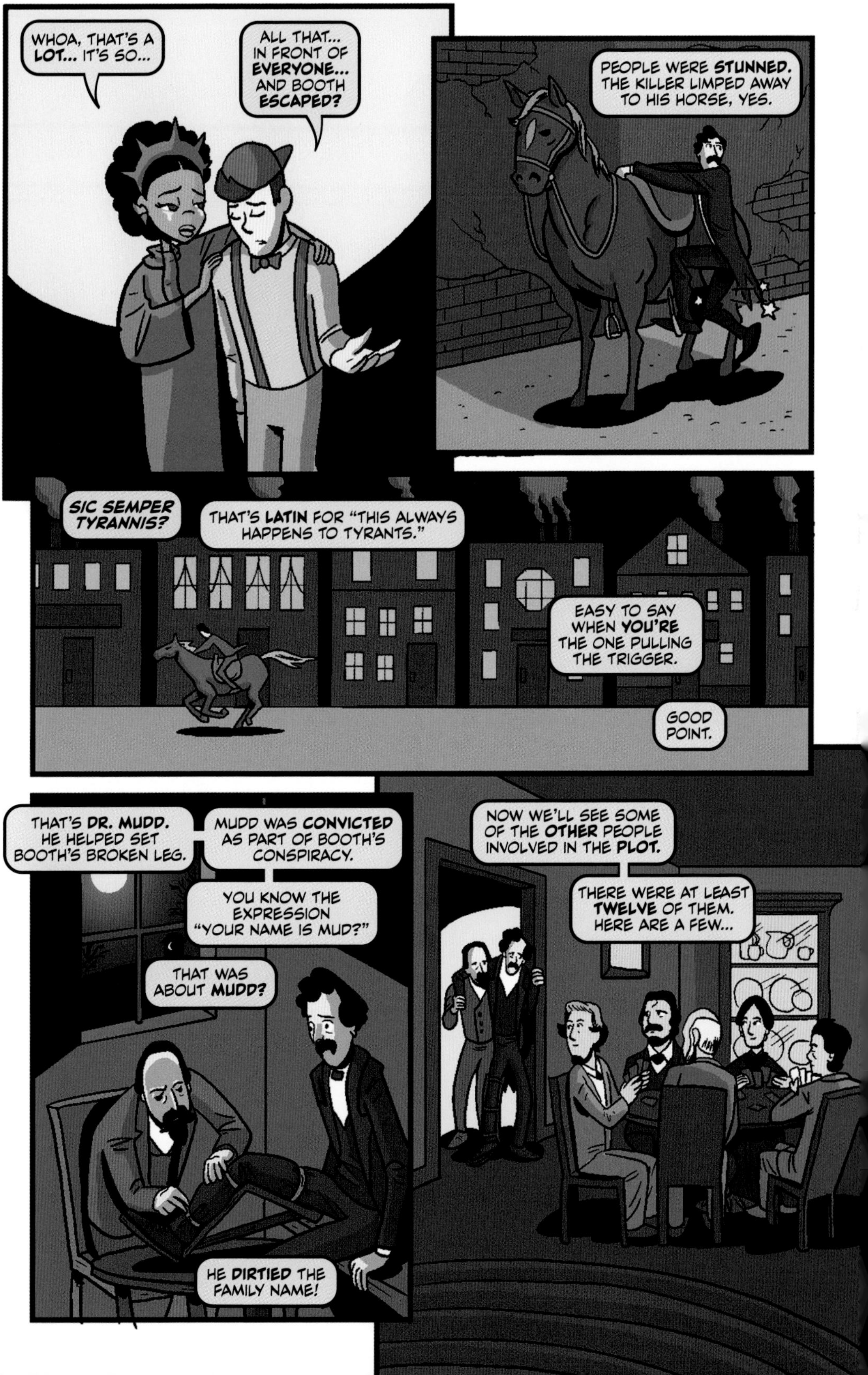
WHOA, THAT'S A LOT... IT'S SO...
ALL THAT... IN FRONT OF EVERYONE... AND BOOTH ESCAPED?
PEOPLE WERE STUNNED. THE KILLER LIMPED AWAY TO HIS HORSE, YES.
SIC SEMPER TYRANNIS?
THAT'S LATIN FOR "THIS ALWAYS HAPPENS TO TYRANTS."
EASY TO SAY WHEN YOU'RE THE ONE PULLING THE TRIGGER.
GOOD POINT.
THAT'S DR. MUDD. HE HELPED SET BOOTH'S BROKEN LEG.
MUDD WAS CONVICTED AS PART OF BOOTH'S CONSPIRACY.
YOU KNOW THE EXPRESSION "YOUR NAME IS MUD?"
THAT WAS ABOUT MUDD?
HE DIRTIED THE FAMILY NAME!
NOW WE'LL SEE SOME OF THE OTHER PEOPLE INVOLVED IN THE PLOT.
THERE WERE AT LEAST TWELVE OF THEM. HERE ARE A FEW...

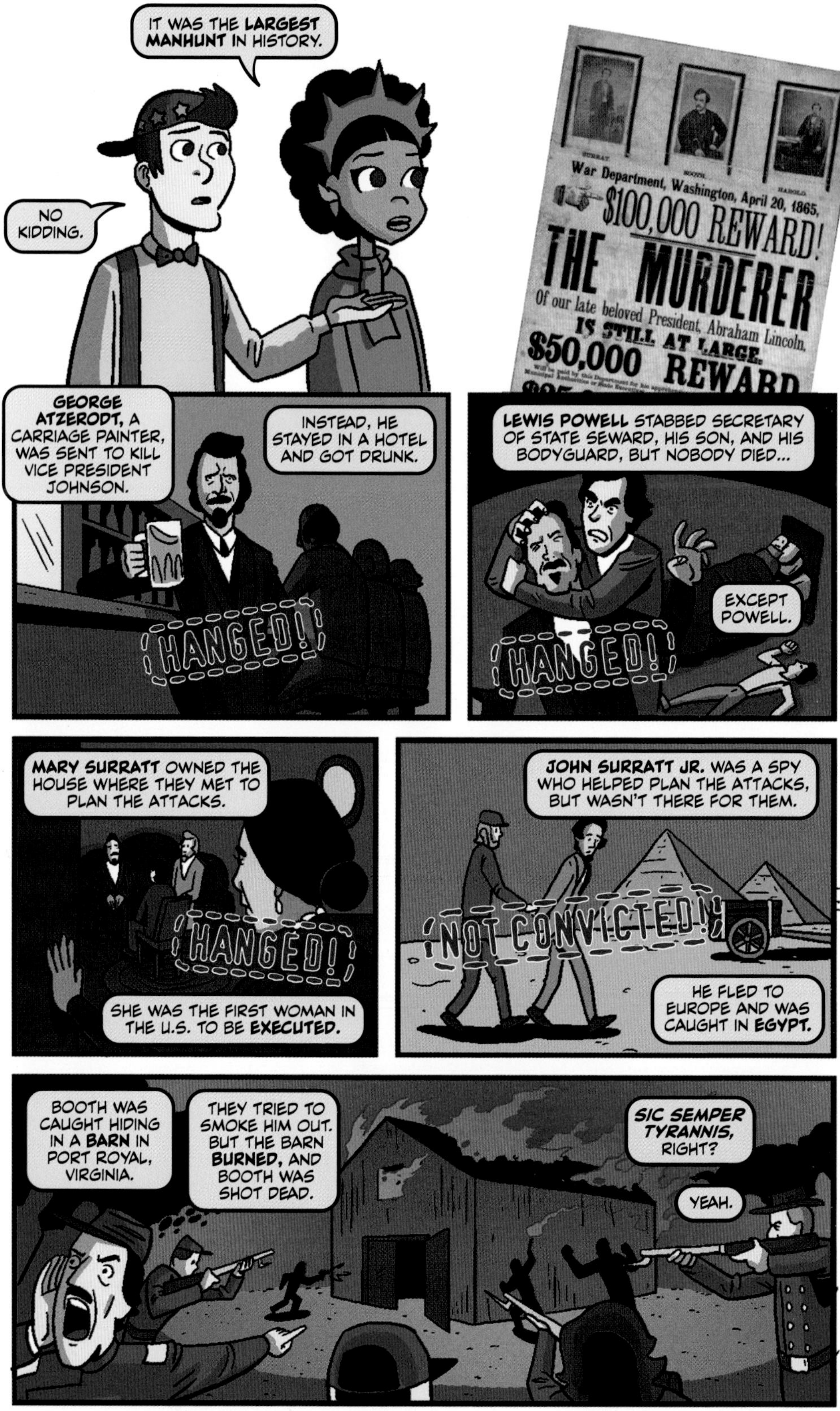

IT WAS THE **LARGEST MANHUNT** IN HISTORY.
NO KIDDING.
War Department, Washington, April 20, 1865,
$100,000 REWARD!
THE MURDERER
Of our late beloved President, Abraham Lincoln,
IS STILL AT LARGE.
$50,000 REWARD
GEORGE ATZERODT, A CARRIAGE PAINTER, WAS SENT TO KILL VICE PRESIDENT JOHNSON.
INSTEAD, HE STAYED IN A HOTEL AND GOT DRUNK.
HANGED!
LEWIS POWELL STABBED SECRETARY OF STATE SEWARD, HIS SON, AND HIS BODYGUARD, BUT NOBODY DIED...
EXCEPT POWELL.
HANGED!
MARY SURRATT OWNED THE HOUSE WHERE THEY MET TO PLAN THE ATTACKS.
HANGED!
SHE WAS THE FIRST WOMAN IN THE U.S. TO BE **EXECUTED.**
JOHN SURRATT JR. WAS A SPY WHO HELPED PLAN THE ATTACKS, BUT WASN'T THERE FOR THEM.
NOT CONVICTED!
HE FLED TO EUROPE AND WAS CAUGHT IN **EGYPT.**
BOOTH WAS CAUGHT HIDING IN A **BARN** IN PORT ROYAL, VIRGINIA.
THEY TRIED TO SMOKE HIM OUT. BUT THE BARN **BURNED,** AND BOOTH WAS SHOT DEAD.
SIC SEMPER TYRANNIS, RIGHT?
YEAH.

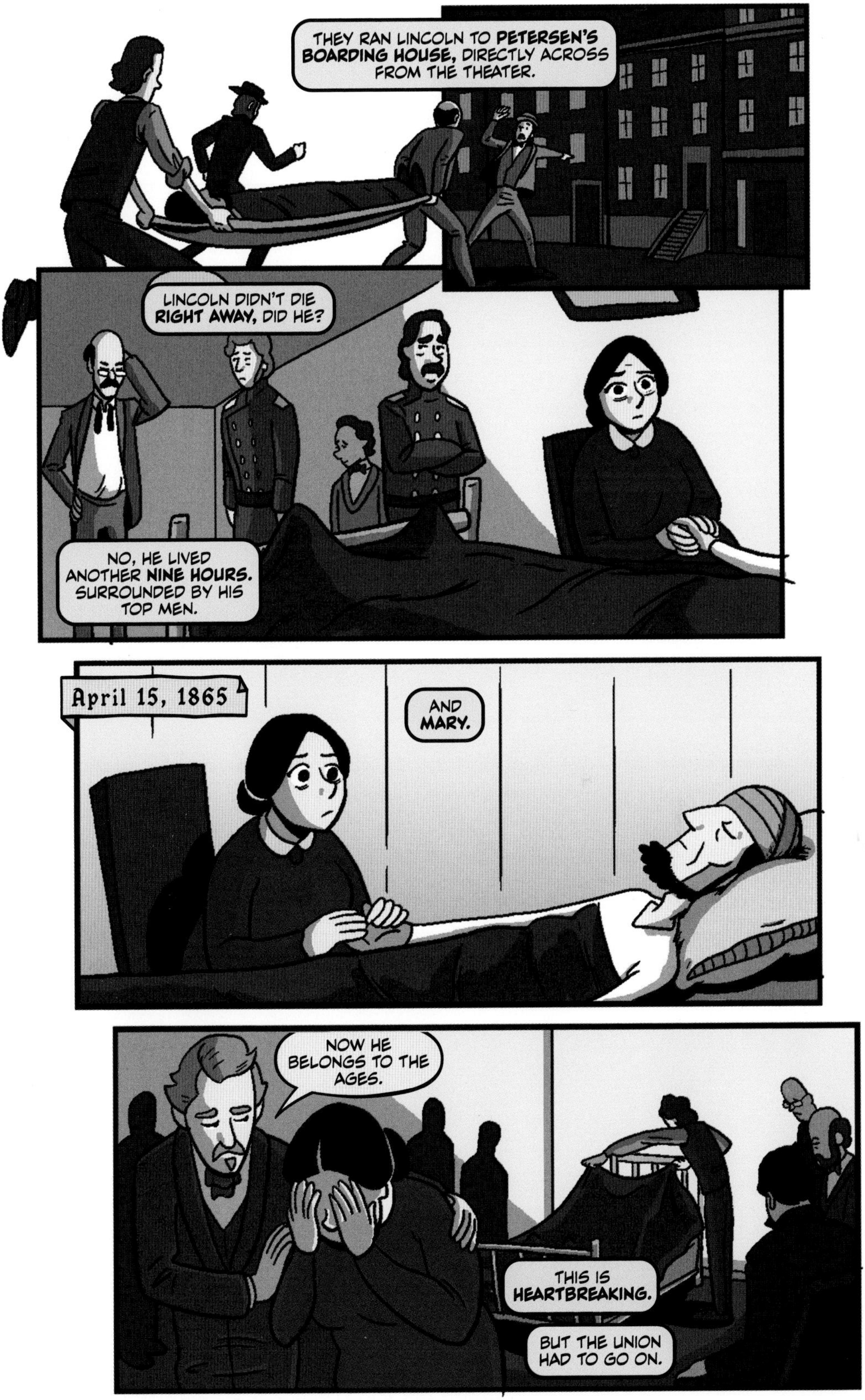
THEY RAN LINCOLN TO PETERSEN'S BOARDING HOUSE, DIRECTLY ACROSS FROM THE THEATER.
LINCOLN DIDN'T DIE RIGHT AWAY, DID HE?
NO, HE LIVED ANOTHER NINE HOURS. SURROUNDED BY HIS TOP MEN.
April 15, 1865
AND MARY.
NOW HE BELONGS TO THE AGES.
THIS IS HEARTBREAKING.
BUT THE UNION HAD TO GO ON.

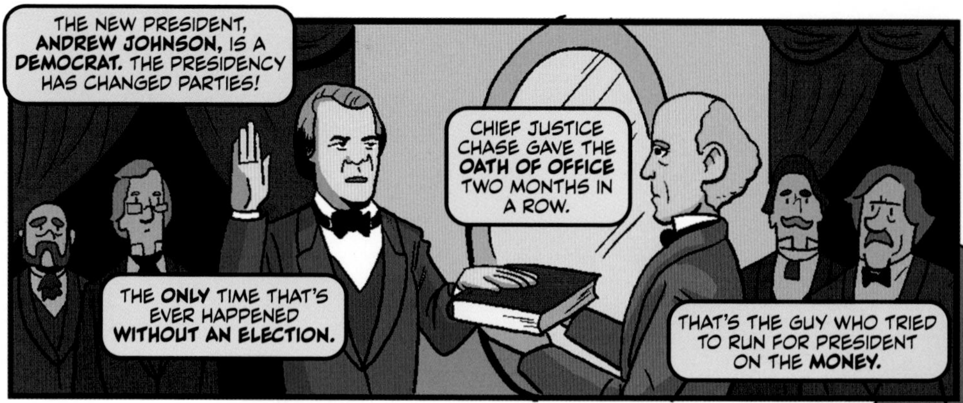
THE NEW PRESIDENT, ANDREW JOHNSON, IS A DEMOCRAT. THE PRESIDENCY HAS CHANGED PARTIES!
CHIEF JUSTICE CHASE GAVE THE OATH OF OFFICE TWO MONTHS IN A ROW.
THE ONLY TIME THAT'S EVER HAPPENED WITHOUT AN ELECTION.
THAT'S THE GUY WHO TRIED TO RUN FOR PRESIDENT ON THE MONEY.

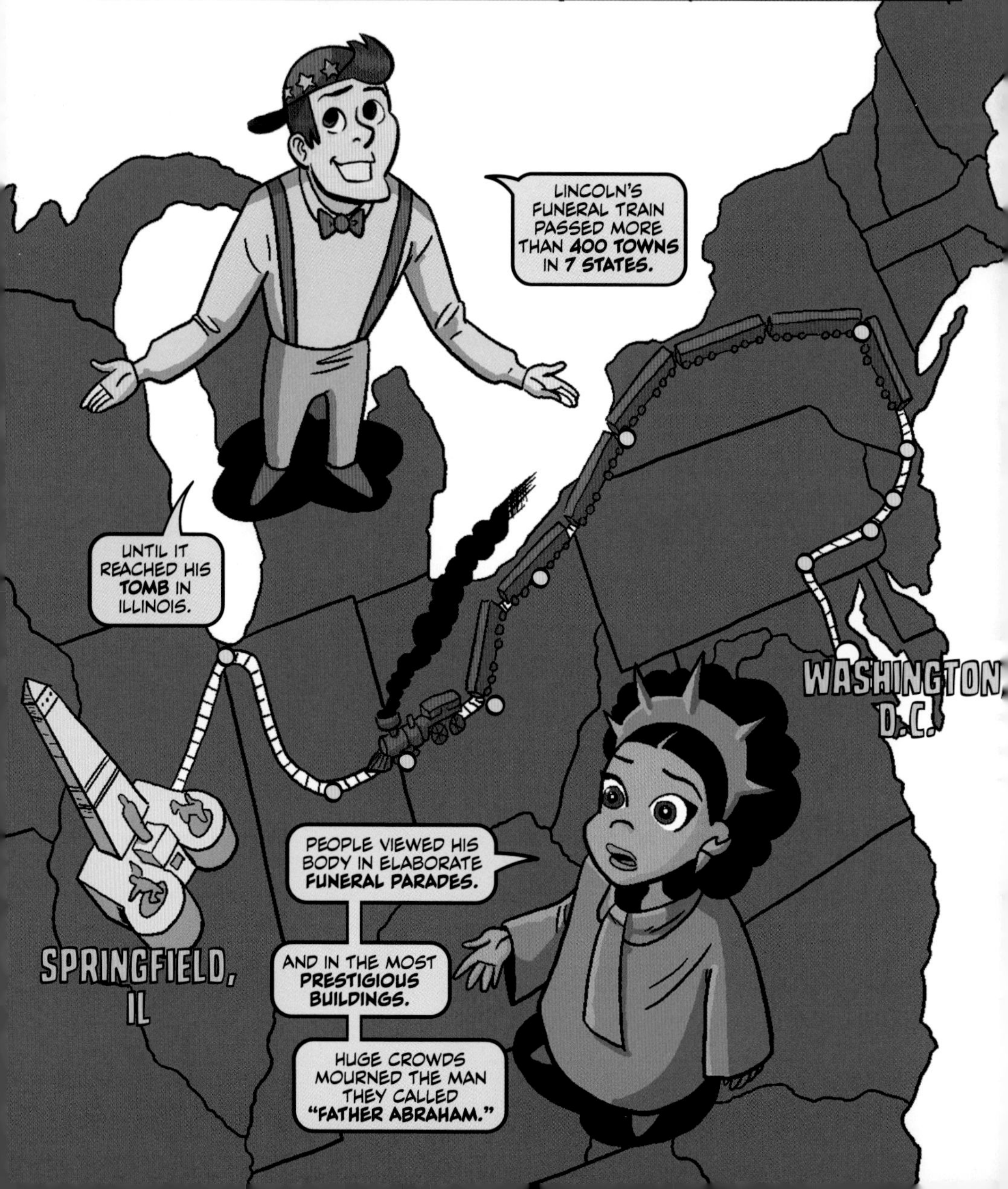
LINCOLN'S FUNERAL TRAIN PASSED MORE THAN 400 TOWNS IN 7 STATES.
UNTIL IT REACHED HIS TOMB IN ILLINOIS.
WASHINGTON D.C.
SPRINGFIELD, IL
PEOPLE VIEWED HIS BODY IN ELABORATE FUNERAL PARADES.
AND IN THE MOST PRESTIGIOUS BUILDINGS.
HUGE CROWDS MOURNED THE MAN THEY CALLED "FATHER ABRAHAM."

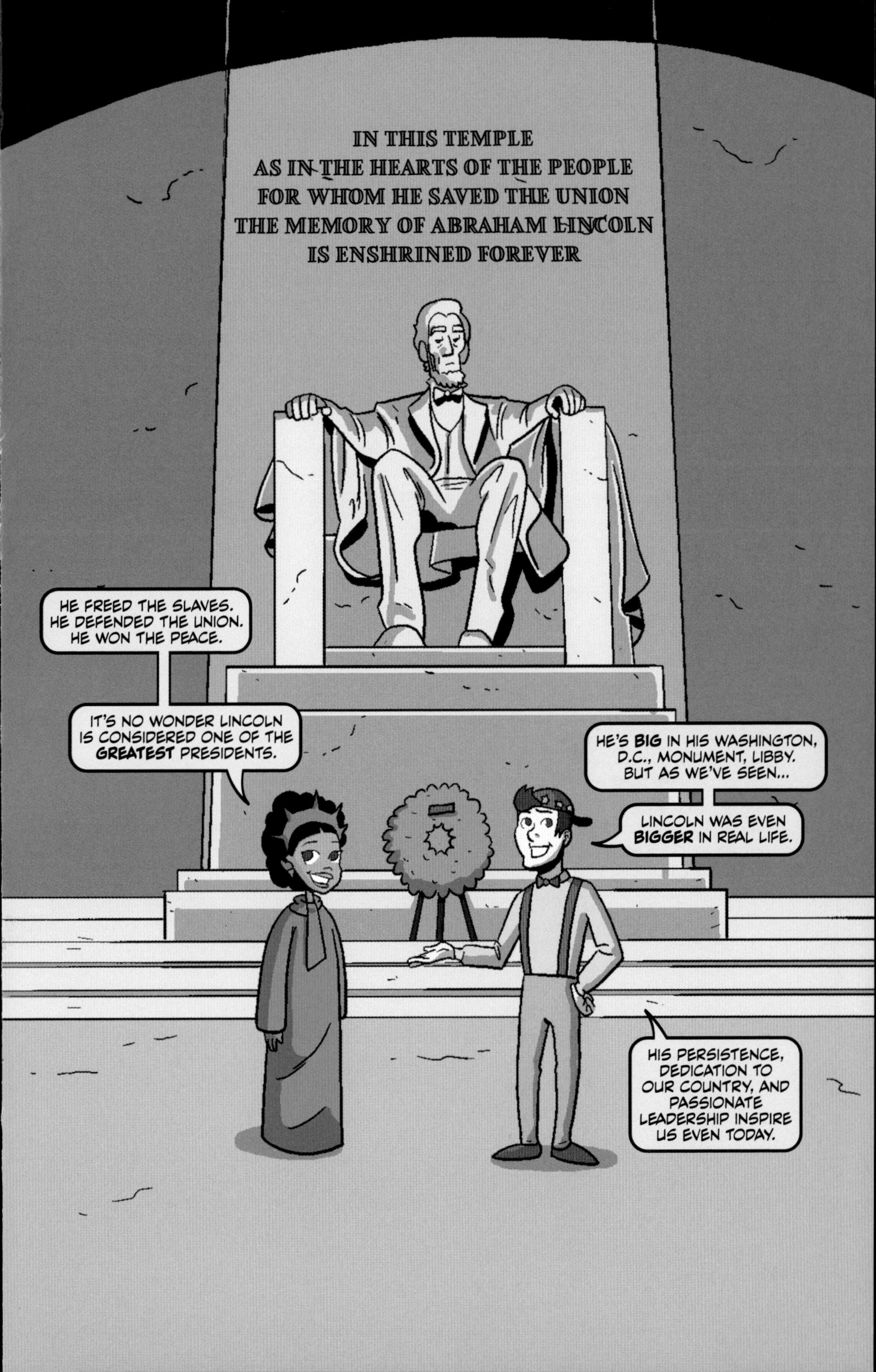
IN THIS TEMPLE
AS IN THE HEARTS OF THE PEOPLE
FOR WHOM HE SAVED THE UNION
THE MEMORY OF ABRAHAM LINCOLN
IS ENSHRINED FOREVER
HE FREED THE SLAVES. HE DEFENDED THE UNION. HE WON THE PEACE.
IT'S NO WONDER LINCOLN IS CONSIDERED ONE OF THE **GREATEST** PRESIDENTS.
HE'S **BIG** IN HIS WASHINGTON, D.C., MONUMENT, LIBBY. BUT AS WE'VE SEEN...
LINCOLN WAS EVEN **BIGGER** IN REAL LIFE.
HIS PERSISTENCE, DEDICATION TO OUR COUNTRY, AND PASSIONATE LEADERSHIP INSPIRE US EVEN TODAY.

LEADERS AGAINST SLAVERY

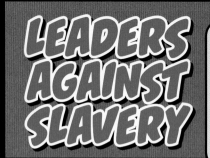

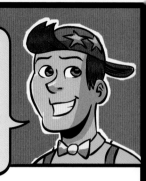

ABRAHAM LINCOLN FREED THE SLAVES, BUT HE WAS ONLY ONE OF **MANY** PROMINENT ABOLITIONISTS WHO SOUGHT TO FREE **ALL PEOPLE** FROM SLAVERY. THE PROUD LIST OF OTHER **CIVIL RIGHTS PIONEERS** INCLUDE...

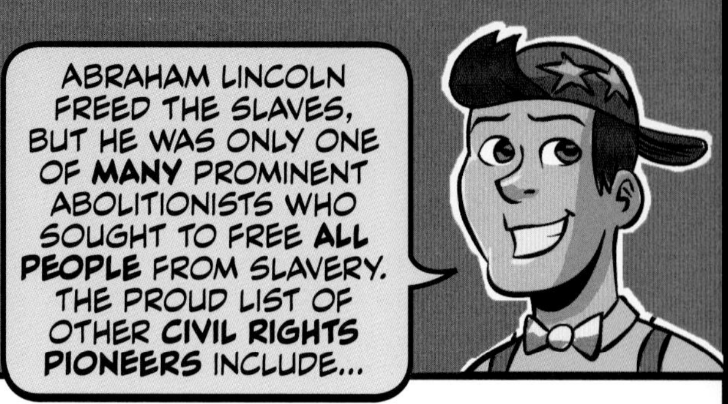

HARRIET TUBMAN (1820?-1913): After escaping slavery in 1849, she returned several times and rescued more than 300 slaves along the Underground Railroad. She was the first woman to lead a raid with the U.S. Army.

FREDERICK DOUGLASS (1818-1895): An escaped slave, Douglass educated himself, and in Rochester, NY, published the *North Star,* an abolitionist newspaper. He was a prominent speaker and was appointed to several public offices.

JOHN BROWN (1800-1859): He believed violence would bring abolition. He caused riots, freed and armed slaves, battled pro-slavery Southerners, and was hanged for treason after a raid and attack on the armory at Harper's Ferry, West Virginia.

SOJOURNER TRUTH (1787-1883): Born into slavery, she escaped in 1826, helping recruit black troops for the army. She spoke for women's rights as well, giving her famous Ain't I a Woman speech at the Ohio Women's Rights Convention.

HARRIET BEECHER STOWE (1811-1896): The white, wealthy author of the best-selling novel, *Uncle Tom's Cabin.* Stowe's book was a powerful weapon for the antislavery movement, making her a prominent voice in politics.

HENRY WARD BEECHER (1813-1887): Harriet's brother was a fire-and-brimstone minister in Brooklyn, NY, who used his pulpit to spread abolitionism, and used his church as a safe haven on the Underground Railroad. Lincoln attended his services.

WILLIAM LLOYD GARRISON (1805-1879): Founder of the *American Anti-Slavery Society,* he edited *The Liberator,* a powerful newspaper that advocated abolition and women's rights. Garrison despised the pro-slavery aspects of the Constitution.

ABRAHAM LINCOLN TIMELINE

1809 Abraham Lincoln is born in Hardin County (now known as LaRue County), Kentucky, on February 12.

1828 Lincoln takes two flatboat journeys down the
1831 Mississippi, observes deep-South slavery firsthand.

1832 Lincoln loses his first run for office, the Illinois General Assembly, and serves in the Black Hawk War as a captain, a private, then a spy.

1834 At age 24, Lincoln is elected to the Illinois General Assembly with the Whig party.

1836 Lincoln earns his law degree, and soon becomes the junior law partner of John Todd Stuart.

1842 Now a traveling circuit lawyer, Lincoln marries Mary Todd, his partner's cousin

1846 Lincoln is elected to U.S. Congress, soon gains his reputation by directly criticizing President Polk. Lincoln will later lose elections for U.S. Senate in 1855, and for U.S. vice president in 1856.

1858 Lincoln debates Stephen O. Douglas for the U.S. Senate, delivers his House Divided speech, yet loses the election.

1861 Abraham Lincoln is sworn in as the nation's 16th president; 39 days into his presidency, the Civil War begins amid fighting at Fort Sumter, South Carolina.

1862 As the war bogs down, Lincoln issues his Emancipation Proclamation, freeing slaves.

1863 After a long war and tremendous losses at Gettysburg, PA, Lincoln commemorates more than 50,000 fallen soldiers in his famous "Gettysburg Address."

1864 As the North claims more victories, and the South is in retreat, Lincoln is reelected.

1865 On April 9, General Robert E. Lee surrenders and the Civil War is over.

1865 Five days later, at Ford's Theatre, John Wilkes Booth assassinates Abraham Lincoln.

GLOSSARY

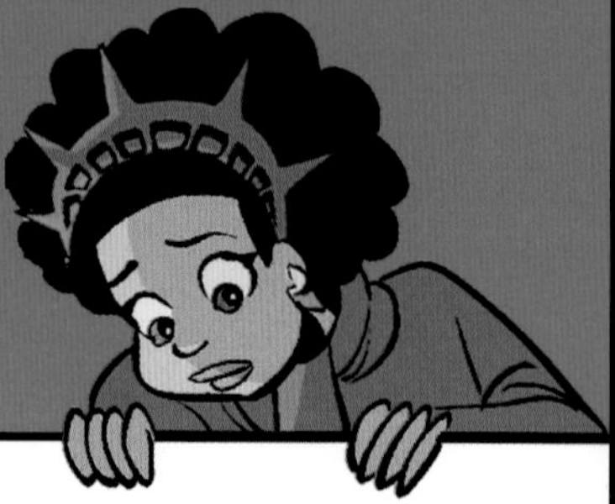

ABOLITIONIST: A person who supports the abolition, or end, of slavery.

CIRCUIT LAWYER: A lawyer who travels a circuit, or route, to areas that do not have lawyers of their own.

CIVIL WAR: A war between different regions, factions, or other groups in the same country.

DEBATE: A formal discussion of opposing views in a public forum.

ELECTORAL VOTES: A system of votes cast by representatives, rather than directly by voters.

EMANCIPATE: To set someone free from the control of someone else.

GENERAL ASSEMBLY: A congress for a state or other political entity.

NOMINATE: To propose a person for an elected office or other responsibility.

PROCLAMATION: An announcement made in a formal, official manner.

SECEDE/SECESSION: To secede is to officially withdraw from a political group or organization.

TYPHUS: A disease transmitted by lice, causing high fever, skin rash, and sometimes death.

FIND OUT MORE

BOOKS

Benoit, Peter. *Abraham Lincoln (Cornerstones of Freedom).* New York: Children's Press, 2012.

Harness, Cheryl. *Abe Lincoln Goes to Washington 1837-1865.* Washington, DC: National Geographic Publishing, 2008.

Herbert, Janis. *Abraham Lincoln for Kids.* Chicago, IL: Chicago Review Press, 2007.

Otfinoski, Steven. *Abraham Lincoln (Encyclopedia of Presidents).* New York: Scholastic Library Publishing, 2004.

Pascal, Janet B. *Who Was Abraham Lincoln? (Who Was? Series).* New York: Penguin Workshop, 2008.

Stone, Tanya Lee. *Abraham Lincoln.* New York: DK Publishing, 2005.

VIDEO

Spielberg, Steven, dir. *Lincoln.* Glendale, CA: DreamWorks Studios, 2012.

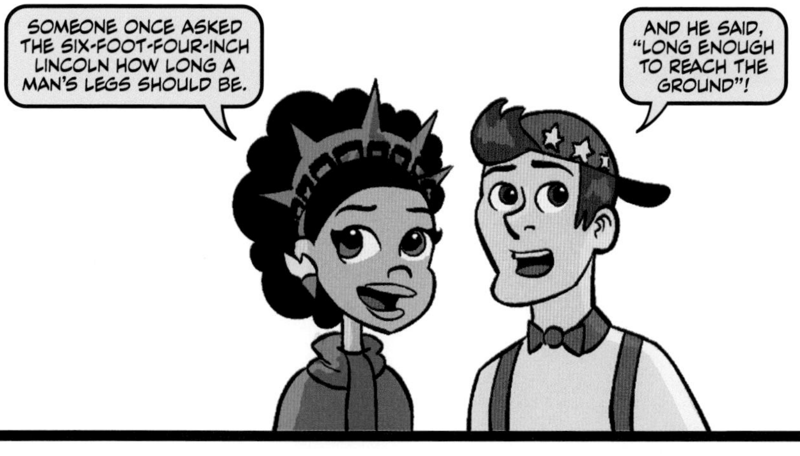

SOMEONE ONCE ASKED THE SIX-FOOT-FOUR-INCH LINCOLN HOW LONG A MAN'S LEGS SHOULD BE.
AND HE SAID, "LONG ENOUGH TO REACH THE GROUND"!

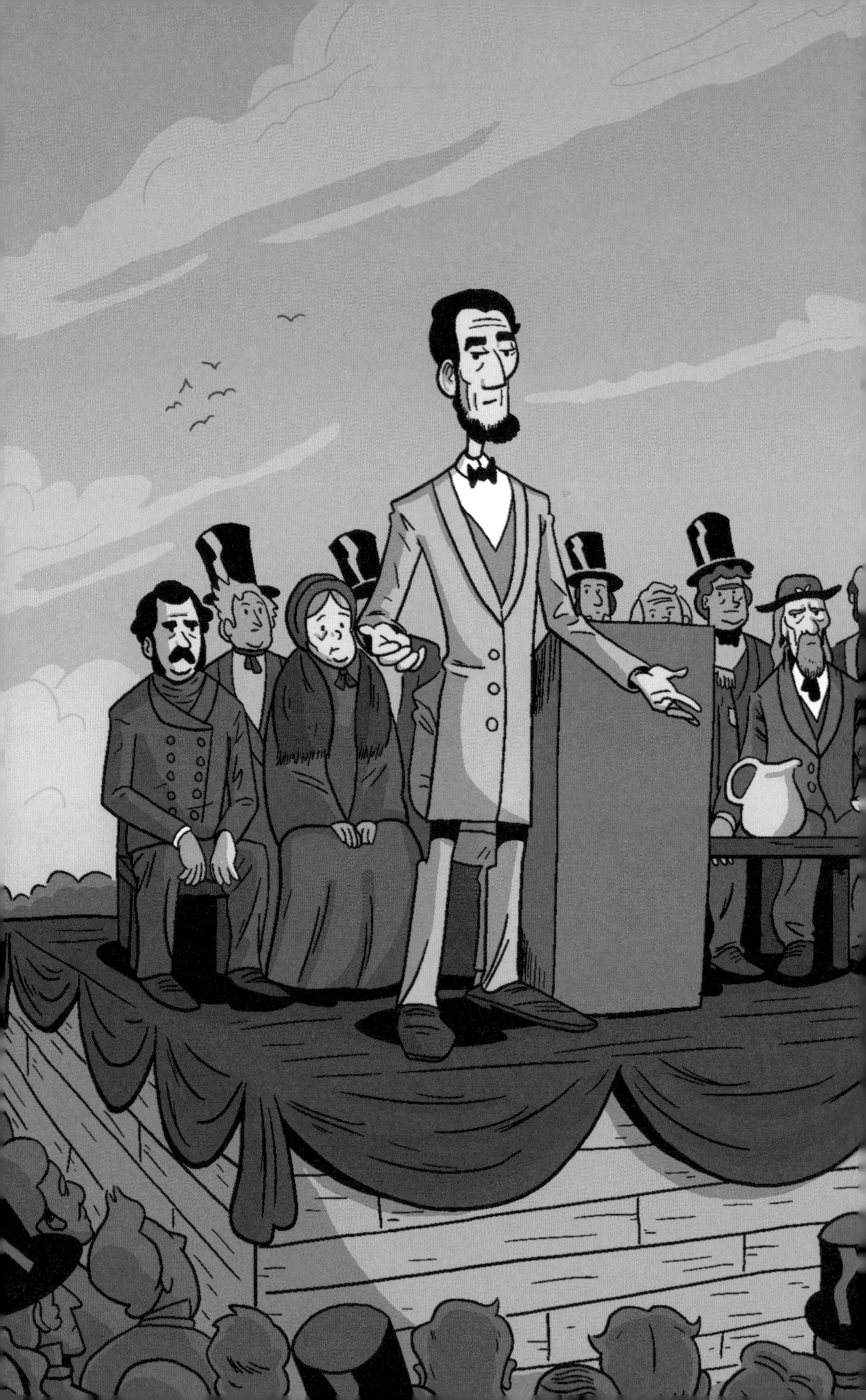